4/07

COOKING IN
# EUROPE, 1250–1650

**The Greenwood Press**
**"Daily Life Through History" Series**

The Age of Charlemagne
*John J. Butt*

The Age of Sail
*Dorothy Denneen Volo and James M. Volo*

The American Revolution
*Dorothy Denneen Volo and James M. Volo*

The Ancient Egyptians
*Bob Brier and Hoyt Hobbs*

The Ancient Greeks
*Robert Garland*

Ancient Mesopotamia
*Karen Rhea Nemet-Nejat*

The Ancient Romans
*David Matz*

The Aztecs: People of the Sun and Earth
*David Carrasco with Scott Sessions*

The Byzantine Empire
*Marcus Rautman*

Chaucer's England
*Jeffrey L. Singman and Will McLean*

Civil War America
*Dorothy Denneen Volo and James M. Volo*

Colonial New England
*Claudia Durst Johnson*

Early Modern Japan
*Louis G. Perez*

The Early American Republic, 1790–1820:
Creating a New Nation
*David S. Heidler and Jeanne T. Heidler*

18th-Century England
*Kirstin Olsen*

Elizabethan England
*Jeffrey L. Singman*

The Holocaust
*Eve Nussbaum Soumerai and Carol D.
Schulz*

The Inca Empire
*Michael A. Malpass*

The Industrial United States, 1870–1900
*Julie Husband and Jim O'Loughlin*

Jews in the Middle Ages
*Norman Roth*

Maya Civilization
*Robert J. Sharer*

Medieval Europe
*Jeffrey L. Singman*

The Medieval Islamic World
*James E. Lindsay*

The Mongol Empire
*George Lane*

Native Americans in the Twentieth Century
*Donald Fixico*

Nature and the Environment in Twentieth-
Century American Life
*Brian Black*

The Nineteenth Century American Frontier
*Mary Ellen Jones*

The Nubians
*Robert S. Bianchi*

The Old Colonial Frontier
*James M. Volo and Dorothy Denneen Volo*

Renaissance Italy
*Elizabeth S. Cohen and Thomas V. Cohen*

The Roman City: Rome, Pompeii, and Ostia
*Gregory S. Aldrete*

Science and Technology in Colonial
America
*William E. Burns*

Science and Technology in Nineteenth-
Century America
*Todd Timmons*

The Soviet Union
*Katherine B. Eaton*

The Spanish Inquisition
*James M. Anderson*

Traditional China: The Tang Dynasty
*Charles Benn*

The United States, 1920–1939: Decades of
Promise and Pain
*David E. Kyvig*

The United States, 1940–1959: Shifting
Worlds
*Eugenia Kaledin*

The United States, 1960–1990: Decades of
Discord
*Myron A. Marty*

Victorian England
*Sally Mitchell*

The Vikings
*Kirsten Wolf*

World War I
*Neil M. Heyman*

# COOKING IN
# EUROPE,
# 1250–1650

Ken Albala

*The Greenwood Press "Daily Life Through History" Series*
*Cooking Up History*
*Ken Albala, Series Editor*

**Greenwood Press**
Westport, Connecticut • London

**Library of Congress Cataloging-in-Publication Data**

Albala, Ken, 1964–
    Cooking in Europe, 1250–1650 / by Ken Albala.
        p.   cm. — (Greenwood Press "Daily life through history" series,
Cooking up history ISSN 1080–4749.)
    Includes bibliographical references and index.
    ISBN 0–313–33096–4
    1. Cookery, European—History.   I. Title.   II. Series.
    TX723.5.A1A43 2006
    641.59409—dc22        2006004782

British Library Cataloguing in Publication Data is available.

Library of Congress Catalog Card Number: 2006004782
ISBN: 0–313–33096–4
ISSN: 1080–4749

First published in 2006

Greenwood Press, 88 Post Road West, Westport, CT 06881
An imprint of Greenwood Publishing Group, Inc.
www.greenwood.com

Printed in the United States of America

The paper used in this book complies with the
Permanent Paper Standard issued by the National
Information Standards Organization (Z39.48–1984).

10  9  8  7  6  5  4  3  2  1

**Copyright Acknowledgments**

The author and publisher gratefully acknowledge premission for use of the following material:

Illustrations by Lisa Cooperman.

 The publisher has done its best to make sure the instructions and/or recipes in this book are
correct. However, users should apply judgment and experience when preparing recipes, especially parents and teachers working with young people. The publisher accepts no responsibility for the outcome of any recipe included in this volume.

# CONTENTS

List of Recipes                                             *vii*

List of Recipes by Country                                  *xv*

List of Recipes for Special Occasions                       *xxiii*

Glossary                                                    *xxv*

Series Foreword                                             *xxxi*

Preface                                                     *xxxiii*

Acknowledgments                                            *xxxvii*

1. Introduction                                             1

2. The Middle Ages, 1300–1450                               29

3. The Renaissance                                          71

4. Late Renaissance and Elizabethan Era                     97

Notes                                                       *137*

Bibliography                                                *139*

Index                                                       *145*

# ✌ LIST OF RECIPES

This list is organized in the same order as recipes appear in the book. Cities are listed here when a country listed did not yet exist in the Middle Ages or Renaissance. When a cookbook is printed, the reference is to place of publication rather than residence of the author. For England, the city of publication is always London; for France, Paris. For other specific locations, refer to the bibliography. The authors of many medieval cookbooks are unknown, in which case they are listed by title or a conventional name such as Anonimo Veneziano, which means anonymous Venetian.

## Middle Ages

### Cold Foods

1. Cold Sage (Chicken Salad)—*Viandier* (France) — 30
2. Blaunche Brawen (White Pork Paté)—Harleian (England) — 30
3. Cold flounder—Rupert of Nola (Spain/Naples) — 31
4. Gelatin of Every Meat—Anonimo Veneziano (Venice, Italy) — 31

### Soups

5. Brouet rousset (Russet Broth)—*Viandier* (France) — 32
6. Chicken broth variations—*Liber de Coquina* (Italy?) — 33
7. For to make potage of oysters—*Liber Cure Cocorum* (Northern England) — 34

8. Jacobin Soup—Chiquart (Savoy) 35
9. Soup which is called Pinyonada (Pine Nut Soup)—
   Rupert of Nola (Spain/Naples) 36

**Meat**

10. Hericoc of Mutton—*Viandier* (France) 36
11. Venoison of fresh deer—*Viandier* (France) 37
12. Roast Pork—*Tractatus de modo preparandi et condiendi omnia
    cibaria* (France?) 37
13. Lamb or veal—Chiquart (Savoy) 38
14. For powme dorrys (Golden Apples of Pork)—*Liber Cure Cocorum*
    (Northern England) 38
15. Stwed Beeff (Beef Stew)—Harleian (England) 39
16. A Janet of Young Goat—Rupert of Nola (Spain/Naples) 40
17. A Dish of Roasted Cat—Rupert of Nola (Spain/Naples) 40
18. To Stuff a Shoulder or Other Part (Mutton)—
    Anonimo Toscano (Tuscany, Italy) 41

**Fowl**

19. Peacocks—*Viandier* (France) 41
20. Roast Chicken—*Tractatus de modo preparandi et
    condiendi omnia cibaria* (France?) 42
21. Stuffed Goose Neck—*Tractatus de modo preparandi
    et condiendi omnia cibaria* (France?) 42
22. Chykonys in bruette (Chickens in Broth)—Harleian (England) 43
23. Rose (of Capon)—*Liber Cure Cocorum* (Northern England) 43
24. Armored Chicken—Rupert of Nola (Spain/Naples) 44

**Fish and Seafood**

25. Fresh Salmon—*Viandier* (France) 45
26. Oysters—*Tractatus de modo preparandi et condiendi
    omnia cibaria* (France?) 45
27. Good Tuna Casserole—Rupert of Nola (Spain/Naples) 45
28. Lamprays bake (Lamprey Pie)—Harleian (England) 46

**Vegetables**

29. Fava Beans—*Tractatus de modo preparandi et condiendi
    omnia cibaria* (France?) 47
30. Little Leaves—*Liber de Coquina* (Italy?) 48
31. White Leeks—Chiquart (Savoy) 49
32. Caboges (Cabbage)—Harleian (England) 50
33. Tansy—Harleian (England) 50
34. Tiny Leaves and Fennel—Anonimo Toscano (Tuscany, Italy) 51

35. Compost Good and Perfect—Anonimo Veneziano (Venice, Italy)  51
36. Eggplant Casserole—Rupert of Nola (Spain/Naples)  52
37. Royal Fava Beans—Rupert of Nola (Spain/Naples)  53

**Starches and Pasta**

38. Gruyau (Barley Gruel)—*Viandier* (France)  54
39. Furmente—*Liber Cure Cocorum* (Northern England)  54
40. For fraunche mele (Bread Pudding)—*Liber Cure Cocorum* (Northern England)  55
41. Farro of Spelt—Anonimo Toscano (Tuscany, Italy)  56
42. Parlem de Fideus (Noodle Soup)—Rupert of Nola (Spain/Naples)  57

**Eggs and Dairy**

43. Green Broth of Eggs and Cheese—*Viandier* (France)  57
44. How to roast cheese—*Tractatus de modo preparandi et condiendi omnia cibaria* (France?)  58
45. Malaches whyte (Egg Tart)—*Forme of Cury* (England)  58
46. Slices of Fresh Cheese—Rupert of Nola (Spain/Naples)  58
47. Stuffed eggs—Anonimo Veneziano (Venice, Italy)  59

**Sauces**

48. A jaunette sauce for fish—*Viandier* (France)  59
49. Mustard—*Tractatus de modo preparandi et condiendi omnia cibaria* (France?)  60
50. Pur verde sawce (Green Sauce)—*Liber Cure Cocorum* (Northern England)  60
51. Good Sauce for Chickens—*Anonimo Veneziano* (Venice, Italy)  61
52. Civet or Black Sauce for Boar—*Anonimo Veneziano* (Venice, Italy)  61

**Fruits**

53. Fried Apples—*Tractatus de modo preparandi et condiendi omnia cibaria* (France?)  62
54. On Lombard Compost—*Liber de Coquina* (Italy?)  62
55. Rysshews of fruyt—*Forme of Cury* (England)  63
56. Strawberye—Harleian (England)  63
57. Good Codonyat (Quince)—Rupert of Nola (Spain/Naples)  64

**Fruit**

58. Crepes Large and Small—*Viandier* (France)  64
59. Fygey—*Forme of Cury* (England)  65
60. To Candy Green Almonds, Unripe Peaches and Green walnuts, being little young ones, neither too hard or soft, etc.— Anonimo Veneziano (Venice, Italy)  65

61. To Make Nun's Bozolati—Anonimo Veneziano (Venice, Italy)     66
62. Frytours (Fritters)—Harleian (England)     66
63. Garbies a la Catalana—Rupert of Nola (Spain/Naples)     67

**Drinks**

64. To degrease all wines—*Viandier* (France)     68
65. Wine comments—*Tractatus de modo preparandi et condiendi omnia cibaria* (France?)     68
66. Vin Cocto (Cooked Wine)—Anonimo Veneziano (Venice, Italy)     69

## RENAISSANCE

**Cold Food**

67. To Make Prosciutto—Messisbugo (Ferrara, Italy)     72

**Soups**

68. Hemp Seed Soup—Martino (Rome, Italy)     72
69. Garlic Soup—*Livre fort excellent de cuisine* (France)     73
70. Digestive Pottage—*Livre fort excellent de cuisine* (France)     73
71. Italian Pottage—Messisbugo (Ferrara, Italy)     74
72. To Make a white broathe—*A Proper Newe Booke of Cokerye* (England)     74

**Meat**

73. To make rolls of meat from Veal or other good meat—Martino (Rome, Italy)     75
74. Hare with Pappardelle (Noodles)—Romoli (Florence, Italy)     75

**Fowl**

75. Soffrito of Meat, or of Pigeons, or of Chickens or of Kid—Martino (Rome, Italy)     76
76. Roasted Capon—*Livre fort excellent de cuisine* (France)     76
77. Dodine blanche (Ducks in White Sauce)—*Livre fort excellent de cuisine* (France)     77
78. Pheasant, Capon or Pigeon, Breast of Veal or other meat stewed in a pot, in the oven—Messisbugo (Ferrara, Italy)     77

**Fish**

79. A Large Sea Bass—Martino (Rome, Italy)     78
80. Pike in English Sauce—*Livre fort excellent de cuisine* (France)     78
81. Carp Fritters—*Livre fort excellent de cuisine* (France)     79
82. Caviar to eat fresh and to keep—Messisbugo (Ferrara, Italy)     79

83. Singular Way to cook and garnish Shrimp—Romoli
    (Florence, Italy)                                                80

## Vegetables

84. How to Cook Mushrooms—Martino (Rome, Italy)                      80
85. Tart of lupins, fava beans, fagioli beans, asparagus or onions,
    artichokes or another thing—Messisbugo (Ferrara, Italy)         81
86. A Tarte to provoke courage either in a man or Woman—
    *The Good Huswifes Handmaide for the Kitchen* (England)          81

## Starches

87. Rice with Almond Milk—Martino (Rome, Italy)                      82
88. To make ten plates of "maccheroni"—Messisbugo (Ferrara, Italy)   83
89. To make Ravioli for Meat and Lean Days, for 10 plates—
    Messisbugo (Ferrara, Italy)                                     84
90. To Make Pancakes—*The Good Huswifes Handmaide
    for the Kitchen* (England)                                      84
91. Fried Fresh Butter—*Livre fort excellent de cuisine* (France)    85

## Eggs and Dairy

92. Eggs on the Grill—Martino (Rome, Italy)                          85
93. To make egges in Moneshyne—*A Proper Newe Booke
    of Cokerye* (England)                                           86
94. Jasper of Milk—*Livre fort excellent de cuisine
    de Cuisine* (France)                                            86
95. Frittata simple, green, filled and difficult—Messisbugo
    (Ferrara, Italy)                                                87

## Sauces

96. Cameline Sauce—Martino (Rome, Italy)                             87
97. White Agliata (Garlic Sauce)—Martino (Rome, Italy)              88
98. Hell Sauce—*Livre fort excellent de cuisine* (France)           88
99. Sauce for roast beef—*Livre fort excellent de cuisine* (France) 89
100. To Make the Sauce called Cordial to place over cooked
     fish—Romoli (Florence, Italy)                                  89
101. A Pyke Sauce for Pyke, Breme, Perche, Roche, Carpe,
     eles, Floykes, and al maner of brouke fyshe—*A Proper
     Newe Booke of Cokerye* (England)                               90

## Sweets

102. Cherry and Rose Tart—Martino (Rome, Italy)                      90
103. Chestnuts—*Livre fort excellent de cuisine* (France)           91

104. To Make a Compote of Melon Peels or Peels of Gourd,
     or Turnips, or whole unripe peaches in a conserve for
     Lent—Messisbugo (Ferrara, Italy)                          91
105. To Make a Tart of Prunes—*A Proper Newe Booke of Cokerye*
     (England)                                                 92

### Sweets

106. To Make Mostaccioli of sugar—Messisbugo (Ferrara, Italy)   92
107. To make 10 puff-pastry pizzas—Messisbugo (Ferrara, Italy)  93
108. Counterfeit Snow—*Livre fort excellent de cuisine* (France) 93
109. For to make wardens in conserve—*A Proper Newe Booke
     of Cokerye* (England)                                     94

### Drink

110. Vermillion Wine—Grataroli (Switzerland)                   95

## LATE RENAISSANCE AND ELIZABETHAN ERA

### Cold Foods

111. To Make Mortadella from lean meat of domestic pork
     leg, wrapped in a caul—Scappi (Rome, Italy)              97
112. To preserve Cucumbers—Lancelot de Casteau
     (Liege, Belgium)                                         100
113. Divers Sallets boyled—Murrell (England)                  100

### Soups

114. To Make a Soup of Melons with Meat Broth—Scappi
     (Rome, Italy)                                            101
115. To Make a Lombard Soup with meat broth—Scappi
     (Rome, Italy)                                            102
116. For White Pease Pottage—Dawson (England)                 102
117. Cauliflower Soup—Lancelot de Casteau (Liege, Belgium)    103
118. How to make Truffle Broth—Maceras (Spain)                103
119. Capirotada Soup—Martínez Montiño (Spain)                 104

### Meat

120. To roast on a spit or braise a loin of beef, or of cow—Scappi
     (Rome, Italy)                                            104
121. To pot roast a whole stuffed leg of lamb—Scappi (Rome, Italy) 106
122. To make Spanish balles—*The Good Huswifes Handmaide
     for the Kitchen* (England)                               106

123. How to make Chuets—A.W. (England)                               107
124. How to cook another dish called Albujauanas
     (Mutton Patties)—Maceras (Spain)                               107

**Fowl**

125. To Roast the Cock and Hen of India, which in some places
     in Italy is called a peacock of India (Turkey)—Scappi
     (Rome, Italy)                                                  108
126. To Stew Larks or Sparrowes—*The Good Huswifes
     Handmaide for the Kitchen* (England)                           109
127. To stue a Capon in Lemmons—A.W. (England)                      110
128. How to make an escabeche of partridge—Maceras (Spain)          110
129. To make blancmange—Lancelot de Casteau (Liege, Belgium)        111
130. A mallard smored, or a hare, or old cony—*Markham* (England)   111

**Fish and Seafood**

131. To Make Stuffed Calamari Soup—Scappi (Rome, Italy)             112
132. To Make Stuffed Rolls of Tuna Meat Cooked on a
     Spit—Scappi (Rome, Italy)                                     113
133. To Seeth Stock fish—*The Good Huswifes Handmaide
     for the Kitchen* (England)                                    114
134. Stuffed crayfish or sea crabs—Lancelot de Casteau
     (Liege, Belgium)                                              114
135. Little fish—Maceras (Spain)                                   114
136. To Sowce Oysters—Murrell (England)                            115
137. Frog Pie—Martínez Montiño (Spain)                             115

**Vegetables**

138. To cook Stuffed Eggplants in days of Lent—Scappi (Rome, Italy) 116
139. To make a soup of Red Chickpeas—Scappi (Rome, Italy)          117
140. To Make Fried Toast of Spinach—Dawson (England)               117
141. Fava Bean Tart—Lancelot de Casteau (Liege, Belgium)           118
142. Carrot Salad—Martínez Montiño (Spain)                         118

**Starches and Pasta**

143. To Make a Minestra of Cracked Millet or Panic—Scappi
     (Rome, Italy)                                                 119
144. To Make a Tart of Tagliatelli or Lasagne cooked in fat meat
     broth or in milk—Scappi (Rome, Italy)                        119
145. To make ravioli—Lancelot de Casteau (Liege, Belgium)         120
146. How to make wheat starch—Maceras (Spain)                     121
147. Buttered Loaves—Murrell (England)                            121

**Eggs and Dairy**

148. To Make Cannoncini of fresh eggs—Scappi (Rome, Italy)  122
149. To poach egg yolks in sugar—Scappi (Rome, Italy)  122
150. Huevos rellenos (Stuffed Eggs)—Maceras (Spain)  123
151. To make Stuffed Eggs—Lancelot de Casteau (Liege, Belgium)  123
152. Fried Quesadillas of Curds—Martínez Montiño (Spain)  124

**Sauces**

153. Royal Sauce—Scappi (Rome, Italy)  125
154. Carrot Sauce—Scappi (Rome, Italy)  125
155. To make a green sauce—Scappi (Rome, Italy)  126
156. Mustard of Cremona—Lancelot de Casteau (Liege, Belgium)  127

**Fruit**

157. To conserve cherries in jelly—Scappi (Rome, Italy)  127
158. To bake peaches—*The Good Huswifes Handmaide for the Kitchen* (England)  128
159. A Plate of all fruits (with eggs)—Martínez Montiño (Spain)  128
160. Apple Tart—Lancelot de Casteau (Liege, Belgium)  129
161. To make a marmalade of oranges—Markham (England)  129

**Sweets**

162. To Make Fritters, in the Roman dialect called Zeppolle—Scappi (Rome, Italy)  129
163. To Make Manus Christi—Partridge (England)  130
164. To make Farts of Portingale—A.W. (England)  131
165. Buñuelos—Granado (Spain)  131
166. To Make Flaky Spanish Pastry—Lancelot de Casteau (Liege, Belgium)  131
167. A Tart of Milk—Maceras (Spain)  132
168. A most delicate and stiffe sugar-paste, whereof to cast Rabets, Pigeons, or any other little bird or beast, either from the life, or carv'd molds—Plat (England)  133

**Drinks**

169. To Cook water with anise, sugar and cinnamon—Scappi (Rome, Italy)  133
170. To make hippocras—Markham (England)  134
171. How to help bastard being eager—Markham (England)  134

# ⚛ LIST OF RECIPES
# BY COUNTRY

Identifying authors by country from the Middle Ages to the Elizabethan Era is actually a little trickier than it sounds. First, there was no such country as Italy yet and people generally identified with their city-state or region first. Similarly, there was no Belgium, and although Liege, where Lancelot de Casteau worked, was then part of the Holy Roman Empire, he wrote in French. Even more confusing, Rupert of Nola wrote in Catalan for the Aragonese court, which then ruled Naples. Nola is a place in southern Italy, but Rupert's cooking is thoroughly Catalonian, with Catalonia now part of Spain. For the sake of convenience, authors are listed by the country that now exists. The numbers refer to recipe number. If no recipes are listed from a particular period under a country, it usually means none was written. The purpose of this list is so that one might construct an entire meal from a particular time and place.

## FRANCE

### Middle Ages

|  |  |
|---|---|
| 1. Cold Sage (Chicken Salad)—*Viandier* | 30 |
| 5. Brouet rousset (Russet Broth)—*Viandier* | 32 |
| 10. Hericoc of Mutton—*Viandier* | 36 |
| 11. Venoison of Fresh Deer—*Viandier* | 37 |
| 12. Roast Pork—*Tractatus de modo preparandi et condiendi omnia cibaria* | 37 |

20. Roast Chicken—*Tractatus de modo preparandi et condiendi omnia cibaria* ... 42

21. Stuffed Goose Neck—*Tractatus de modo preparandi et condiendi omnia cibaria* ... 42

25. Fresh Salmon—*Viandier* ... 45

26. Oysters—*Tractatus de modo preparandi et condiendi omnia cibaria* ... 45

29. Fava Beans—*Tractatus de modo preparandi et condiendi omnia cibaria* ... 47

38. Gruyau (Barley Gruel)—*Viandier* ... 54

43. Green Broth of Eggs and Cheese—*Viandier* ... 57

48. A jaunette sauce for fish—*Viandier* ... 59

49. Mustard—*Tractatus de modo preparandi et condiendi omnia cibaria* ... 60

53. Fried Apples—*Tractatus de modo preparandi et condiendi omnia cibaria* ... 62

58. Crepes Large and Small—*Viandier* ... 64

64. To degrease all wines—*Viandier* ... 68

65. Wine comments—*Tractatus de modo preparandi et condiendi omnia cibaria* ... 68

### Renaissance

69. Garlic soup—*Livre fort excellent de cuisine* ... 73

70. Digestive Pottage—*Livre fort excellent de cuisine* ... 73

76. Roasted Capon—*Livre fort excellent de cuisine* ... 76

77. Dodine blanche (Ducks in White Sauce)—*Livre fort excellent de cuisine* ... 77

80. Pike in English Sauce—*Livre fort excellent de cuisine* ... 78

81. Carp Fritters—*Livre fort excellent de cuisine* ... 79

91. Fried Fresh Butter—*Livre fort excellent de cuisine* ... 85

94. Jasper of Milk—*Livre fort excellent de cuisine* ... 86

98. Hell Sauce—*Livre fort excellent de cuisine* ... 88

99. Sauce for roast beef—*Livre fort excellent de cuisine* ... 89

103. Chestnuts—*Livre fort excellent de cuisine* ... 91

108. Counterfeit Snow—*Livre fort excellent de cuisine* ... 93

## ENGLAND

### Middle Ages

2. Blaunche Brawen (White Pork Paté)—*Harleian* ... 30

7. For to make potage of oysters—*Liber Cure Cocorum* (Northern England) ... 34

14. For powme dorrys (Golden Apples of Pork)—*Liber Cure Cocorum* (Northern England)        38

15. Stwed Beeff (Beef Stew)—Harleian        39

22. Chykonys in bruette (Chickens in Broth)—Harleian        43

23. Rose (of Capon)—*Liber Cure Cocorum* (Northern England)        43

28. Lamprays bake (Lamprey Pie)—Harleian        46

32. Caboges (Cabbage)—Harleian        50

33. Tansy—Harleian        50

39. Furmente—*Liber Cure Cocorum* (Northern England)        54

40. For fraunche mele (Bread Pudding)—*Liber Cure Cocorum* (Northern England)        55

45. Malaches whyte (Egg Tart)—*Forme of Cury*        58

50. Pur verde sawce (Green Sauce)—*Liber Cure Cocorum* (Northern England)        60

55. Rysshews of fruyt—*Forme of Cury*        63

56. Strawberye—Harleian        63

59. Fygey—*Forme of Cury*        65

62. Frytours (Fritters)—Harleian        66

## Renaissance

72. To Make a white broathe—*A Proper Newe Booke of Cokerye*        74

86. A Tarte to provoke courage either in a man or Woman—*The Good Huswifes Handmaide for the Kitchen*        81

90. To Make Pancakes—*The Good Huswifes Handmaide for the Kitchen*        84

93. To make eggs in Moneshyne—*A Proper Newe Booke of Cokerye*        86

101. A Pyke Sauce for Pyke, Breme, Perche, Roche, Carpe, eles, Floykes, and al maner of brouke fyshe—*A Proper Newe Booke of Cokerye*        90

105. To Make a Tart of Prunes—*A Proper Newe Booke of Cokerye*        92

109. For to make wardens in conserve—*A Proper Newe Booke of Cokerye*        94

## Late Renaissance and Elizabethan Era

113. Diverse Sallets boyled—Murrell        100

116. For White Pease Pottage—Dawson        102

122. To make Spanish balles—*The Good Huswifes Handmaide for the Kitchen*        106

123. How to make Chuets—A.W.        107

126. To Stew Larks or Sparrowes—*The Good Huswifes Handmaide for the Kitchen*        109

127. To stue a Capon in Lemmons—A.W.     110

130. A mallard smored, or a hare, or old cony—Markham     111

133. To Seeth Stock fish—*The Good Huswifes Handmaide for the Kitchen*     114

136. To Sowce Oysters—Murrell     115

140. To Make Fried Toast of Spinach—Dawson     117

147. Buttered Loaves—Murrell     121

158. To bake peaches—*The Good Huswifes Handmaide for the Kitchen*     128

161. To make a marmalade of oranges—Markham     129

163. To Make Manus Christi—Partridge     130

164. To make Farts of Portingale—A.W.     131

168. A most delicate and stiffe sugar-paste, whereof to cast Rabets, Pigeons, or any other little bird or beast, either from the life, or carv'd molds—Plat     133

170. To make hippocras—Markham     134

171. How to help bastard being eager—Markham     134

## Spain

### Middle Ages

3. Cold flounder—Rupert of Nola (Spain/Naples)     31

9. Soup which is called Pinyonada (Pine Nut Soup)—Rupert of Nola (Spain/Naples)     36

16. A Janet of Young Goat—Rupert of Nola (Spain/Naples)     40

17. A Dish of Roasted Cat—Rupert of Nola (Spain/Naples)     40

24. Armored Chicken—Rupert of Nola (Spain/Naples)     44

27. Good Tuna Casserole—Rupert of Nola (Spain/Naples)     45

36. Eggplant Casserole—Rupert of Nola (Spain/Naples)     52

37. Royal Fava Beans—Rupert of Nola (Spain/Naples)     53

42. Parlem de Fideus (Noodle Soup)—Rupert of Nola (Spain/Naples)     57

46. Slices of Fresh Cheese—Rupert of Nola (Spain/Naples)     58

57. Good Codonyat (Quince)—Rupert of Nola (Spain/Naples)     64

63. Garbies a la Catalana—Rupert of Nola (Spain/Naples)     67

### Late Renaissance and Elizabethan Era

118. How to make Truffle Broth—Maceras     103

119. Capirotada Soup—Martínez Montiño     104

124. How to cook another dish called Albujauanas (Mutton Patties)—Maceras     107

128. How to make an escabeche of partridge—Maceras     110

135. Little fish—Maceras     114

137. Frog Pie—Martínez Montiño                                     115
142. Carrot Salad—Martínez Montiño                                 118
146. How to make wheat starch—Maceras                              121
150. Huevos Rellenos (Stuffed Eggs)—Maceras                        123
152. Fried Quesadillas of Curds—Martínez Montiño                   124
159. A Plate of all fruits (with eggs)—Martínez Montiño            128
165. Buñuelos—Granado                                              131
167. A Tart of Milk—Maceras                                        132

## ITALY

### Middle Ages

4. Gelatin of Every Meat—Anonimo Veneziano (Venice)              31
6. Chicken broth variations—*Liber de Coquina*                    33
8. Jacobin Soup—Chiquart                                          35
13. Lamb or veal—*Liber de Coquina*                               38
18. To Stuff a Shoulder or Other Part (Mutton)—Anonimo Toscano
(Tuscany)                                                        41
30. Little Leaves—*Liber de Coquina*                              48
31. White Leeks—Chiquart (Savoy)                                  49
34. Tiny Leaves and Fennel—Anonimo Toscano (Tuscany)             51
35. Compost Good and Perfect—Anonimo Veneziano (Venice)          51
41. Farro of Spelt—Anonimo Toscano (Tuscany)                     56
47. Stuffed eggs—Anonimo Veneziano (Venice)                      59
51. Good Sauce for Chickens—Anonimo Veneziano (Venice)           61
52. Civet or Black Sauce for Boar—Anonimo Veneziano (Venice)     61
54. On Lombard Compost—*Liber de Coquina*                        62
60. To Candy Green Almonds, Unripe Peaches and Green
walnuts, being little young ones, neither too hard or soft, etc.—
Anonimo Veneziano (Venice)                                       65
61. To Make Nun's Bozolati—Anonimo Veneziano (Venice)            66
66. Vin Cocto (Cooked Wine)—Anonimo Veneziano (Venice)           69

### Renaissance

67. To Make Prosciutto—Messisbugo (Ferrara)                       72
68. Hemp Seed Soup—Martino (Rome)                                 72
71. Italian Pottage—Messisbugo (Ferrara)                          74
73. To make rolls of meat from Veal or other good meat—
*Martino* (Rome)                                                 75
74. Hare with Papardelle (Noodles)—Romoli (Florence)             75
75. Soffrito of Meat, or of Pigeons, or of Chickens or of Kid—
Martino (Rome)                                                   76

78. Pheasant, Capon or Pigeon, Breast of Veal or other meat
    stewed in a pot, in the oven—Messisbugo (Ferrara)          77
79. A Large Sea Bass—Martino (Rome)                             78
82. Caviar to eat fresh and to keep—Messisbugo (Ferrara)       79
83. Singular Way to cook and garnish Shrimp—Romoli (Florence)  80
84. How to Cook Mushrooms—Martino (Rome)                       80
85. Tart of lupines, fava beans, fagioli beans, asparagus or onions,
    artichokes or another thing—Messisbugo (Ferrara)          81
87. Rice With Almond Milk—Martino (Rome)                       82
88. To make ten plates of "maccheroni"—Messisbugo (Ferrara)   83
89. To make Ravioli for Meat and Lean Days, for 10 plates—
    Messisbugo (Ferrara)                                      84
92. Eggs on the Grill—Martino (Rome)                          85
95. Frittata simple, green, filled and difficult—Messisbugo (Ferrara) 87
96. Cameline Sauce—Martino (Rome)                            87
97. White Agliata (Garlic Sauce)—Martino (Rome)             88
100. To Make the Sauce called Cordial to place over cooked
     fish—Romoli (Florence)                                  89
102. Cherry and Rose Tart—Martino (Rome)                    90
104. To Make a Compote of Melon Peels or Peels of Gourd,
     or Turnips, or whole unripe peaches in a conserve for
     Lent—Messisbugo (Florence)                             91
106. To Make Mostaccioli of sugar—Messisbugo (Ferrara)     92
107. To make 10 puff-pastry pizzas—Messisbugo (Ferrara)    93

**Late Renaissance and Elizabethan Era**

111. To Make Mortadella from lean meat of domestic pork leg,
     wrapped in a caul—Scappi (Rome)                        97
114. To Make a Soup of Melons with Meat Broth—Scappi (Rome)  101
115. To Make a Lombard Soup with meat broth—Scappi (Rome)    102
120. To roast on a spit or braise a loin of beef, or of cow—
     Scappi (Rome)                                          104
121. To pot roast a whole stuffed leg of lamb—Scappi (Rome)  106
125. To Roast the Cock and Hen of India, which in some places
     in Italy is called a peacock of India (Turkey)—Scappi (Rome) 108
131. To Make Stuffed Calamari Soup—Scappi (Rome)            112
132. To Make Stuffed Rolls of Tuna Meat Cooked on a Spit—Scappi
     (Rome)                                                 113
138. To cook Stuffed Eggplants in days of Lent—Scappi (Rome)  116
139. To make a soup of Red Chickpeas—Scappi (Rome)          117
143. To Make a Minestra of Cracked Millet or Panic—Scappi (Rome) 119
144. To Make a Tart of Tagliatelli or Lasagne cooked in fat meat
     broth or in milk—Scappi (Rome)                         119

148. To Make Cannoncini of fresh eggs—Scappi (Rome)     122
149. To poach egg yolks in sugar—Scappi (Rome)     122
153. Royal Sauce—Scappi (Rome)     125
154. Carrot sauce—Scappi (Rome)     125
155. To make a green sauce—Scappi (Rome)     126
157. To conserve cherries in jelly—Scappi (Rome)     127
162. To Make Fritters, in the Roman dialect called Zeppolle—
     Scappi (Rome)     129
169. To Cook Water with anise, sugar and cinnamon—Scappi (Rome) 133

## BELGIUM

### Late Renaissance and Elizabethan Era

112. To preserve Cucumbers—Lancelot de Casteau (Liege)     100
117. Cauliflower Soup—Lancelot de Casteau (Liege)     103
129. To make blancmange—Lancelot de Casteau (Liege)     111
134. Stuffed crayfish or sea crabs—Lancelot de Casteau (Liege)     114
141. Fava Bean Tart—Lancelot de Casteau (Liege)     118
145. To make ravioli—Lancelot de Casteau (Liege)     120
151. To make Stuffed Eggs—Lancelot de Casteau (Liege)     123
156. Mustard of Cremona—Lancelot de Casteau (Liege)     127
160. Apple Tart—Lancelot de Casteau (Liege)     129
166. To Make Flaky Spanish Pastry—Lancelot de Casteau (Liege)     131

## SWITZERLAND

### Late Renaissance and Elizabethan Era

110. Vermillion Wine—Grataroli     95

# ⚜ LIST OF RECIPES FOR SPECIAL OCCASIONS

**Novelty Dishes (Subtleties)**

14. For powme dorrys (Golden Apples of Pork)—*Liber Cure Cocorum*
    (Northern England)                                            38
17. A Dish of Roasted Cat—Rupert of Nola (Spain/Naples)           40
94. Jasper of Milk—*Livre fort excellent de cuisine* (France)     86
108. Counterfeit Snow—*Livre fort excellent de cuisine* (France)  93
168. A most delicate and stiffe sugar-paste, whereof to cast Rabets,
    Pigeons, or any other little bird or beast, either from the life,
    or carv'd molds—Plat (England)                                133

**Holidays and Fast Days**

30. Little Leaves—*Liber de Coquina* (Italy?)                     48
59. Fygey—*Forme of Cury* (England)                               65
89. To make Ravioli for Meat and Lean Days, for 10 plates—
    Messisbugo (Ferrara, Italy)                                   84
104. To Make a Compote of Melon Peels or Peels of Gourd, or
    Turnips, or whole unripe peaches in a conserve for
    Lent—Messisbugo (Florence, Italy)                             91
133. To Seeth Stock fish—*The Good Huswifes Handmaide for the
    Kitchen* (England)                                            114
138. To cook Stuffed Eggplants in days of Lent—Scappi (Rome, Italy) 116

**Illness**

7. For to make potage of oysters—*Liber Cure Cocorum* (Northern England     34

38. Gruyau (Barley Gruel)—*Viandier* (France)     54

129. To make blancmange—Lancelot de Casteau (Liege, Belgium)     111

169. To Cook water with anise, sugar and cinnamon—Scappi (Rome, Italy)     133

# GLOSSARY

ALKANET: The powdered root of a plant *(Alkanna tinctoria)* used as a reddish-purple dye in medieval cuisine.

ALMOND MILK: Substitute for regular milk used during Lent or any time of year. Made by pounding blanched almonds with a few drops of water to prevent the oil separating, then soaking in hot water overnight, lastly straining.

AMBERGRIS: Perfume coughed up from the intestines of whales and found washed up on beaches. It is very difficult to find today and unbelievably expensive, as in the past, which was precisely why it was used in cooking.

BARBERRIES: Wild sour red oblong berry *(Berberis vulgaris)* native to Europe often cooked with savory dishes, in conserves, or used as a garnish.

BLANCMANGE: Literally, "white food," originally made of pounded capon breast, sugar, rosewater, and almond milk. In later centuries it becomes a sweet almond dessert without chicken.

BORAGE: Fresh green herb *(Borrago officinalis)* with a light cucumber-like taste and sweet, edible purple flowers, thought to enliven the heart and drive away sorrow in the past.

BOTARGO: Dried salted mullet roe (egg sack) eaten as an appetizer thinly sliced.

BRAZIER: Little iron container with a grate that holds hot coals, on which pots or pans can be placed to gently simmer.

BREAD CRUMBS: Rather than dry commercial bread crumbs, keep good stale bread on hand and grate or crush as needed for a thickening agent, or to make stuffing and dumplings. Sometimes fresh bread crumb is called for, in which case remove crust or pull the interior from a loaf of bread.

CANELLA: See **Cinnamon.**

CAPON: Castrated male chicken. The procedure makes the bird grow fatter, as did feeding in coops. The preferred form of chicken.

CASSIA: See **Cinnamon.**

CASSIA BUDS: Dried bud of the cassia tree, resembling small cloves, but tasting like cinnamon.

CASSOLA: Round ceramic dish used to cook directly over a low flame or placed in the coals or in the oven. Normally glazed only on the inside. A modern casserole will work for most recipes but not those cooked over direct flames. Sold in Spanish and Italian cookware shops.

CAUL: Fatty visceral lining of the pig. Used to wrap around dry meats during roasting to keep them moist and also formed around chopped meat to create little meatballs or sausages.

CHAFING DISH: Metal pan set over hot coals to keep food warm. Normally used for serving rather than cooking.

CINNAMON: True cinnamon, native to Sri Lanka, is the delicate aromatic bark of a tree in the laurel family rolled into quills and dried. In most vernacular languages, the word *canella* refers to either cinnamon or cassia, which is closely related and brasher tasting. What is sold in the United States preground as cinnamon is actually cassia. Confusingly, canella today refers to a New World species *(Canella winterana)*. Unless cassia is specifically called for in a recipe, the word *cinnamon* has been used here for the sake of familiarity.

CITRON: Relative of the lemon, used primarily for its aromatic peel, which was often candied.

CLOVES: Spike-like bud of a plant native to the Moluccas in present-day Indonesia, used decoratively stuck into foods or finely ground.

COMFITS: Candy-coated spices such as aniseed, or other confections, used to sweeten the breath after a meal. Sometimes used as a garnish on savory dishes.

CUBEBS: Small, pepper-like spice from Asia with a short spike or "tail" on one end. Used both in pharmacy and cuisine.

CURRANTS: Small, tart berry, red, black or white *(Ribes)*. The name was also applied to Raisins of Corinth—tiny dried grapes that are still sold as currants.

CURY: Old English for "cookery."

DUTCH OVEN: Extremely versatile cast-iron pot with lid, three legs, and usually a wire handle. Hot coals can be placed on the concave lid to cook from all sides.

ENTREMETS: French for "between dishes," referring to small courses that appear between large courses with multiple dishes.

FLAN: Egg-based custard usually incorporating milk or cream and today usually gently baked, set in a *bainmarie,* or water bath.

FRY: This word referred to cooking in a shallow layer of fat in a pan and includes what we would call today sautéing. Deep-fat frying was fairly rare, though it could have been used for fritters and the like.

GALINGALE (GALANGAL): Fiery, slightly tougher relative of ginger, used dried and powdered in the Middle Ages but rarely thereafter. Available fresh or dried (preferable for medieval cooking) in Southeast Asian groceries.

GRAINS OF PARADISE: Meleguetta pepper, a small pungent seed from West Africa, vaguely similar to black pepper, used in a variety of medieval spice mixtures. It became almost completely unknown in European cookery by the late seventeenth century.

HYSSOP: Fresh evergreen herb *(Hyssopus officinalis)* used as a seasoning since Biblical times. Inexplicably absent from North American cookery.

ISINGLASS: Gelatin made from the air bladder of fish such as sturgeon and cod.

LAMPREY: Long, eel-like fish *(Petromyzon marinus)* with sharp teeth arranged in a circle, with which it latches onto its prey and drains it of blood. Popular in medieval cookery, especially baked into pies.

LARDO: Cured strips of pork fat, unsmoked. Not to be confused with lard, which is rendered and spreadable, though both were used in the past.

LEACH: To slice, and any food served in solid form sliced and cold.

LENT: Period of fasting in spring between Christian Advent and Ash Wednesday when no meat, eggs, or dairy products could be eaten. Towns and individuals could purchase dispensations from this rule, however, and by the sixteenth century, the rules were relaxed or abolished in some Protestant countries.

LONG PEPPER: Close relative to black pepper, but in form a small, finger-like catkin, and a little hotter. Once the most highly sought-after form of the spice. Available in Indian groceries.

MACE: See **Nutmeg.**

MANCHET: Small loaf of white bread used by wealthy English families. Normally used in cookery with the crust removed.

MARROW: Unctuous interior of bones, often used to enrich and moisten pie fillings and stews. Butter is an alternative, often suggested in old recipes.

MARZIPAN: Thick paste of crushed almonds and sugar, often used in pies and even savory recipes.

MASTIC: Resinous gum from a tree related to the pistachio that grows on the Island of Chios in Greece. Used ground in baked goods and flavored wines or chewed as "gum."

MEDLAR: Little apple-like fruit *(Mespilus germanica)* used in cooking and conserves that must be eaten when extremely ripe or nearly rotten as commentators in the past claimed.

MINESTRA: Italian thick soup with chunky contents.

MORTADELLA: Large cooked sausage made of finely ground pork studded with fat and whole peppercorns made traditionally in Bologna, Italy. It is the ancestor of what is known in the United States as bologna.

MORTAR AND PESTLE: Sturdy footed deep bowl of wood, stone, or brass, used with a blunt stick to pound spices, sauces such as "pesto," and other foods. Indispensable to medieval and Renaissance kitchens.

MOSTACCIOLI: Crisp biscuit or cookie originally made with grape juice or must but later with more expensive spices and aromatics. Often crushed into stuffing and sauces or used as a garnish.

MUSK: Perfume taken from the scent glands of a deer native to Siberia. Formerly used in food but today rarely used in any context. There is no substitute, so omit when recreating old recipes.

MUST: Freshly squeezed juice of wine grapes often containing skins and seeds when reduced; thereafter strained to make sapa.

NUTMEG: From the Moluccas in what is today Indonesia, among the most popular spices in Medieval cooking and thereafter. Used in sweet and savory dishes until a few centuries ago. Always use whole nutmeg freshly grated or carefully sliced with a sharp paring knife. Mace is the yellow aril covering the "nut," which has a distinct flavor.

PANIC: Variety of millet commonly used to make polenta before the arrival of corn into Europe.

PARBOIL: Because culinary texts so often called for foods to be boiled until half done, one must assume that this word meant exactly the same as it does today, to boil just until firm, rather than thoroughly boil.

PARMIGIANO: In the United States pale imitations of this hard grating cheese are called parmesan. Use only that stamped "Parmigiano-Reggiano" and always grate fresh. Universally appreciated throughout Europe since the Middle Ages, as were similar cheeses from Piacenza and Lodi, today labeled "Grana Padano."

PEASE: Original singular form of "pea," or a dish made from peas.

PESTO: Green sauce typically associated with Liguria on the northwest coast of Italy, today made with basil, pine nuts, parmigiano, and olive oil pounded in a mortar with a pestle, which is the origin of its name. Ancestors of this sauce contained other herbs and were thickened with bread and made sour with vinegar, verjuice, or lemon.

PIPKIN: Small, rotund, three-legged earthenware pot with a handle. Designed to be placed over a pile of hot coals.

POTTAGE: In England, any thick soup or sometimes stew, normally consisting of a starch and sometimes meat and vegetables.

PROSCIUTTO: Air-dried cured but unsmoked ham from Parma and elsewhere in Italy. Today eaten thinly sliced and raw, but often cooked in the past or used as a cooking ingredient.

PUDDING: Virtually any food boiled in an intestine or stomach, or pudding bag made of cloth. Can be sweet or savory, based on batter, crumbs, or other starch, or even meat when they more closely resemble sausages.

QUINCE: Astringent and aromatic apple-like fruit *(Cydonia vulgaris)* that must be cooked to be edible. Often boiled down and made into a paste, like the Spanish *membrillo*, which is sliced and eaten like cheese, or cooked in marmalade.

ROAST: To cook on a spit before a fire, in a hearth, or outdoors. The word has become practically meaningless today because there is roasting in an oven and even pan roasting on a stovetop.

ROSEWATER: Almost universal flavoring in medieval and Renaissance cuisine. Use Middle Eastern or Indian rosewater rather than the concentrated and expensive French rosewater sold in tiny blue bottles.

SANDALWOOD: Powdered wood of a tree from India, used to dye food red. Use sparingly as it can be astringent.

SAPA: Boiled-down grape must (squeezed juice). Used as a cooking ingredient in the past much the same way honey or later molasses would be used. Can be purchased from Italian suppliers, often labeled "saba," or made by reducing grape juice to one-half its volume or until thick.

SEETHE: Archaic word meaning "to boil gently."

SIEVE: To press through a hoop strung with horsehair or other material, today normally metal (*tamis* in French), designed to create fine purées or to remove seeds or spices from thick sauces. Today a conical strainer with fine mesh will work, as will a food mill or a processor to create fine purées.

SOFFRITO: Fried dish. Today also refers to a combination of aromatics such as onions, carrots, and celery, and sometimes tomatoes, fried as the first step to preparing another dish.

SPIKENARD: Root of an Indian plant with a resiny aromatic flavor. Sometimes called just "nard."

SPIT: Long iron rod, often with fastening clamps or prongs, used to roast practically anything before a fire. Could be cranked by hand when mounted on a stand, or turned by a spring-loaded or weighted mechanism. Some even used the force of rising air to turn a primitive turbine, which was connected to gears.

STOCKFISH: Dried cod that must be pounded and soaked before use. Similar to bacala or salted dried cod. A staple during Lent when meat products were forbidden.

SUMAC: The dried and powdered berries of a tree *(Rhus coriaria)* used to make dishes sour, not to be confused with poison sumac which is white.

TESTA: (*testo* in Italian) Ceramic cooking pot with a concave lid into which coals are heaped. Used for slowly braising food or even baking. A Dutch oven works the same way.

TRENCHER: Flat, rectangular plate made either of a slice of bread, wood, or in wealthier households, pewter or silver. Normally food would be served from a common dish and placed on the trencher. By the sixteenth century these are gradually replaced by round, rimmed plates. This ultimately facilitates serving foods in more liquid sauces.

VERJUICE: Juice of unripe grapes or sometimes other sour fruit such as crabapples where grapes were unavailable. It is both astringent and sour and thus quite different from vinegar, which was nonetheless sometimes called for as a substitute. Several wineries produce verjuice, mostly in France, but also in California and Australia. If unripe grapes are available, squeeze when still green (hence the name, which means "green juice") or use tart white table grapes freshly squeezed as a substitute.

# SERIES FOREWORD

*The beasts have memory, judgment and all the faculties and passions of our mind, in a certain degree; but no beast is a cook.*

This quip by the eighteenth-century Scottish biographer James Boswell defines the essence of humanity in a way his contemporaries would have found humorous but also thought provoking. It is neither an immortal soul, reason, nor powers of abstraction that separate us from animals but the simple ability to use fire to transform our daily fare into something more palatable and nutritious. We are nothing more than cooking animals. Archaeological evidence bears this out; it is our distant Neanderthal relatives, whose sites offer the earliest incontrovertible evidence of cooking. From those distant times down to the present, the food we eat and how it is prepared has become the decisive factor in the survival of both individuals and whole civilizations, so what better way to approach the subject of history than through the bubbling cauldron?

Growing and preparing food has also been the occupation of the vast majority of men and women who ever lived. To understand ourselves, we should naturally begin with the food that constitutes the fabric of our existence. Yet every culture arrives at different solutions, uses different crops and cooking methods, and invents what amount to unique cuisines. These are to some extent predetermined by geography, technology, and a certain amount of luck. Nonetheless every cuisine is a practical and artistic expression of the culture that created it. It embodies the values and aspirations of each society, its world outlook as well as its history.

This series examines cooking as an integral part of important epochs in history, both as a way to examine daily life for women and men who cooked, and as a way to explore the experiences of people who ate what was served. Cookbooks are thus treated here as primary source documents that students can interpret just as they might a legal text, literary or artistic work, or any other historical evidence. Through them we are afforded a glimpse, sometimes of what transpired in the great halls of the powerful, but also of what took place in more modest households. Unlike most forms of material culture, we can also recreate these dishes today to get an immediate and firsthand experience of the food that people in the past relished. I heartily encourage you to taste the past in these recipes, keeping in mind good taste is not universal and some things are simply impossible to make today. But a good number of dishes, I assure you, will both surprise and delight.

We begin the series with six volumes stretching from ancient times to the twentieth century, including European and American regions, written by experts in culinary history who have done a superb job of interpreting the historical texts while remaining faithful to their integrity. Each volume is designed to appeal to the novice cook, with technical and historical terms amply defined, and timely advice proffered for the adventurous time traveler in the kitchen. I hope your foray into the foods of the past is nothing less than an absolute delight.

Ken Albala
University of the Pacific

# 𝒲 PREFACE

Today we can travel to far-off places and taste foods from around the world. Interesting new restaurants open every day, and cookbooks explain how to prepare exotic recipes. In specialty shops and even in supermarkets, adventurous eaters can find unfamiliar ingredients and can prepare dishes from countless brilliant cuisines. The past, however, is not so accessible. But imagine if we could go back in time 500 years to the lavish banquets of kings and queens, not only to read about their meals from a safe distance, but to cook and taste the very same recipes they did. What would we think? Would it be as exciting as the new Thai or Peruvian restaurant? Would we enjoy the food or find it strange, frightening, or even repulsive? The answer is both. Some recipes have scarcely changed in hundreds of years. Though cooking technology was very different in the past, a roast chicken is still basically just that. On the other hand, most of us are unfamiliar with the spiced, sweet and sour flavor combinations preferred in the past, the smooth-pounded textures, the variety of organ meats and familiar animal body parts, and especially the customs surrounding food. But that is no reason not to try these foods. In lieu of time travel, this cookbook is an invitation to learn about the food of medieval and Renaissance Europe by studying the recipes and cooking (and even enjoying) some of the favorite dishes from these eras.

Some recipes will definitely not appeal to our taste or sensibilities. This book does not sanitize them for modern palates. In fact, apart from a few ingredients that are nearly impossible to find or illegal to sell, almost everything in this book is perfectly edible and delicious. Some of the recipes are included only because they are typical of the time or were royal favorites. Clearly no one today will cook a peacock re-sewn into its feathers or bake a porpoise, let alone prepare whole stuffed calves' heads. These are here to teach us about what people in the past liked to eat. Readers should feel free to cook whatever sounds interesting, and taste everything else with the imagination.

Most of the recipes require readily available ingredients and can be made easily without compromising the flavors of the past. Of course, there is no way of knowing exactly what food tasted like years ago. Animal and plant species have changed over time, cooking methods are completely different, and many of our basic staples have been radically transformed in the past century. For example, homogenized, pasteurized 2 percent milk from cows raised on industrial feed, hormones, and antibiotics probably tastes very different from milk fresh from the udder and unadulterated. Those of us without access to our own herd will just have to make do with store-bought milk.

Complete authenticity is impossible, but cutting too many corners teaches us nothing about the past. Therefore, the recipes here have not been tinkered with or "adapted" for the modern kitchen. If something tasted good to people in the past it will probably taste good now, even though we may be unaccustomed to archaic flavor combinations. Most importantly, the authors of cookbooks from the past, although we cannot be sure they were professional cooks, should always be trusted. Except when mistakes in copying manuscripts or typographical errors have rendered a text unintelligible, the directions in old cookbooks usually make perfect sense; they are just written very differently from modern recipes. They are nonetheless usually clear and easy to follow.

The directions therefore have not been rearranged in modern recipe format or altered to make them say what it seems the author intended. Each recipe includes an explanation of unfamiliar terms and how one can get as close as possible to the original, but this must partly be guesswork. Most medieval and Renaissance cookbooks were written for professionals, who did not need explicit instructions. To arbitrarily insist on a specific quantity or temperature as modern recipes do seems to miss the point entirely that cooks in the past followed no such rules. They measured temperature by touch. Cooking times were measured by the time it took to recite a prayer or not at all. Cooks tasted as they went along, smelled, and looked carefully at food until it was properly browned. They learned through practice, not by following directions to the letter. This is the only way to really cook.

So, to get a true feeling for this cuisine, one must be willing to experiment a bit, season to taste and take the suggestions provided here as only that. Some will prefer a lot of spice, others more sugar; some will want a dish thick, others thinner. It was the same with the original readers of these cookbooks, and there is no right or wrong way to make these recipes. Only when a cookbook author has specified measurements would it be best to follow the recipe as given. The commentaries provided here after each recipe are only suggestions, interpretations of the authors' intentions when explicit instructions are not provided, so that the recipe can be made in a modern kitchen. But again, the recipes are in no way tampered with to please modern palates.

The instructions also begin with the assumption that readers will not be experts in the kitchen, so some basic guidelines are provided. Some procedures, such as pounding and sieving and proper roasting, are actually quite simple but are likely to be unfamiliar. Few of us have large mortars, horsehair sieves, or roasting spits. So alternative ways to achieve decent results will be discussed, but when unnecessary modern conveniences will be avoided. A microwave oven many be very useful today, but there is absolutely no reason to use it in reconstructing historic recipes. A regular oven or barbecue grill will unfortunately not produce exactly the same results as an open flame in a hearth, but for many recipes the oven will be adequate, if not historically accurate.

The issue of rare ingredients is a little more difficult to resolve. There are certain spices and condiments that just cannot be found on the grocery shelf. They are available on a number of reliable Internet suppliers' sites, sources of which are listed on page 26. Try getting your hands on grains of paradise or cubebs or galangal. In a pinch, pepper and ginger will do but will not give you exactly what the author intended. Some unfamiliar ingredients can be made at home or bought. For example, verjuice, the juice of unripe grapes, is manufactured by several wineries. It can also be squeezed from tart table grapes. Lemon juice is not a good substitute. Almond milk is today sold as a dairy substitute alongside soy milk, but it can and should be made at home. Substitutions are sometimes unavoidable and cooked-down grape juice will work for sapa. But again, the more substitutions made and the more corners cut, the less the finished dish tells us about the past. And once you start adding ingredients that would have been unavailable in the past or unheard-of conveniences, then the point of authentic recipes is lost. New World foods should come nowhere near medieval cookery. If you ever see a potato, tomato, corn, chili, or any plant from the Americas, including turkey, in a dish that claims to be medieval, it is completely bogus. These foods are even absent from most Renaissance cookery. Tomatoes do not appear in a cookbook until the very end of the seventeenth century. Although botanists knew about them earlier and some people may have tasted them, they appear nowhere in this book. As for kitchen equipment, the blender is very convenient but really does not yield the same results as a mortar. To make a comparison, a medieval song accompanied by an electric guitar might be very pleasant and intriguing, but what does it tell us about medieval music?

A gothic cathedral with neon lights might be very beautiful, but do we learn anything about medieval taste from it?

As a rule recipes are reproduced here in the exact form they first appeared. The English sources, when readable, have been left in the original spelling as well, sometimes with modern English translations when the language is very old and difficult. Elizabethan English has been left intact and with a little reading out loud should pose no problems. All abbreviations and archaic letters have been spelled out. This is not intended to be a critical edition of these texts, so there is no scholarly apparatus apart from a citation for the source. (A superscript Roman numeral "V" with the source page refers to "verso" in the original when a book has a number only on every right-side or "recto" page.) Unusual terms are explained as well. All recipes taken from foreign languages have been translated specifically for this book. The translations are as literal as possible without excessive rearranging, which often obscures the author's intentions. Punctuation, however, has sometimes been added for clarity. The recipes cover English, French, Italian, Spanish, Catalan, and Latin sources.

The recipes come from cookbooks as early as the fourteenth century up to the beginning of the seventeenth century, or the time of Shakespeare. They are divided into three sections: the Middle Ages, roughly about 1300 to the 1450s when printing was invented; the Renaissance, up to about 1570; and the late Renaissance, when cookbooks were larger and more comprehensive and even sometimes illustrated. Cookbook authors whose works have already been translated in excellent editions have been generally avoided. For example, an author like Chiquart Amiczo, chef to the Duke of Savoy in the early fifteenth century, can be found in English translation but is difficult to find in the original French. It was necessary therefore to essentially retranslate whatever recipes could be found. Such authors have been included for the sake of complete coverage, but whenever possible this book focuses on texts that have either never been translated into English or are hard to find in print.

It must also be understood that these historical cookbooks represent a relatively small proportion of what was eaten by most people. They necessarily reflect the food of the elite, and to some extent wealthy townspeople. Figuring out what the poor ate is really the job of the archaeologist. Historians limit themselves to interpreting written sources. There will be little discussion of biographical or bibliographical details, textual variants, or other such matters, which are only of concern to specialists. These pages are devoted to the recipes themselves, discussing what they reveal about the past and how one might reconstruct them today. The ultimate goal here is to learn about people of the past through their food and through tasting a reasonable approximation of it when possible.

# ACKNOWLEDGMENTS

Writing this book has been a remarkable and unusual undertaking. It required three separate sets of skills: training as a professional historian, passion as a cook, and a lifelong interest in languages. It has been extremely gratifying to see these meet in one project. But I would be remiss if I did not acknowledge my gratitude to the many people who made this work possible, not least of which the cookbook authors of the past. This is really their work; my job was merely one of translation and interpretation.

I have drawn on the studies of many scholars who deserve recognition. Foremost are the food historians who created this field: Terence Scully, Constance Heiatt, Jean-Louis Flandrin, Bruno Laurioux, Massimo Montanari, and many others whose names can be found in the bibliography. Thanks also to the many translators and interpreters who have preceded me. Although everything here has been newly translated specifically for this volume, I would sometimes have been lost without the benefit of comparison. Terence Scully, once again; as well as Barbara Santich; Odile Redon; Françoise Sabban and Silvano Serventi and their translator, Edward Schneider; Karen Hess; Jeremy Parzen; Robin Caroll-Mann; James Prescott; Cindy Renfrow and Louise Smithson; and many others deserve thanks.

Enormous thanks also to the publishers and Webmasters who have made these texts available in their original languages: Arnaldo Forni Publishers, Thomas Gloning, the Fons Grewe Web site at Barcelona, Early English Books Online, Prospect Books, and the Southover Press as well as the many Web sites about medieval and Renaissance food, such as those by Greg Lindahl,

Ivan Day, Martha Carlin, Robert Dirks, Henry Notaker, and Mark S. Harris. Thanks also to the countless librarians through the years who have helped me use their collections, at the Vatican, Bodleian Library, Wellcome Library, the Schlesinger Library at Radcliffe, the Folger Shakespeare Library, the Library of Congress, the Bancroft at Berkeley, and as always, the library here at the University of the Pacific.

I would also like to thank my students at Boston University with whom I slogged through many of these recipes in a beautiful demo kitchen. Our success confirmed my suspicion that these cookbook authors should always be trusted. Thanks to my food history class at the University of the Pacific, who at least got to read and critique many of these recipes, if not taste them.

Thanks also to Wendi Schnaufer at Greenwood for signing me on to edit this series, and for once again proving to be a great person to work with.

Thanks to those who were forced to eat many of these things—my family and friends.

And lastly to my dad, to whom this work is dedicated, a man who lived to eat.

# 1

## 🖎 INTRODUCTION

### Medieval, Renaissance, and Elizabethan Cuisine

#### Overview

* Arab and Persian origins of Medieval cuisine
* New ingredients: eggplant, spinach, artichokes, rice, lemons
* Sweet and sour dishes with dried fruits and vinegar
* Heavy use of spices and sugar
* Condiments: almond milk, verjuice, rosewater
* Pounded sauces based on bread or nuts
* Perfumed and colored foods

To a certain extent, the cookery of the High Middle Ages and Renaissance up to the seventeenth century can be considered one unified cuisine. There were of course changes, shifts in taste preference and techniques and many geographical variations. Some ingredients came into fashion or slowly lost favor through this period. But it is nonetheless safe to say that someone eating in the fourteenth century would enjoy much the same basic repertoire of dishes as someone 300 years later. Culinary historians sometimes draw a sharp distinction between medieval and Early Modern food, but there is really no reason to separate the two. The dramatic changes come in the latter seventeenth century, when new techniques and many new foods and drinks—coffee, tea, and chocolate among them—completely revolutionize European foodways. Medieval cuisine, or more properly cuisine of the Late

Middle Ages, as we are really discussing only the last few centuries of the medieval era, was somewhat different from Early Modern cuisine, described in cookbooks published (and printed) after 1500. But there are just as many similarities and continuities connecting the former to the latter. The most significant change is not a different culinary style, but the expanded readership that came with increasing literacy and affordable printed books. In many cases these new readers demanded different kinds of recipes. They could not afford whole porpoises or venison and they wanted recipes for fewer guests and less expensive ingredients. This accounts for many of the changes in European cookery. So too do purely economic factors such as the profitability of dairy cattle and the increasing prevalence of milk products in cuisine after 1500. Purely accidental factors, such as the Portuguese control of the direct spice trade with Asia and their unwillingness to have inferior spices compete with their supply of pepper, meant that some ingredients like chili peppers remained rare in Europe and others, like grains of paradise, gradually disappeared.

There were many changes, as hopefully will become apparent in the recipes themselves in each section. But the discussion that follows can still be taken as relevant to a basic cooking style that prevailed in Europe from the thirteenth century or so all the way through the mid-seventeenth century.

To a great extent this cuisine was inherited from or was an adaptation of Middle Eastern and Persian cuisine. Just as spices, sugar, and dried fruits were bought from Muslim merchants in the eastern Mediterranean, so too were cooking techniques and flavor preferences. This was a cuisine that used many spices together in dense clusters of flavor. Sugar and sour ingredients were often used in combination, along with nuts. Food was often pounded into fine smooth textures. Interestingly, it was this cuisine that was carried with Muslim expansion into India with the Moghuls where it remains today. It was also carried into Spain and flourished under the Abbasid Caliphate of Cordoba after the eighth century. The Muslim settlers brought with them many new ingredients, too; for example, eggplants, spinach, artichokes, rice, lemons, and sugar. In Spanish all these words are descended from Arabic. Even after the Moors, as they are often called, were driven from Spain, their cuisine persisted and was in many ways carried over to the New World. We rarely consider that a molé poblano from Mexico is a distant cousin of the Northern Indian Curry, but the pounded nuts, fruits, and spices are clear rudiments of their common origins. In any case, medieval and Renaissance cuisine were still part of this greater Mediterranean food culture.

## SPICES

The use of spices, which ultimately came from either India and Ceylon in the case of pepper and cinnamon or the Moluccas in what is today Indonesia in the case of cloves and nutmeg, definitely derives from Middle Eastern cookery. It has often been said that it was crusaders in their brief sojourn in the Holy Land as rulers who brought back the taste for spices, dried fruits, and nuts. This is an oversimplification, and in fact there had been contact and trade between Europe and the Middle East prior to the crusades. It was wealth and luxuries of the East that enticed the crusaders in the first place and led them to conquer what is today Israel, Lebanon, and much of the surrounding area as well. Still, it is true that trade increased dramatically after the Crusades and continued despite the collapse of the crusader kingdoms. Venice, with some competition from the Genoese and Pisans, for the most part carried the spices and luxury goods from eastern ports, and of course brought fabulous wealth to Italian merchants.

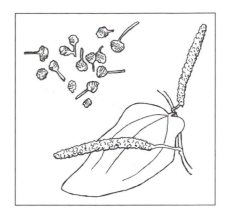

*Cubebs.*

The spice repertoire of the average medieval cook was far more extensive than any used today in the West. Along with those mentioned were cassia, which is a relative of cinnamon and is actually what is sold today in the United States labeled cinnamon, cassia buds, as well as grains of paradise or meleguetta pepper from the West Coast of Africa, long pepper and what was called tailed pepper or cubebs. Cubebs have a tiny pointy spike, but otherwise look like black pepper. All these have very subtly distinctive flavors and aromas. Ginger, always in dried form and ground, was also a major spice as well as its cousin galangal, which is spicier; some modern cookbook authors describe it as mustard-like and pungent. Galangal can be bought in any Southeast Asian grocery store. There was also spikenard, sandalwood (in powder to make foods red), alkanet (a purplish red food dye), and rosewater, which was used in both sweet and savory dishes. These can still be found in Indian or Middle Eastern grocery stores. Sugar of course, then rare and precious, has since become ubiquitous. Like today, it came in many different shades, the whitest being considered the finest.

## UNFAMILIAR FLAVORS AND PRACTICES

A few now-unfamiliar ingredients were also staples in the medieval and Renaissance kitchen. Verjuice is the juice of unripe grapes or sometimes other fruits like crab apples in Northern Europe. It is tart and astringent and a tiny amount goes a long way in livening up almost any dish. If you are not lucky enough to own grape vines or live near vineyards, sour table grapes are similar, but it is preferable to buy verjuice from a manufacturer. Sometimes recipes call for whole unripe grapes as well. Another staple ingredient, sapa, or as it is called today saba in Italy, is cooked-down grape

*Subtleties—flaming peacock.*

must, which is freshly pressed grapes. It is thick syrup, like molasses, that adds a remarkable depth of flavor. It can easily be made by reducing grape juice, preferably freshly squeezed. In consistency it is like good balsamic vinegar, which incidentally is made from a sapa base. Reduced wine, boiled down by one half or more, is another ingredient that is worth making at home and keeping on hand. Good vinegar is indispensable to this cuisine, white wine vinegar is best, although there were also flavored vinegars such as rose and cinnamon, which can be made at home by merely steeping the ingredients in vinegar. Be sure roses have not been treated or sprayed if you intend to consume them.

Although almonds themselves were first imported from the East and later grown throughout the Mediterranean, the use of almond milk appears to have been a European invention. It is essentially blanched and ground almonds soaked in hot water overnight and then strained. It has much the same consistency as coconut milk and is basically made the same way. It was used as a substitute for regular milk during Lent and other fast days, when dairy products were prohibited. It can also be made from pine nuts, which need not be strained, but merely pounded with water added until thick and smooth.

Medieval and Renaissance cooks also enjoyed perfumed food, particularly toward the end of the period covered here. They achieved this with flower waters distilled from rose, orange, and jasmine, but even with actual perfumes such as ambergris and musk. Ambergris is a secretion of whales' intestines washed up on beaches; musk is taken from the scent glands of deer in central Asia. These two substances were used in perfumery into modern times but are almost completely unobtainable today. In cuisine they were generally replaced with vanilla, which some people compared with amber. By the time vanilla was widely available in Europe, such scents had been relegated to sweet foods only, though.

Coloring food was also a favorite practice, especially in the Middle Ages. This could be done with simple ingredients like parsley or beet greens; egg yolks and saffron for yellow; or such extravagant items as silver and gold leaf. These are completely edible but have no flavor. Edible silver leaf can be bought in Indian specialty shops and is called vark. The same goes for ground pearls, which were obviously eaten only for dramatic effect and cost. Vegetable dyes were also used in food, powdered sandalwood for red and later cochineal, made from tiny insects, from the New World.

Fantastic presentation dishes, or "subtleties," as they were called in England, were also favorites at medieval feasts. One could have birds re-sewn into their feathers spewing flames. This trick was done by soaking a wad of cloth in alcohol or camphor, lighting it, and putting it in the bird's beak. The rhyme "four and twenty blackbirds baked in a pie" also has a real culinary origin. An empty shell was baked, the top removed and live birds or even rabbits were put inside, only to escape when the pie was opened and served. These marvels, and especially sugar sculptures depicting classical heroes or battle scenes by the sixteenth century, formed the centerpiece of any great banquet.

## FOOD AND CULTURE

* Fasting: No meat or dairy products during Lent and on Fridays
* Dieting to achieve balance of "humors"
* Manners: elegant, food eaten with fingers
* Forks become more common in the sixteenth century, though not everywhere

## INFLUENCE OF RELIGION

Another crucial factor that influenced all medieval cuisine, and even continued to be followed in many Protestant places after the Reformation, is the restriction on meat and animal products (but not fish) during Lent, usually during Advent, and where strictly observed on all Fridays and sometimes another day of the week as well. In Catholic countries these dietary restrictions were suspended by the Vatican II Council some 40 years ago, though many people still continue to eat fish on Fridays. The significance of these rules for ordinary people in the past was that for a stretch of 40 days between Ash Wednesday and Easter, roughly February to March, no meat could be consumed. For the poor this meant surviving on vegetables, starches, ubiquitous beans, and preserved products such as dried cod or pickled herring. For the wealthy, it meant an entire alternate culinary repertoire based entirely on seafood, usually large and fresh species such as sturgeon or salmon, oysters, and delicate, light-textured freshwater fish. It was no deprivation, but in fact, a welcome change of menus that encouraged experimentation. Many Lenten foods were mock versions of regular meat-day meals. At the end of the fifteenth century, these restrictions appear to have loosened because we suddenly find butter among the ingredients allowed, and in fact used in profusion. After the Protestant Reformation, many regions abandoned the rules altogether, but in England they remained for political reasons, allegedly to support the fishing industry.

## Influence of Health Concerns

Medieval and Renaissance diners were also, perhaps surprisingly, very concerned about their health and diet. They used a system of medicine inherited from the ancient Greeks to evaluate foods to determine what effect the foods would have on the body. This system is known as the theory of humors, or humoral physiology. It supposes that there are four basic fluids that regulate the human body: blood, phlegm, choler, and black bile. Each of these was described, in order, as being hot and moist, cold and moist, hot and dry, and cold and dry. Foods, too, were categorized with these same qualities, so that a cucumber could be called cold and moist and it was thought that eating cucumbers would cause the body to become cold and moist. Regulating food intake, as well as exercise and other external factors, to maintain a mean body temperature and humidity was the aim of the whole system—to achieve *eukrasis* or a balance of humors. Each individual thus had to pay attention to his or her own humoral makeup or "complexion" to decide which foods would be best.

To a certain extent, cuisine was influenced by this system. Foods that were considered too extreme in certain qualities would be cooked with or "tempered" by ingredients that would correct them. A cold phlegmatic food would be corrected by adding hot and dry spices. Equally the texture of a food could be corrected. For example a cold and phlegmatic fish, thought difficult to digest and apt to clog the body's passageways, would be improved with the addition of a sour cutting ingredient such as lemon juice, which would scour the body's passages. Cooking methods too were believed to be correctives, making tough foods more digestible, moistening dry foods with boiling, and drying moist foods with roasting.

Now to what extent these considerations influenced actual recipes is a matter for debate. It is clear that diners regularly ignored physicians' warnings on dietary matters, and physicians consistently complained about how aristocratic diners ignored all dietary rules, particularly in the matter of eating too much food and too many different types of food in one sitting. Physicians did not write these recipes or organize banquet menus. Nonetheless, there are many flavor combinations that appear to have their origin in this dietary logic, and the preference for sharply contrasting sweet and sour flavors appears to have at least some connection to humoral theory. Rather than a direct causal relationship, it seems that, just as today, those people who did follow dietary rules gradually influenced what was being served. Even if cooks often confused the original precepts, they at least hoped they could offer health-conscious guests foods they would eat. The same process occurs today as restaurants and food manufacturers rush to offer Atkins-friendly choices. In a few years there will be another bandwagon to jump on. Then as today, cuisine is influenced by, though rarely originates in, dietary rules. In the end, it is always taste that matters most.

## MANNERS AND TABLEWARE

The topic of manners must be addressed when reconstructing meals of the past. It is true that medieval diners used their fingers to eat, much as people still do throughout the Middle East and Africa. It would be a terrible mistake, though, to assume that they were outright slobs spattered in grease and tossing food around. All evidence suggests that, at least at aristocratic tables, diners were very much concerned with cleanliness and propriety. Napkins were an essential part of the dining experience, though sometimes the tablecloth served the same function. It is perfectly possible to eat daintily with your fingers; in fact it is easier to do so than with cutlery, which distances the person, perhaps unnecessarily, from the tactile pleasure of feeling the food and bringing it to the mouth. Medieval diners also had small dishes of sauces into which they customarily dipped pieces of food that were always carved before being presented. That is, one would never rip apart a huge joint of meat with the bare hands. It would be elegantly placed before the diner, not on a plate but rather on a thin slice of bread with the crust removed, or on a trencher.

*Pitcher.*

There was some cutlery, though—spoons for soups and stews and knives that were often brought to the table by the individual diner and were his personal possession. Sometimes rectangular metal plates were used for service or ceramic plates and bowls. Cups, either metal, ceramic, or increasingly toward the end of the period, glass, were also standard. Normally, however, a glass would be presented, its contents drunk, and then it would be taken away to be cleaned. Increasingly, through the Early Modern period, tableware and serving utensils became opulent objects for display. In fact a large part of a family's vested earnings could be tied up in set of silver. Even down the social scale, such tableware became an important and treasured possession, and increasingly made of pewter or a more durable material rather than wood.

The issue of forks is somewhat more contentious. There are examples of forks stretching through the Middle Ages. These are usually two-pronged utensils, shorter versions of carving forks, that were definitely used to skewer tidbits such as candied fruits in syrup and other foods which one would not want to touch. They were not, however, used as a regular eating utensil until the late fifteenth and early sixteenth centuries in Italy, and thereafter in the

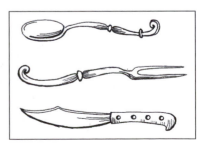

*Utensils.*

rest of Europe. Naturally, the advent of the fork meant that foods could more often be sauced before presentation, or could be presented in ways that were unusual in the Middle Ages. The influence of the fork on the cuisine of Europe is generally underestimated, but it does seem crucial to understanding how cuisine ultimately shifts entirely after the late seventeenth century.

Table manners themselves are also debated among food historians. A sharp contrast between the filthy and disgusting medieval diner and the cultured, elegant Renaissance courtier who would no longer pick his nose or pull half-chewed food from his mouth at the table can no longer be justly made. Merely because manners and etiquette books proliferated in the age of printing does not mean that there were no manners before and that people had absolutely no threshold for revulsion. We can say confidently, however, that more and more people were interested in learning how to behave properly at the table, and that this became a concern for a wider range of people, not merely the wealthiest. What exactly this means and why it happened is still widely debated, but is it is nonetheless clear that eating became a far more regulated and indeed civilized affair in the sixteenth and seventeenth centuries than it was in those preceding. Elegant manners, like clothes, speech, and general deportment, became the mark of a refined and cultured upbringing. Without these, there was no entrance into elite society.

## Basic Ingredients and Recipe Types

European elites ate a wide variety of foods from countless species of plants and animals. Cookbooks tend to focus on meat because it was the most expensive and prestigious of foods, and the most complicated to cook, but there are many recipes for vegetables and lowly starches as well. These, of course, made up the bulk of ordinary people's diet, but aristocrats and wealthy townspeople, the readers of cookbooks, were not above eating them. Every meal at every level of society included bread and wine, or beer in the north—even in the morning.

The ingredients that were available and commonly eaten in Europe changed very little between 1300 and 1600. This might seem surprising given that many new foods were discovered in the Americas after 1492. Most of these were grown only as botanical specimens and it is not until the very end of the seventeenth century that recipes appear that include items like tomatoes and peppers. Even those foods that were adopted in certain regions, such as corn and new species of beans and squash, made no appearance in cookbooks and we can only guess how they were cooked. Corn was probably ground and boiled like other grains as a porridge or polenta. New World beans were cooked exactly like favas and black-eyed peas. Potatoes appear very rarely, mostly in the British Isles, and even then it is probably sweet potatoes rather than white potatoes from Peru that they were using. Turkeys, on the other hand were accepted almost immediately, but it is not always clear if authors are referring to the American species or the African guinea fowl, which often went by the same name.

The recipes in each section beginning with the next chapter are organized either by major food type or by type of dish. That is, soups are gathered together, as are desserts, dishes based on fowl, vegetables, and so on. It is important to remember, though, that courses were not organized as in modern meals. Cold foods tended to start a meal and sweets came near the end, but otherwise there is little in common with the way we eat today.

## COLD FOODS

Meals did often begin with cold foods, but these rarely appear in medieval and Renaissance cookbooks. This is either because they were purchased or perhaps more importantly, they were not included among the responsibilities of the cook and kitchen, which provided hot prepared dishes. That is, foods that required no cooking were often supplied by a separate officer, the credenziero in Italy, the butler, pantler, or various other officials elsewhere. Most important among these is bread. Everywhere, throughout the centuries covered by this book, bread would have been present at the table. The wealthiest people ate thin crustless slices of white bread, which were presented ceremoniously on a long flat blade and served as a plate onto which other foods could be placed, eaten daintily with the fingers, of course. By the late fifteenth and sixteenth centuries, plates began to replace the bread trencher, but bread was still always present. Nobles ate fine soft white bread or manchet as it was called in England, while ordinary people ate darker coarser bread, the amount of bran increasing among poorer families. In the north rye bread was common, or sometimes a combination of wheat and rye—called maslin.

Along with bread there was also, in Italy, an entire course or several courses devoted only to cold foods, what we would call appetizers and palate cleansers. They usually came at the start of a meal, but often between courses as well, though in France an *entremet*, as it was called, was often a hot savory dish between other courses. The only thing these foods had in common was that they were cold; they could be made of meat, fowl, fish, pastry, and even sweets. For example, a typical first cold course might consist of prosciutto, a cold chicken pie, pickled fish, salads, sugar sculptures, and so on. This was not the pattern everywhere, and in fact in England, the custom was to start with roasts and heavier foods and move toward lighter ones at the end of the meal. In any case, there were many cold foods in medieval and Renaissance cuisine and not surprisingly, the recipes for them are comparatively scarce.

## Soups

Soups were without doubt one of the major mainstays of the popular diet throughout Europe for the entire period covered in this book, and certainly long after as well. The poorer the family, the greater their dependence on soup—in which could be put any type of vegetable, grain, or meat. In fact, it was often customary to just keep a soup pot over the hearth, continually adding ingredients at hand, indefinitely. Beans could be added, cabbage and leafy greens, practically anything. Soups were also eaten any time of day, in the morning in the rustic farmhouse, or as an evening's supper, made of left over ingredients. Soups also varied according to thickness, and recipes usually distinguish between thin bouillons and broths and thicker pottages—or what in Italian were called *minestre,* as in the modern word *minestrone.* Also, many of these recipes are what was called "sops"—the ancestor of our word *soup* and the meal soupper or supper. The sop is a slice of bread at the bottom of the bowl that soaks up the liquid, making it a more substantial dish, appropriate for a late evening meal or a large first course. The recipes that have survived are naturally intended for wealthier households and were made for a single meal, but were usually based on a bouillon which would be on hand as a kitchen staple. It is best, naturally, to make a broth or stock yourself at home—and it is fairly easy to do, though time-consuming. Essentially a chicken or beef with bones is boiled slowly with aromatic vegetables such as onions, celery, and carrots for several hours and is then strained. There were also vegetable-based broths, even one based on dried peas. These were used as bases for soups and other dishes. We can never know, however, exactly what went into these bases, and cookbook authors merely assume they will be available in every good kitchen. For modern cooks canned broth is a quick alternative. Bouillon cubes are usually too salty and hide the flavor of almost any ingredient.

## Meat

Throughout the entire period covered by this book, meat was invariably the centerpiece of any formal meal, with the exception of fast days. Recipes in cookbooks, designed for wealthy readers, always focused on meat. This is because meat was usually the most complicated food to prepare and the one on which cooks lavished their greatest attention. It does not follow, though, that medieval and Renaissance diners only ate meat and nothing else. Nonetheless, it is still hard to deny that meat is what interested people most. Counter to our impression that noble diners preferred large whole animals roasted on a spit, and preferably huge hunted beasts like boar or venison, most recipes call for meat to be cut up during the cooking process, if not pounded into a smooth puree. It may also be that simple roasts required no recipe and therefore it is the more complicated creations that appear in cookbooks.

Among the meats, wild animals were favored for their intense gamey flavor, which matched well with spices and piquant sauces. But domestic meats were also very common, pork and beef, but also lamb and mutton (from mature sheep), as well as kid, or baby goat. There were regional differences, as well as changes in preference over time. In general, beef was more common in Northern Europe, while southern Europeans tended to depend more heavily on younger animals such as lamb and veal. These are not hard-and-fast rules, though, and most cookbooks offer at least a few recipes for every meat available.

Some historians have also stressed that the late fourteenth and fifteenth centuries were the heyday of meat eating in Europe for all social classes. Interestingly, in the Late Middle Ages, a period of relatively low population following the first outbreak of bubonic plague in 1348, meat was relatively inexpensive. That is, due to general economic prosperity among those fortunate to survive, a greater proportion of the average household budget could be spent on meat. This situation changed gradually in the sixteenth century as the population grew and more money had to be spent on basic and inexpensive staples such as grains, legumes, and vegetables. In wealthy households, meat remained a central feature, though, and even a symbol of status. Increasingly it was only the rich who could afford to serve meat at every meal, except in Catholic countries when it was forbidden during Lent and other fast days.

## FOWL

Chickens, wild fowl, and even waterfowl such as ducks, heron, swan, and crane were considered among the most elegant of all foods that appeared in medieval and Renaissance banquets. Even tiny little birds such as thrushes and fig peckers were perennial favorites. In the case of wild birds, these were captured by falcons, one of the favorite pastimes of European nobles. The white flesh of domestic fowl was also highly appreciated and was thought to be easily digested. Capons, or castrated male roosters, were considered the lightest of fowl, and along with pheasant,

*King at feast.*

perfectly apt for delicate palates. Peacock, especially served resewn into its feathers, was a standard presentation dish as well. Practically every bird was eaten in some form—roasted, pounded, and placed into pies or sautéed with other ingredients. By the sixteenth century, turkeys also appeared and took their place alongside other domestic fowl.

## FISH AND SEAFOOD

Fish were among the most important food items in medieval and Renaissance households, both poor and wealthy, primarily because of the restrictions on meat and animal products during Lent and on various fasting days throughout the calendar. Except for people who lived near the sea or near freshwater lakes, fresh fish, because of the demand, were generally too expensive for anyone but the rich. It is also clear that certain species were preferred on elegant tables, sturgeon above all, but also eels and a variety of light-textured and white-fleshed fish, such as flounder and carp. In most households, and especially those inland, they would have eaten dried or salted cod, pickled herrings, or sardines.

Fish was normally cooked, whether boiled or roasted, with ingredients thought to dry its excessively moist and therefore unhealthy flesh. Acidic ingredients were also thought to help cut through the "gluey humors" and thus make them more digestible. Using lemon juice on fish may originate in this medicinal logic. Otherwise, cooking fish was quite different from today, and rather than accentuate the flavor with sauces based on fish stock, the idea was to add sharp-tasting ingredients that would contrast with the flavor of the fish. Dairy products were rarely used with fish, for the very reason that they are both cold and moist and this was thought to create a dangerous combination, likely to upset a person's humoral balance.

## VEGETABLES

Vegetables were nearly as important as fish for fast days, and of course the poorer the household the greater proportion of the average meal would be made up of vegetables such as cabbage and turnips as well as various legumes. They do not figure prominently in some cookbooks, except when baked in pies. Presumably cooks only needed directions for complicated procedures, but not for simple preparations. The exception to this is in Italy and Spain, where vegetables of all kinds were highly esteemed. Nonetheless, many vegetables do not appear in cookbooks because they were served as salads or were prepared simply. This is the case with artichokes and asparagus, which were among the most highly prized vegetables. In Italy they were also served separate from the main courses in their own course as "fruits." The recipes for vegetables that do exist, in any case, show that they were not regarded as lowly food and were eaten everywhere in Europe, even in places where meat took center stage in a meal.

## STARCHES

Although bread provided the bulk of starchy calories for most Europeans, there were also other dishes commonly made of wheat, barley, and other grains. In England the pudding was standard. This was not a sweet creamy dessert, but a starch or in fact any ingredient, cooked in an intestine or stomach. Pasta featured prominently in Italian cooking throughout these centuries and everywhere boiled whole or crushed grains were a staple. Rice was something relatively new, usually cooked with sugar, but eaten as a side dish nonetheless.

## EGGS

Eggs were possibly the most ubiquitous food in European cuisine of the past and were eaten by people of every social class at any meal. Eggs were never considered common or pedestrian, but rather one of the most healthy and convenient foods available. They were often given to sick people as a restorative as well. Furthermore, as a seemingly exhaustible resource, hens in a coop must have been an extremely common sight, far more common than a chicken on the table. Eggs feature prominently in cooking, as a thickener for sauces and as the preferred binding agent for stuffing and fillings, and egg yolks were sometimes added just to make a dish golden and richer. They are also included in many pies and tarts—relatives of what we

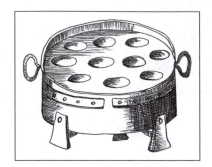

*Pan for frying eggs.*

would call custards and quiches. Some cookbooks include eggs in practically every dish. The repertoire of egg recipes was no less extensive than our own, perhaps even more so. Old food reference books even distinguish between subtle differences in the texture of cooked eggs, from "drinkable," to soft-boiled or "trembling," to hard-boiled, not to mention poached, fried, scrambled, coddled, stirred into soups, roasted and even threaded onto a spit and cooked before a fire. Even more amazing is a recipe that instructs how to make one egg as big as twenty that involves cooking the yolks in a bladder and then placing that in the center of the whites in a larger vessel to cook.

Along with eggs, dairy products were an important staple in European cooking. This was particularly the case in regions where cattle were raised. Dairy products were featured more prominently in cookbooks in the sixteenth century and thereafter, probably because cattle rearing became especially profitable as the population grew, demand increased, and it became more cost-effective to leave land for pasture than to rent it to tenants. Cheese is found in recipes throughout the late Middle Ages and Renaissance, and some cheeses were already known by name, parmigiano being the most famous, but there were many others as well. Another reason why dairy products became more prevalent, according to some historians, is because cooks paid less attention to physicians who warned that hard cheese can be difficult to digest and that milk mixed with meats or seafood can corrupt inside the body, causing stomachaches and various other ailments. Whatever the cause, the use of cream in cooking was unusual until the very end of the period covered here.

## SAUCES

Sauces were an integral and essential part of the art of cookery in the past. Sometimes they were poured over a dish before service but often were presented in several little bowls scattered around the table that diners could choose from to suit their taste. Unlike today, sauces were rarely based on butter or cream. More often they were sour vinegar– or verjuice-based, thickened with bread crumbs and intended to contrast in flavor with the main dish. They were almost always heavily spiced as well, or laden with garlic and herbs. Rarely were they made from the same ingredient as the food being sauced, and the stock-based sauce thickened with a combination of flour and butter or a roux is an invention of the latter seventeenth century and is nowhere to be found in medieval or Renaissance kitchens. Thick, fat-based sauces like mayonnaise and hollandaise were also missing. Sometimes a sauce would be based on drippings, often from a roasting fowl or joint of meat, or broth would be included, but to these were often added spices and sour ingredients along with sugar. So these sauces were very different from what we think of as gravy today. Fortunately, most sauces were very simple to make and required a last-minute combination of a few staple ingredients. Some, however, were closer to what we think of as jellies and jams, sweetened and fruit-based and often more like an Indian chutney than a European sauce. Cranberry sauce with turkey is perhaps a remnant of an archaic type of sauce, for which American ingredients have been substituted. One might say, though, that Americans eat this more as a side dish than a sauce. Mint sauce with lamb is also a descendant of these sauces, as is an Italian pesto.

The change from medieval to modern sauces was not abrupt, though. Butter increasingly made its way into European cookery in the sixteenth century. Spices slowly went out of favor thereafter and sugar gradually replaced many of the more sour sauces. But it does seem that when comparing medieval sauces with modern ones, they are startlingly different. For example, we rarely add coloring to our sauces, sweet spices like cinnamon and cloves we prefer in desserts, and a sweetened sauce on fish leaves us perplexed. These flavors will seem very foreign to us, but they are certainly worth trying, especially since you can make several and avoid those you might not like.

## FRUIT

Recipes for fruit appear much less frequently in old cookbooks than those for meat, fowl, and other ingredients. This is partly because most fruits were usually consumed fresh and needed no recipe. In Italy in particular there was an entire course dedicated just to fruit, although this was broadly defined to include items such as olives and artichokes. When recipes are offered they are usually for fruit pies, which could be eaten anywhere in a meal, or for conserves and candied fruit, which normally came at the very end of the meal. Fruit was also often cooked with other foods, raisins or prunes along with meats, grapes with fowl, and in many other surprising and interesting combinations.

Wealthy diners definitely did eat and appreciate a wide variety of fruits, even though physicians often warned against the dangers of eating too many fruits, or taking them in the wrong part of a meal. In fact, a long-standing argument among physicians concerned when to eat such corruptible fruits as melons and peaches. Some contended that at the beginning of a meal the fruit

*Medlars.*

would be forced into the liver and veins by other food before it was fully digested, causing clogs in the body and fevers. Others insisted that fruits eaten at the end of the meal would float on top of other foods, corrupting and sending noxious fumes up to the head. This is why they generally recommended drinking wine or other alcoholic beverages with fruit, to act as a preservative in the stomach.

Despite these warnings, it is clear that people ate fruits whenever they pleased, both at the beginning and toward the end of the meal, just before sweets. They also consumed an extremely wide variety of fruits, many of which are relatively unfamiliar today. Small sour and wild varieties such as azaroles, medlars, and various berries were cooked or made into jelly. Dried fruits such as dates, raisins, and figs, along with citrus, at least in the north, were usually imported and were considered among the most valuable and elegant of foods.

## SWEETS

Sweet foods that we would normally eat only at the end of a meal or as a snack were customarily eaten throughout the meal in the Middle Ages and Renaissance—as well as at the end. This explains why sweet dishes are scattered throughout this book. Not only was sugar added to foods that we would probably not consider edible sweetened, but sugar was one the most valuable and desired products in elite cookery and by the sixteenth century was practically ubiquitous. A good proportion of recipes in most cookbooks were sweetened regardless of the main ingredient. There were nonetheless many sweet foods served at the end of a meal that filled exactly the same function as desserts do today. Comfits, or small candies such as sugar-coated spices or preserved fruits, were very fashionable to close a banquet. Confusingly, many of these fruit conserves we would expect to find at the breakfast table.

## DRINKS

References to drinks are rare in cookbooks of the Middle Ages and Renaissance. This makes sense as the most common beverages required no cooking and were totally outside the responsibilities of the cook. A separate wine steward normally took charge of wines and oversaw how they were mixed with water. Wine was the beverage of choice for elite households everywhere, especially sweet imported wines from the Mediterranean, such as malmsey or malvasia and sack—what we today call sherry. Many of these wines are still made today, Madeira being a good example of a wine made much the same way as it was in the past. There were also local wines of every color, made on estates and monasteries throughout Europe, and in fact there were far more wineries in Northern Europe than there are today. Most of the major wine regions of Europe were exactly the same as those still producing wines. For example, Bordeaux already had a brisk export trade in wine. Some vineyards in Italy, Spain, and France had been producing wine since antiquity.

Water was not typically drunk by those who could afford to do otherwise. There is a very good reason for this: most water was polluted and could carry a whole array of pathogens. There were no efficient purification systems, and most people got water directly from a well or running stream. Alcoholic beverages were much safer to drink as the antiseptic property of alcohol kills many germs. This may be why wine was usually mixed with water—not to make the wine weaker, but to make the water safer. People certainly understood the dangers of drinking water, and even though they knew nothing about germs, physicians recommended that water be boiled.

Ale and, by the fifteenth century, beer flavored with hops were also common in Northern Europe. So too was cider in various pockets throughout Europe—in the west of England, in Normandy, and in places in Spain. Cider, made from small hard and astringent apples, had a relatively low alcoholic content and was mostly consumed by common folk rather than nobles. Mead or various flavored versions of honey wine also came in and out of fashion throughout the period covered here, and recipes do sometimes appear in guides to household management and other culinary literature.

Far more frequently, though, there are recipes for what we might call flavored wines. Contrary to today when the idea of adding anything to wine (especially water) seems abhorrent, in the past, spices and herbs enhanced the value of wine. Mulled wine is the sole surviving descendant of literally dozens of flavored aromatic wines of the Middle Ages.

The late Middle Ages also witnessed the introduction of distillation, and a whole separate subgenre of how to make and flavor alcohol flourished, especially after the advent of printing. The ancestors of many of the liqueurs and spirits found on shelves today were already made by the sixteenth century. Alcohol flavored with juniper berries, a rudimentary gin, grain-based vodka in Eastern Europe, and not long after the discovery of the New World, rum, were all eventually common drinks. Aqua Vitae—or the water of life (in Gaelic *usque beatha* or whiskey) was the first distilled spirit, made from wine, and was used primarily as medicine, but eventually recreationally as well. In Dutch it was called *brantwijn*—from which we get the word *brandy.* In culinary literature, however, more typical are sweetened aperitifs and cordials, flavored with herbs, flowers, fruit, and even exotic spices.

The recipes for drinks in each section can be made with de-alcoholized wine if one likes, or with juice. As it is illegal to distill alcohol at home, recipes for spirits have not been included, only those that require adding flavorings or cooking wine. Also included are a few recipes for correcting faults in wine, apparently something that happened frequently enough to warrant comment.

## MEAL STRUCTURE

The recipes in each section are arranged chronologically in subsections based on the prime ingredient, rather than their place in the meal. This is because, unlike today, the meal structure was not based on a progression of different kinds of recipes from appetizers to soup to fish to meat to desserts and coffee. One would often find savory and sweet dishes in every course. Or an entire course would be composed of roasted dishes, whether made of meat, fowl, or fish. Pies could be found in any and every course. Fruits and vegetables were often served just before the end in a fruit course. In some places, particularly in Italy, hot and cold courses would alternate, or there would be a table or credenza set with cold foods, what are today called antipasti, such as cold cuts, cheeses, pastries, and olives. The meal structure actually underwent a very subtle and complicated development over time and differed greatly from place to place. It is probably best today to serve everything at once, or with a larger group to divide into two courses with boiled and sauced food in the first and roast food in the second course, but keeping in mind that there should be several different types of food in every course so that diners have a choice. Although there were no desserts per se since sweet dishes appeared throughout the meal, it was customary, after the fruit course, to serve comfits or candies, preserves, and spices. These were thought to improve the digestion and breath, and of course they tasted good.

To reconstruct a typical medieval or Renaissance meal it is most important to remember that food was served in what we would call family style, on platters placed on the table and never arranged on individual plates in the kitchen. There should be one or several individuals whose job it is just to carve and serve the food. In Renaissance Italy, everything would have been carved. Even small fruits and tiny fowl were carved in mid air perched on a fork. Everywhere the carver was an important position. There should also be separate pages to fill drinks or offer the basin to wash hands ceremoniously. A scalco, or what we would call head waiter or maitre d', who was certainly not a menial servant but rather an aristocratic member of the household who organized the entire banquet, would place the food on the plates of individual diners. Toward the sixteenth century, these officers of the mouth proliferated and the ceremonies of eating became increasingly complex, but never would an aristocratic diner be expected to serve him- or herself. Noble equals were honored by being given the privilege of doing so.

*Carver.*

The time for a grand meal will also strike us as rather odd. The largest meal of the day, dinner, was eaten around 11 a.m. or noon. It gradually shifted later and later in the day until finally, long after the period studied here, it was eaten at night. In the Middle Ages and Renaissance, however, the evening meal is supper and is generally a smaller affair and with fewer courses than dinner. Banquets, on the other hand, were special occasions and they could really take place any time of day, but people were generally accustomed to eat their larger meal early in the day. Laborers might eat a very small meal in the morning, but breakfast was not common. Lunch was unheard of. In some places smaller snacks—forming a meal called merenda, taken late in the afternoon, might hold people until the evening.

Assuming the meal is not during Lent or on a fast day, each course, anywhere from two or three to twelve or more, should contain both flesh and fish, pies and pastries, and always bread—either in thin slices with the crust removed, or rolls. A typical menu from the sixteenth century looked liked this. There is a certain logical progression, but certainly very unlike modern service. In creating your own banquet, of course, recipes can be taken from any of the chapters that follow. As in most banquets, there is a set scene made out of food arranged before diners arrive. In the menu that follows, it is figures of Hercules made out of sugar, fighting the mythical hydra made out of pheasant with seven heads attached, and a bull made from a baby goat with silver horns. Also, there were eight separate plates of every dish described. That probably meant a plate for each table of about six or eight people, so this was a grand meal for maybe as many as sixty people. Even if one prepared such a meal for one table, it is obvious that incredibly vast amounts of food are required.[1]

## ✦ APRIL

Banquet made by the Illustrious Signor Count Ludovico Manfredi, for most Serene Princes and Excellent Lords, Knights, and Ladies, with eight plates, furnished with two tablecloths, with beautiful paintings and strewn with flowers, in the evening.

## First Cold Course

Pastries of goat, with a Hercules of pastry on top

Endive salad with balls of cheese

Salad of sprouts with halved hard boiled eggs

Lettuce with dabs of caviar

Slices of beef pie with slices of citron

Aspic [meat-based gelatin] with partridge meat underneath

Flaky little pastries filled with blancmange [pounded chicken with spices, sugar, and almond milk]

Beef tongue in long slices with pitted olives

Pastry roses filled with marzipan [sweetened almond paste]

Peacock in white sauce stuck with bacon

Boar's Head covered in pomegranate seeds

Salami split lengthwise and sliced with gilded citron leaves interspersed

Prosciutto julienned over fried bread, and slices of boiled prosciutto [Italian ham]

Capons in pastry with white sauce, stuck with cinnamon sticks and gilded myrtle leaves

Cold quails on a spit interspersed with yellow sausage

Slices of pork loin soaked in vinegar with toast

Cherry sauce

## Second Course, hot and all roasted

Peacock roasted covered with fried oysters, with oranges

2 Pheasants per plate covered with slices of fried squid, with lemons

Kid covered with golden pears fried

Shoulder of lamb

Beef chuck roast larded, and in caul fat [net-like visceral lining of a pig]

Sweet foccaccia of flaky pastry filled with beaten turtledove

## Third Course again roasted

Partridges six per plate with slices of lemon

Tarts of apple

Tongue of beef larded with sauce

Figpeckers with lemon

Young Turkeys, two per plate

Little pastries of minced capon

Veal loin with oranges

Leg of goat with garlic and rosemary

Bastard Sauce [spicy sauce based on sweet wine]

Flaky pastries, empty

Veal liver, larded, cut in mouthfuls with sauce

Cow's Belly larded, but first boiled, on a spit, with sauce

Fritters of blancmange

Large Olives

### Fruit Course

Honeyed Milk
Wafer cones
Tarts of black lupins [relative of beans]
Quinces hollowed and filled with sugar, cinnamon and baked in an oven
Truffles
Chestnuts
Cooked pears in slices with fulignati [wine sauce?]
Raw pears
Apples, two sorts
Cheese from Lodi [city near Milan, Italy]
Cardoons [stalks related to artichokes]
Fresh grapes
Pitted olives

### Hands washed and towel dried, then present the confections, first seven labors of Hercules in Sugar that appear on plates

Cherry Jelly in little majolica vases
Citron halves in syrup
Artichokes in sugar, dry
Pistachio biscuits
Filled Portuguese flans [egg custards]
White Portuguese cannelloni [tube-shaped pastry], gilded
Little red cannelloni, silvered
Boxes of quince paste cut into mouthfuls with whole cinnamon sticks
Boxes of marmalade
Almond Comfits [candy-coated almonds]
Little Marzipan gnocchi [dumplings]
Anise
Little mallets [presumably for breaking the sculptures before eating them]
Napkins and knives
Toothpicks

## FINDING A RECIPE

To help the reader find the type of recipe desired, three lists have been included in the front matter. The first is a List of Recipes as they appear in the book, organized by time period and by type of food. Next is a List of Recipes by Country, further categorized by time period. The third is a List of Recipes for Special Occasions, grouped by novelty dishes, holidays and fast days, and illness.

## GETTING STARTED—EQUIPMENT

* mortar and pestle
* sieve or strainer
* roasting spit
* cast-iron or earthenware pots
* standard cooking utensils

None of the recipes in this book require expensive or complicated equipment. There are, however, two, perhaps three, special items that were absolutely central to the medieval and Early Modern kitchen. A mortar and pestle was used in a vast array of dishes and to make almost all sauces. The type typically carried today in kitchenware shops is significantly smaller than a medieval cook would have used and holds maybe a cup or two of ingredients that can be comfortably pounded. Wooden mortars are cheap and work well but tend to pick up flavors, especially spices and garlic, often used in the recipes. Marble is a much better choice, and so are stone mortars. A huge, rough-hewn stone mortar can be purchased in an Indian shop for about $15. Large, smooth Thai mortars are also a good option as are Mexican ones, though an authentic *metate* is made of porous stone that is too soft for serious pounding and is really intended for avocados, tomatoes, and such. The medieval cook would have used a brass mortar that holds maybe a gallon or more—large enough to hold a whole chicken or a good handful of spices. These are practically indestructible and are still made today but are extremely expensive; even a small brass mortar can cost a fortune. In place of a mortar a food processor should work.

The other item essential to getting started is a sieve. In the past this would have been a round hoop strung with horsehair or coarse fabric through which foods were pressed, creating a smooth puree. This sort of sieve is still used today in classic French kitchens and is called a *tamis*; it is usually strung with a fine metal or nylon mesh screen. A food mill makes a good substitute—it is a round metal container with a perforated disk at the bottom and a crank that passes food, but not seeds and larger pieces of food, through the holes. A conical "china hat" sieve or a regular fine mesh sieve also works well. Food can be pushed with a spoon, the back of a ladle, or a special wooden cone that fits inside. For pureeing liquids, a blender is an acceptable substitute and even an immersion blender works well. But both the texture and even flavor are a little different using a mortar and sieve, and the labor involved is really minimally greater than using a machine—and of course it gives you a better idea of historical cooking methods.

Last among unusual implements, a proper spit is something truly invaluable. A hand-turned spit, a long metal rod onto which food is skewered and held in place with pins or brackets, should be placed next to rather than over a moderate fire, either in front of the fireplace or outside beside a fire pit. To test some of the recipes in this book, a mechanical turnspit that needs winding every 15 minutes was used. It can be purchased from http://www.spitjack.com. It comes with extensive instructions and is well worth the hefty price. It is a little tricky to position properly in front of a standard fireplace, but the fiddling is well worth the time. A drip pan must be used beneath, both for basting and to catch the drippings, which can be used as a gravy base—though this is more typical of cookery after the period covered here. The flavor of food properly "roasted" before a fire cannot be described; there is really nothing like it. A cooking fire, ideally made with hardwood like apple or oak, should be

*Woman with mortar and pestle.*

started a good hour or two before one intends to cook. The flames are thus very hot and steady. A rotisserie on a barbecue can come close, but cooking directly over a fire is somewhat different. Grilling, a technique that was indeed used in the past, is also quite different. The food cooks much quicker, and of course leaves grill marks and charred parts. There are a few excellent books that can get you started with hearth cooking if you are so inclined—William Rubel's *The Magic of Fire* is highly recommended. For most recipes an oven will also work, though naturally the flavor will be much simpler and less interesting.

Cooking with pots over a hearth is also something worth trying if one takes proper precautions. Tin-lined copper was preferred in wealthy households by the sixteenth century, and these can still be found in high-end cookware shops, but they are very expensive and difficult to maintain. Cast iron is cheap, sturdy, and completely authentic. The only real difficulty is getting started with seasoning the pans. Manufacturers, such as Lodge, provide directions and even sell preseasoned cookware. Still it is very important to remember to never leave cast iron wet or it will rust, especially in the first year or so of use. Wipe it completely dry and rub with oil or bacon fat before storing. Second, and this will clash with everything you have been told about cleanliness, soap should never come near cast iron. Use a scrubby sponge to remove stuck-on particles of food, but never soap, which removes the seasoning. Cooking over a fire really helps develop a shiny surface, which after a year or so works better than the best teflon nonstick pan.

To cook over a fire, or more typically over hot coals, one needs other kinds of equipment—little tripods or spiders on which to place pots or pots with legs designed exactly for this purpose—such as a Dutch oven—lifting irons or tongs, notched stands for iron

*Pig roasting.*

spits, and if one really want to be authentic, a large crane arm built into the hearth so that pots or a cauldron can be suspended directly over the fire and swung out for tasting or serving. In many historic houses across the country one can see proper hearth cooking in action, and it is really not very different from campfire cookery except that it is done inside. Moreover, colonial American cooking technology is not terribly different from that used in the Middle Ages and Renaissance. Colonial Williamsburg in Virginia and Plimoth Plantation and Old Sturbridge Village in Massachusetts, as well as dozens of other historic sites, are great places to see hearth cooking in action.

If you choose not to go this route, of course any standard pots and pans work fine on conventional gas or electric stoves. But there is one type of cookware definitely worth trying if you can: earthenware. Low-fired pottery, although it breaks if dropped, is cheap and surprisingly sturdy both in the oven and directly over a gas flame, or in fact in the hearth. Be sure to use low-fired pottery intended for use as cookware, not decorative pots. Pottery cookware usually has a clear glaze only on the inside. High-fired stoneware and porcelain, although much stronger, are more thoroughly vitrified, i.e., more like glass, and therefore shatter with sudden temperature changes, both in the oven and even sometimes in the freezer. Earthenware, however, expands and contracts easily and conducts heat nicely. Pottery cooking vessels can be bought at Spanish food shops, and online at The Spanish Table (http://www.spanishtable.com) and Tienda.com (http://www.tienda.com), or at some Italian cookware shops. These vessels were often called for specifically in old cookbooks, for acidic sauces that might react with iron pots. Furthermore, most poorer households used earthenware vessels for all their cooking. Both covered casseroles and simple round straight-edged pans without handles are a delight to cook with. So too is a little pipkin—a rotund pot with three legs and a handle. If you know someone who can make pottery, the possibilities are endless—but again, to use over direct flame, the clay must be low-fired earthenware with a clear food-safe glaze inside. For cooking in the oven, stoneware and porcelain casseroles are fine.

## OVENS

For all recipes that require baking, a regular oven can be used. Baking was actually not a very common technique and was mostly used for bread and pastries, especially in wealthy households. Something important to remember is that bread would always be baked in a fairly hot oven before other foods. This was done by building a fire directly in the oven, which was either a brick or stone box next to the hearth or a free-standing, dome-shaped structure outside. When sufficiently heated, the ashes would be swept out and the floor of the oven swabbed out with a wet cloth on a pole. Bread would be baked first for an hour or more, and later pies or pastries or other foods would go in. What this means is that when an oven is called for, it would be fairly low in temperature. Sometimes a cookbook author will specify to use a hot oven or use a moderate oven. When unspecified, take as a rule baking between 325 and 350 degrees. To start, the oven might have been as hot as 800 degrees, which is how hot a proper pizza oven should be. Bread would have been baked cooler than this. The bricks would cool over time, and then other foods would be cooked at lower temperatures. However, if using an oven as a substitute for roasting, it is best to use higher temperatures, perhaps 400 to 425 degrees. A wooden or metal peel—a long pole with a sturdy flat end—was used for placing bread or other foods in the oven.

## OTHER KITCHEN TOOLS

Other equipment used—and many of these items are illustrated in Bartolomeo Scappi's *Opera*—might have included a small-holed grater—both for grating bread used as a sauce thickener, but also for spices such as nutmeg or for cheese. Scappi also used a variety of fluted pastry wheels to give decorative edges to crusts. Ladles and cooking spoons are naturally indispensable, and modern versions are fine. Olive wood spoons are preferable for their rusticity, though they are harder to maintain than stainless steel. Plastic seems completely out of place in historic recipes. A large mesh basket skimmer is also useful for frying, as is a whisk for beating egg whites or whipping cream, though this was common only at the end of the period covered here.

By the stovetop it is also handy to have a small dish of coarse sea salt for seasoning by the pinch, a pepper grinder—which is always preferable to preground pepper—and a few small mortars for pounding spices, garlic and herbs, or whatever. As for other utensils, tongs, spatulas, peelers, and the like are inauthentic, but if you are accustomed to them there is no real reason for them to be banished for historic cooking.

The cook of the past would have owned and used as many knives as we use today. For example, one illustration in Scappi shows no fewer than 14 different shapes, for cutting tarts or pastry, opening oysters, dismembering joints. Two-pronged forks for holding meats were also essential, especially when carving, which was often done while holding the bird or roast up in the air on a fork. There were, in fact, entire books devoted to carving. String and pins for sewing fowl or tying up roasts are also necessary and are specifically called for in many recipes. Barding needles are somewhat harder to find. They were used for attaching long strips of fat to the exterior of roasts by threading them in and out of the surface. Attaching smaller strips through holes and knotting them works well too, and this procedure is what is often depicted in still-life paintings.

Scappi's book also illustrates what is called a mezzaluna in Italy today. It is a curved blade with two handles rocked back and forth to chop herbs or other ingredients. He also used rolling pins, one ingeniously made with sharp ridges for cutting noodles out of a sheet of dough. The illustrations even show a syringe, used for filling pastries among other things. None of these is necessary today, though, and most likely cooks in the Middle Ages had never used the range of equipment available to Scappi.

## FINDING SPICES

Apart from the basic repertoire of kitchen utensils, a few medieval and Renaissance ingredients are definitely worth hunting down. Since almost anything can be bought online nowadays, a simple search for items such as "grains of paradise" or "cubebs" will bring results. They are even available for sale on Amazon.com. Francesco Sirene, a spicer in Canada, as well as The Goat in the Garden, in California, are reputable suppliers. They also carry drinking vessels, spoons, books and other medieval paraphernalia. These are their Web sites: http://www.silk.net/sirene/ and http://www.thegoatinthegarden.com/.

*Grains of paradise.*

## SAFETY

A final note about kitchen and hearth safety is in order. When cooking before an open flame, it is always best to wear long pants and sleeves, heavy boots, and thick, fireproof mitts that are intended for serious barbecuing. Because one must necessarily reach into the hearth to remove lids (always with a lid lifter or fireplace tongs) or to shift entire pots over the coals or away from the fire, one can never err on the side of over-precaution. One of the most common household accidents of the past was being burned while cooking. It is also best to start off with one pot or one food roasting on a spit. In the past rearranging several items was key to cooking success, and it may be that cooking an entire dinner on a hearth takes years of experience. In the past, it was also often the case that hot coals would be removed and placed in a brazier or

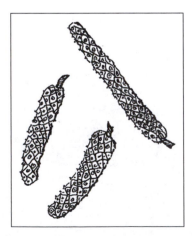

*Long pepper.*

in a flat space near the fire. Modern fireplaces are much smaller as a rule, which makes this impossible, but it can be done if cooking outdoors.

Before a hearth and even in a modern kitchen, supervision for young cooks is absolutely essential, and so is dealing carefully with raw ingredients, especially meat and poultry. It is always best to keep one cutting board for fruits and vegetables and another for meat and poultry—which should be promptly and thoroughly washed in hot soapy water after each use. Hands should also be washed. Apart from the risk of cross-contamination, some smells, particularly of onions and garlic, should be kept away from other produce, so it seems best to use the meat board for these. A heavy wooden board slides around less and lasts a lot longer than a plastic one.

## How to Cook from Old Recipes

The modern recipe format is an invention of the twentieth century. It is advantageous because it offers a list of ingredients with precise measurements and explicit instructions, along with cooking times and temperatures. Modern recipes are written scientifically, even though cooking is for the most part not a science. For some types of food, precise scientific recipes are indispensable. Cakes and many baked goods literally fail unless directions are followed exactly. But cooking throughout all of human history up to the last century used either no recipe, or cooks followed instructions written in a very different format. A modern cook may become exasperated when old recipes offer no measurements or cooking times. Both these factors are, however, always variable and depend on the number of guests, the size or amount of ingredients at hand, and the equipment used. And in all cases, for every recipe contained in this book, measurements are really not important. Some old authors, particularly in the Renaissance, began to offer exact measurements, but even these should be taken "with a grain of salt"—that is, how much spice to use depends on how many people you are feeding, the quantity of the main ingredient, and, of course, your particular taste. So the first word of advice is to trust your instinct. If an old recipe says "take chicken"—one bird will feed about four people. If you are feeding two, a half will do, unless you are especially hungry or want leftovers. This is something you can only learn through experience—no recipe can tell you how much food to make.

Old recipes do not list ingredients, but this is something you can and should do mentally to start. Read through the recipe and assemble what you need at the very beginning. Take out the cooking equipment and put everything in its place so you can follow the recipe without interruption. Chances are you will be cooking several recipes at once, and this is a kind of juggling act which, again, one only perfects with experience. Beginners should try one recipe at a time and later attempt beginning several in succession. Timing several recipes to be finished at the same time is yet another trick.

Since most old recipes are written in a kind of shorthand, you will need to elaborate exactly what is intended before you start cooking. Sometimes an old author is unclear, and in this case the comments provided may offer some assistance. But most of the work of interpretation will have to be done by the reader, which is exactly what the authors of all these old cookbooks intended. They address their comments to "you," and while some of their directions assume the reader is professional cook, most are clear and explicit enough to be followed by everyone.

Take the following recipe from Bartolomeo Scappi, for example.[2]

## TO FRY A CAPON IN VARIOUS WAYS [FIRST OPTION.]

*Cook the capon in water and salt until more than half done, and divide into four quarters, and let it stay for eight hours in a combination of white wine, vinegar, cooked must, pepper, cinnamon, cloves, nutmeg, pounded coriander and crushed cloves of garlic. Remove from the mixture, flour, and fry in melted lard, and when it's fried serve hot with a sauce over it made of the same marinade.*

The commentary for this recipe would explain that cooked must is the sapa or boiled-down grape juice, but otherwise, despite the unusual procedure, it is perfectly simple to follow. A capon is a castrated rooster, but a chicken will also work. How to boil until half done is entirely a matter of guesswork. Gently boiling the chicken whole for about a half an hour will work—but the recipe would not be ruined if you boil it more or less. The marinade should obviously cover the chicken completely in a separate bowl or casserole, and a sprinkle of each spice should be enough, but again, more or less will not matter in the least. Flouring means just a light dusting of flour, and then frying in lard in a pan until browned is also simple enough. What Scappi does not explain is how to make a sauce from the marinade, and here the commentary would suggest thorough boiling and reduction of the marinade in a saucepan and then straining out the spices. The recipe is just precise enough, requires no measurement or cooking time, and in fact liberates the reader to cook as she pleases. The fact that other variations follow suggests that Scappi was truly trying to teach the reader how to be creative, rather than depend on following a recipe to the letter.

Finally a word of advice: trust your instinct, feel free to experiment and have fun. The recipes that follow are fascinating, bizarre, and if nothing else will show that despite all the changes in ingredients and procedures, what tasted good hundreds of years ago still tastes good today. And there is only one way to find that out—by cooking and tasting them. *Bon chance!*

# 2
## ❦ THE MIDDLE
## AGES, 1300–1450

The period covered in this section, when cookbooks began to proliferate, is technically only the Late Middle Ages. There were a few manuscript cookbooks before 1300, most notably the *Libellus de arte coquinaria* (Little Book on the Art of Cooking), which may go back to the twelfth century, but it survives only in several Germanic versions copied and translated around 1300 or thereafter. The real efflorescence of medieval cuisine begins with the cookbook entitled *Viandier*, attributed to Guillaume Tirel, called Taillevent, chef to King Charles V of France. In fact, many of the recipes are found in manuscripts predating Taillevent, and confusingly, many more were added after him, especially in the later printed versions. Nonetheless, the recipes give a good idea of the very opulent cuisine that would be enjoyed by kings and nobility throughout Europe. Down the social scale, a wealthy urban professional known as the Ménagier de Paris composed a household guidebook for his young bride, and he also includes recipes. Elsewhere cookbooks such as the *Forme of Cury* written at the court of Richard II of England; the *Du fait de cuisine* by Chiquart written in Savoy; and the *Libre de Sent Sovi* written in Catalunya in the east of what is today Spain show that the same basic cooking procedures and flavor combinations were enjoyed everywhere with major differences only in the ingredients used. There were also a number of minor cookbooks written in Latin and other vernacular languages. Rupert of Nola's cookbook, *Libre de doctrina per a ben server, de tallar y dol art de coch . . . , (Book of rules to serve well, and the art of cooking)* written in Catalan for the Aragonese court in Naples, was especially influential. The focus in the recipes that follow is on the lesser-known cookbooks because these are harder to find in translation, but examples from others, particularly the *Viandier*, are also included.

## COLD FOODS

### ⇥ 1. COLD SAGE (CHICKEN SALAD) ⇤

*France, 14th c. (Viandier, 136)*

*Take your poultry and put it to cook in water; then let it cool. And then pound ginger, cinnamon buds, grains of paradise and cloves, without straining them, then pound bread, parsley and sage and a bit of saffron with the greens, if you like, to make it bright green and pass it through a sieve; and some sieve hard boiled egg yolks moistened with vinegar. Cut up your poultry in half, quarters or in parts, and place it in a plate with the sauce on top, and on that have hard boiled eggs, cut into morsels with a knife and not crumbled by hand.*

This is listed among Taillevent's (nickname of Guillaume Tirel, chef to Charles V of France) *entremets*, and was thus a cold dish that came between main courses, apparently giving the kitchen staff a little time to prepare another round of hot dishes. This recipe is a kind of proto-chicken salad, although, as with many poultry dishes, the bones are not removed.

### ⇥ 2. BLAUNCHE BRAWEN (WHITE PORK PATÉ) ⇤

*England, 15th c. (Harleian, 34)*

*Take Freysshe Braun, & mynce hem small, & take gode thikke mylke of Almaundys y-blaunchyde, & putte all in-to a potte, & Sugre, & lat boyle alle-to-gederys tyl it be rygt styffe; then caste it uppe, & caste it in a fayre cold basyn, & lette it stonde ther-in tyl it be cold; & then leche ii or iii in a dysshe, & serve forth.*

*Take fresh pork and chop it finely, and take good thick milk of blanched almonds, and put it all in a pot with sugar, and let it boil together until it is very firm. Then take it out and put into a cold basin and let it stand until it is cold, then slice two or three per dish and serve.*

Leche meats were a whole category of medieval cold dishes that were served in slices, some like pâté, others based on fruits or dairy. Most are sweet, though. This variation will only stay together if the meat is very finely chopped and contains some fat. To get even slices it is best if the mixture is pressed firmly into a rectangular bread pan lined with greased parchment paper, chilled for several hours (and of course a refrigerator is easier to use that a basin set in cold water), and then turned out and sliced.

## ⇥ 3. COLD FLOUNDER ⇤

*Spain—Aragonese-ruled Naples, 15th c. (Rupert of Nola, li)*

*. . . To prepare cold flounder. First take the flounder and scale it well, and then open it along the side, then when you want to fry it place on a bit of salt and heat the oil and when it is hot place in the flounder. And as it firms up you quickly turn it to the other side and press your hand on it so that it doesn't curl up while becoming firm. When it's well fried you want to eat it with pepper and lemon slices. And after take some of its oil and enough vinegar and place it on the flounder and place on the other things. And you know something, the flounder is a royal fish and is very good to eat cold as hot.*

Cold fish dishes were another item that might appear as an appetizer in the past, just as they are served as tapas in Spain today. By opening it, the author means filleting the fish off the bone. The *palaya* in the original recipe in Catalan is the Atlantic spotted flounder (*Citharus linguatula*) that is also common in the western Mediterranean. Any small flat fish, including sole, will work well. Rupert's describing flounder as royal, that is fit for royalty, is corroborated by the evidence of physicians who frequently complained about the courtly fashion for eating cold fish, which they believed could cause colds and other disorders.

## ⇥ 4. GELATIN OF EVERY MEAT ⇤

*Italy, 14th c. (Anonimo Veneziano, 16)*

*If you want to make a good gelatin of all meats: of wild pig's flesh, take ears and feet and every thing, and capons, partridges, thrushes, hares, roebuck and pheasants. Take these things and place them on the fire in part water and part vinegar. When it boils and is well skimmed, add spices — pepper, cinnamon, ginger and saffron, not pounded together, enough according to the quantity of meat. And whichever meat is cooked remove, but leave behind the ears and feet because they are of little substance. When everything has been removed, dust all the meat with spices and let your gelatin stay on the fire and take saffron and soak it in the gelatin and arrange the meat in a vessel that you want and line it with bay leaves and place over this gelatin strained with the saffron through a sieve. When it is strained over the meat, take sweet spices and moisten with the same gelatin, and cast it over, and you want it to be colored and deep red. And add salt while boiling, as much as is convenient, and it will be good and beautiful gelatin.*

The idea of a savory meat gelatin may strike American readers as odd as we are used to seeing gelatin flavored with fruit, but it is very typical of medieval and even modern European cooking and today is called an aspic. This is one of the cold dishes—the gelatin sets after being cooled—that was considered an elegant presentation piece. It would take the shape of whatever vessel it was poured into. Gelatins could be clear, too, and came in various colors, though this one contains the cooked meat. The directions specify, though not entirely clearly, that the parts that give the gelatin its body, such as cartilaginous ears and feet, should not be included in the final dish. For those unwilling to deal with ears and feet, the dish can also be made with powdered unflavored gelatin, rich beef broth and chunks of meat with spices. This will give a decent and easy approximation of the original dish.

## SOUPS

### ◈ 5. BROUET ROUSSET (RUSSET BROTH) ◈

*France, 14th c. (Viandier, 59)*

*Take whatever meat you like, and onions sliced in rounds and parsley leaves and place them to fry in lard; and then sieve bread and livers with beef bouillon and wine and boil it with your meat and then finish off with ginger, cinnamon, cloves, grains of paradise, cassia buds, and temper with verjuice; and it will be reddish.*

Although there is an option to use any meat here, it was probably chicken that was used most often as the recipes that accompany this one suggest. Slices of chicken breast work nicely. When these and the onions are lightly browned, the bread, which has been soaked in bouillon and wine, is passed through a sieve with cooked livers and added to the pot with chicken. The spices should all be finely pounded. The only one that is difficult to find today is the cassia buds, which are the dried unripe fruit of a close relative of cinnamon. The proportions of ingredients are entirely a matter of personal taste, but for a few servings, one chicken breast, 12 ounces of broth, and a glass of red wine with a slice of bread soaked in them suffice, as does just a pinch of each spice and a drizzle of verjuice. Liver would have been considered essential to the flavor and texture of the dish, and every chicken comes with one, but today this soup can be made without it. It will still be remarkably delicious.

> ### ✦ 14TH-CENTURY ADVICE FOR A YOUNG BRIDE
>
> Around 1393 a book of household and kitchen advice was composed by an elderly man probably of the mercantile class, known as the Ménagier de Paris. It was intended for his young bride, who he assumed would outlive him and remarry. The woman was most likely a complete beginner in the kitchen, given the nature of the comments. In it he says

"to prevent thy pottage from burning, thou must move it in the bottom of the pot and look that the logs touch not the bottom and if already it have begun to burn, thou must forthwith change it into another pot." He specifies also that the pot should not be allowed to boil over and "into pottages the spices should be well brayed [pounded] and not strained [until] the last moment. In sauces and jelly the contrary."[1]

## ❧ 6. CHICKEN BROTH VARIATIONS ❧

*Italy?, 14th c. (Liber de Coquina, 7)*

*On Provincial broth: for an appetizing broth take chickens cut into quarters, fry with lard and onions. After add a little cold water, and then the liver. [Take] marjoram, rosemary, parsley, savory, saffron. Pound all these and moisten with the broth of the said flesh; and put it to boil with the flesh. After that take spices, cinnamon, cloves, nutmeg, fusticellos, cardamom, galangal, honey, ginger. After, pound its boiled liver with cooked egg yolks, enough to suffice. Moisten with the broth of flesh and make it boil. Then remove from the fire.*

*On martin broth: for martin broth, take chickens and fry like above. And chop parsley with other aromatic herbs, add to the said flesh and a bit of cold water, mix with this. Then bread crumbs moistened with the aforesaid broth and likewise mixed. And let it boil a little and color it with saffron, and if you want add other spices.*

*On Teutonic broth: for German broth, capons or fat chickens and boil well. Toss in parsley, mint, marjoram, rosemary, all beaten with saffron, and moisten with the broth, and let it boil a little.*

*On Gallic Broth: For French broth, boil chicken. Then cleaned almonds well pounded with garlic, moistened with the lean chicken broth, place in another vessel. And when the chicken is cooked, mix the fat of the broth with the rest and boil. After, leave slices of bread in the broth to soak it up arranged in slices like a sunburst with spices sprinkled on top. And serve.*

*On Sarracen Broth: for sarracen broth, take roasted capons and their liver with spices and toasted bread well pounded, moisten with good wine and verjuice. Then cut up the parts of the capons and with the aforementioned boil in a pot, add dates, dried Greek raisins, whole cleaned almonds and enough lard. Color it if you like.*

*On Spanish Broth: for green Spanish broth, take chickens or whatever birds or meat and boil. Then pound well the liver with good spices and green herbs, add beaten eggs. And place in the broth to boil, but the broth should not boil too much.*

Why the author, most likely Italian, associated these specific variations with these peoples is not entirely clear, though some of the ingredients and methods do appear in other cookbooks from these places. Dried fruit was consistently associated with Muslim lands, garlic and almonds with sops with the French. In any case, all are typical in that they require two separate cooking methods, and here the full range of combinations is nicely demonstrated. The chicken is fried, boiled, or roasted and then made into a soup. Exactly how such dishes were eaten is a matter of speculation, as there were no forks. Diners probably used a spoon for the liquid and pulled the chicken meat off the bones with their fingers, perhaps with the use of a knife. Or each serving might have been carved and plated from the larger bowl and then placed into individual bowls. The *fusticellos* mentioned in the first variation may be whole cinnamon sticks, as the word means a little twig or plant stem.

### ⁓ 7. FOR TO MAKE POTAGE OF OYSTERS ⁓

*Northern England, 15th c. (*Liber Cure Cocorum, *17)*

*Perboyle thyn oysters and take hom oute;*
*Kepe welle thy bre with outen doute,*
*And hakke hom on a borde full smalle,*
*And bray in a mortar thou schalle;*
*Do hom in hor owne brothe for goode,*
*Do mylke of almonds ther to by the rode,*
*And lye hit up with amydone,*
*And frye smalle mynsud onyone*
*In oyle, or seethe hom in mylke thou schalle;*
*Do powdur thereto of spyces withalle,*
*And coloure hit thenne with safron gode;*
*Hit is holden restoratyf fode.*

*Parboil your oysters and take them out;*
*Keep well the broth, with out a doubt,*
*And chop them on a board very small,*
*And beat them in a mortar you shall;*
*Add in their own broth for good,*
*Add milk of almonds, I swear,*
*And thicken it with starch,*
*And fry small minced onion*
*In oil, or boil them in milk you shall;*
*Add powder therein of spices withal,*
*And color it then with saffron good;*
*It is considered restorative food.*

This might be considered an ancestor of the oyster or clam chowder, a pottage being a thick soup. In fact there were medieval soups called chawdron—probably derived from the word for cauldron. As the author states, it was considered a fortifying soup, good for invalids and weak people. The medieval English equivalent of saying "I swear" is "by the rood," meaning "by the cross, I swear." The starch called for here would have been wheat starch made by washing and refining flour. Cornstarch, not available in the Middle Ages because corn comes from the New World, is an acceptable but inauthentic substitute.

### ↭ 8. JACOBIN SOUP ↮

*Savoy, modern-day border of Italy and France, 15th c. (Chiquart, 105)*

*And to serve Jacobin Soup, you must have your beautiful capon, and according to the number at the feast, a hundred or two hundred capons that are very fat, and a great deal of other fowl to serve in default of these capons, and they should be roasted well and just right. And when the fat beef is being butchered, take the marrow bone and wash them well and right, then put them to boil in nice clean cauldrons along with good mutton. And then next take a quintal of very good cheese, Crampone and Brie, the finest that can be made and found, and cut these and clean well and just right, and then chop very minutely. And the cook who is appointed to make the said Jacobin soup will take two or three hundred breads and cut this bread into delicate slices and toast them very well, cleanly without burning, so they will be russet, and then place them in nice clean pots, and you should have two nice white clean tables to cut your toasted bread for the Jacobin soup. And then when you have your golden and silver platters lined up, in your platters place your bread nice and sweetly with the cheese on top. And take your capons and disjoint them, that is, remove the wings and legs and remove the back, and then take the white meat of the capon and cut it very finely, and this capon white meat sprinkle over your Jacobin soup. Then take the other parts of the capon, that is, the wings, legs and back and place neatly on top of your Jacobin soup. And take care with your bouillon of beef marrow and mutton that it's nice and sweet, and strain the soup into a big pot, nice and clean, and take a good bunch or bouquet of herbs like sage, parsley, marjoram and hyssop, they must be well cleaned and washed, and put it in your bouillon. And near the table where you will be serving the said soup Jacobin, have a good charcoal fire beneath your pots containing your bouillon so that it continues to boil. And with this bouillon cover your soup Jacobin.*

The Jacobins were a religious order, apparently not known for their austerity. Clearly the ingredients called for here are meant to serve an enormous crowd. The quintal of cheese, for example, equals 120 pounds. Crampone cheese comes from Craponne in the Auvergne, France, and is similar to Gruyere. The dish can easily be made with one roasted capon or chicken and regular beef broth. A slice of toast per bowl and a few spoonfuls of cheese, the rind of the Brie removed, with the chopped chicken breast on top, whole legs and wing sections, and then broth poured over should approximate this dish fairly well. Interestingly, there is no indication that any spices are used in this soup. Chiquart usually cooked at the castle of Chambery which is today in France. Most of Savoy, however, is in Italy.

### ⊰ 9. SOUP WHICH IS CALLED PINYONADA (PINE NUT SOUP) ⊱

*Spain—Aragonese-ruled Naples, 15th c. (Rupert of Nola, xv)*

*Take a good quantity of pine nuts that are cleaned and add almonds and pound completely in a mortar. After they are pounded moisten it with chicken broth and pass it through a sieve. And when it is strained, place in a clean pot and let it boil and place in sugar, all the time stirring with a whisk. And when it is cooked remove from the fire and let it rest a while covered with a cloth and sprinkle sugar over the bowls.*

This smooth, creamy soup survives today in what is called a white gazpacho in Spain, though today it is usually garnished with raisins and pieces of apple and includes garlic and a touch of vinegar. It can be made with either pine nuts or almonds alone as well. It can also be made in a blender very easily, but it is safest to use room-temperature broth and then reheat very gently after blending. It can also be served chilled.

## MEAT

### ⊰ 10. HERICOC OF MUTTON ⊱

*France, 14th c. (Viandier, 40)*

*Take your mutton and place it all raw to fry in lard, and cut it into small pieces, with onions finely chopped and moisten with beef bouillon, and add in wine and verjuice and mace, hyssop and sage and let it boil well together.*

The word hericoc or haricot comes from the verb herigoter "to shred," though here the meat is cut up. The simple, terse form of this recipe is typical of this period. It assumes the cook is experienced enough to know how long to cook the meat and how heavily to season it. Some versions of this recipe specify that the meat should be cut up first, and this is how we would make a stew today. But the scribe may have intended for the meat to be cooked first and then cut up. It is certainly easier to cut this way, and in fact normally a large piece of meat would be par-boiled for precisely this reason. Either way will work, especially as the combination is stewed together afterward. The only ingredient that may pose a problem here is hyssop, which can be easily grown from seed but is hard to find as an herb. It can be omitted, or in a pinch tarragon can be substituted, though it was

rarely used in medieval cooking. If mutton, or adult sheep, is not available, lamb works well here and in other recipes.

### ☙ 11. VENOISON OF FRESH DEER ❧

*France, 14th c. (Viandier, 43)*

*Venoison of deer and fresh young wild goat. Parboil and lard all along, and with mace, and a great deal of wine, cook well and eat with cameline or place in a pastry shell parboiled and larded and eat with cameline.*

Other manuscripts of this recipe suggest that the venison be larded along the inside, which would preserve the look of the deer when presented. Obviously a very big cauldron would be needed to boil the animal whole. Larding is essentially taking small strips of bacon and slipping them through slits made completely through the surface of the animal's flesh and then knotting the strips to keep them fastened. This was designed to keep the meat moist and was used both for roasted meats and for boiled, as well as the variation here in which the whole deer—bones and all—is baked in a huge pie. The cameline sauce called for was standard and consists of ginger, cinnamon, cloves, grains of paradise, mastic, and long pepper, mixed with bread soaked in vinegar. The whole is then strained and seasoned with salt. Mastic is a resin from a tree that grows on the Greek island of Chios and can be bought at Greek grocery stores. It was also used as chewing gum, and we get the word masticate (to chew) from this resin. It was one of the most highly prized spices and in fact Christopher Columbus traded mastic early in his career.

### ☙ 12. ROAST PORK ❧

*France?, 14th c. (Tractatus de modo preparandi et condiendi omnia cibaria, 9)*

*Roast pork flesh: Take (the part) around the kidneys with the loin or next to the spine on the back and if you like toss in wine for a day so that it whitens and becomes more tender and flavorful. And roast on a spit and place a pan underneath with wine and chopped onions to collect the dripping fat. After cut into bits and let it fry a bit with the aforementioned fat and fried onions and season with spices.*

*Some roast more simply, they eat it without seasoning, but with green sauce and sprinkled with salt. There are even those who finely chop pork or beef flesh and place in a drink with a bit of wine or water, completely covered with its own broth or fat; they allow it to boil until fully decocted, often stirring. After they add onions, then season with spices.*

The recipe clearly calls for a pork loin, which is marinated, presumably in white wine if it makes the flesh lighter, and then roasted on a spit. The recipe specifies dripping of fat, so the cut probably includes the skin and fat as well, and is not the very lean loin as would be found in a butcher's shop today. As a modern variant, the loin can be roasted in the oven with some bacon or fat back and onions, then the meat cut into cubes and sautéed in the drippings with spices such as ginger and cinnamon.

### ⤙ 13. LAMB OR VEAL ⤚

*Italy?, 14th c. (Liber de Coquina, 406)*

*A dish of lamb or veal. Take meat from lamb or veal and cut into fine strips the size of two fingers. Then place to cook in boiling water. And when it seems to be boiled, place in sugar, and some of the best wine. After, add in good spices pounded and moistened with the same broth. And when the meat is cooked remove the pot from the fire and put in eggs well beaten in a bowl with a bit of the broth cooled, heat gently and mix the said broth with a spoon.*

As with many medieval recipes, this dish is thickened with eggs that have been "tempered" with the broth to make a sauce. "To temper" meant to balance or fine tune and usually referred to either moistening an ingredient, or even balancing it with seasoning. Here it is done to prevent the eggs from scrambling once they enter the pot with the meat and broth.

### ⤙ 14. FOR POWME DORRYS (GOLDEN APPLES OF PORK) ⤚

*Northern England, 15th c. (Liber Cure Cocorum, 37)*

*Take porke and grynde hit rawe, I kenne*
*Temper hit with swongen egges; thenne*
*Kast powder to make hit on a balle;*
*In playand water thou kast hit schalle*
*To harden, thenne up thou take,*
*Enbroche hit fayre for goddes sake.*
*Endore hit with yolkes of egges then*
*With a fedyr at fyre, as I the kenne;*
*Bothe grene and rede thow may hit make*
*With iuse of herbz I undertake;*
*Halde under a dysshe that nogt be lost,*
*More honest hit is as thou wele wost*

*Take pork and grind it raw, I know*
*Moisten it with beaten eggs; then*
*Cast flour to make it in a ball;*
*In simmering water you shall cast it*
*To harden, then you take it up,*

*Skewer it well for god's sake.*
*Make it golden with egg yolks then*
*With a feather at the fire, as I show you;*
*Both green and red you may make it*
*With juice of herbs I undertake;*
*Hold under a dish that nothing be lost,*
*More frugal it is as you well know.*

The name of this dish means golden apples, of the sort that figure in mythology as the apples of Hesperides that Hercules had to find as his eleventh labor. This is one of the many disguised foods so beloved at medieval courts. It can be made today with ground pork rolled into apple-shaped balls and then rolled in flour. A twig as a stem can be added for further effect. The balls are then lightly poached in water, skewered, and turned slowly before the fire while egg yolk is brushed on to make them golden. The author specifies to catch the drippings, which were probably used as a sauce. Spinach or parsley blanched, chopped, and then wrung through a cloth will make green juice. Sandalwood was probably used in the past to make red coloring, but beet juice will also work. Grate a raw beet and squeeze out the red juice and add it to the pork before forming into balls. The apples can also be baked in an oven at 300 degrees, with the egg yolk brushed on every few minutes until they are golden.

### ☙ 15. STWED BEEFF (BEEF STEW) ☙

*England, 15th c. (Harleian, 72)*

*Take faire Ribbes of ffresh beef, And (if thou wilt) roste hit til hit be nygh ynowe; then put hit in a faire possenet; caste ther-to parcely and oynons minced, reysons of corauns, powder peper, canel, clowes, saundres, safferon, and salt; then caste there-to wyn and a litull vynegre; sette a lyd on the potte, and lete hit boile sokingly on a faire charcoal til hit be ynogh; then lay the fflessh, in dishes, and the sirippe there-uppon, And serve it forth.*

*Take fair ribs of beef, and if you wish, roast it until it is nearly enough, then put it in a fair pot, cast therein parsley and minced onions, currants, ground pepper, cinnamon, cloves, sanders, saffron, and salt. Then add in wine and a little vinegar. Set a lid on the pot and let it boil gently on a fair charcoal (fire) until it is done. Then lay the flesh in dishes with the syrup thereon. And serve it forth.*

Though this sounds bizarre, it would definitely pass in any decent rib joint as braised short ribs in a sweet-and-sour sauce. The adjective "fair" merely means pretty or neat. Roasting the ribs first browns them and lets much of the fat melt away. The spices and currants (that is, tiny raisins, not the fruit currant) along with vinegar give this a sweet-and-sour bite not unlike modern barbecue sauces. The only really difficult ingredient to find is sanders or sandalwood, which would add to the aroma and color, though it is not essential. Ideally this dish should be braised, as the technique is called today, the word itself deriving from the "braises," meaning coals. Cooking over very low heat for two or three hours yields an absolutely tender and succulent dish.

### ◈ 16. A JANET OF YOUNG GOAT ◈

*Spain—Aragonese-ruled Naples, 15th c. (Rupert of Nola, xii)*

*Take the front thigh of a young goat and cook it in a pot. And when it is cooked remove from the pot and cut it into pieces as large as a nut. Then take good salt pork that is fatty and fry the kid with a bit of onion. Then take almonds that are toasted and pound in a mortar with a good piece of the goat's liver cooked on the coals along with the crumb of bread toasted and soaked in white vinegar. And all should be pounded together with a pair of egg yolks for each plate. And when it is all well pounded moisten it with good broth. And after pass it through a sieve and when it is sieved, place it in the pot where it should boil with all fine spices and add likewise the kid in the pot together with the sauce and let it cook. When it is cooked add a bit of chopped parsley in the pot and also sugar. And make it so that the sauce tastes a little of vinegar and place in the grease from the pot in which was first cooked the goat and put in a lot, and thus it is done.*

This recipe is typical of cooking methods and flavor combinations throughout Europe. It shows clearly that Catalunya on the east coast of the Iberian peninsula and the Kingdom of Naples where Rupert of Nola worked were fully in touch with developments elsewhere. The janet has counterparts in French and English sources and normally means a yellow sauce, but this does not seem to be. Clearly this recipe was designed for Christian consumers because it includes pork, which suggests that it is not of Arabic origin, as so many medieval Catalonian dishes were.

Janet of goat being cooked over three-legged pot.

### ◈ 17. A DISH OF ROASTED CAT ◈

*Spain—Aragonese-ruled Naples, 15th c. (Rupert of Nola, xxix)*

*Take a fat cat and slit its throat. And when it is dead remove the head and be sure that no one eats it, for they might go mad. And after skin it well and cleanly open so that it is clean. And when it is clean, take it and place it in a cloth of clean linen and bury it in the earth where it should stay a day and a night. And after remove it from there and place it on a spit before the fire to cook. And while it is cooking baste it with good garlic and oil and when it is greased, beat it well with a rod and do this until it is cooked, greased and beaten. And when it's cooked take and carve it as you would a rabbit and place it on a big plate and take the garlic and oil that's been moistened with good broth so that it's clear, and pour it over the cat. And then eat it, truly a singular dish.*

Judging from the concluding comments, it seems that cat was not a common dish if the author has to convince his readers to try it. His explicit comments about slaughter are also unlike the recipes for other meats, so again cooks were probably not familiar with it. Having said that, most food authorities of the period do attest to the fact that cats were eaten in some regions, presumably Catalunya among them.

### ᴈ 18. TO STUFF A SHOULDER OR OTHER PART (MUTTON) ᴈ

*Italy, 15th c. (Anonimo Toscano, 17)*

*Take a shoulder of mutton and remove the meat from the bone, and take cured pork belly and chop everything together and beat it with a knife on the cutting board. Then take aromatic herbs in good quantity, pound with spices and saffron, and mix it in with the meat and pork. Add fresh cheese, well pounded with egg, in good quantity and moisten so that it will be not too firm or soft. Then take a caul from a pig or sheep and lay it on the table, and place in the center this meat and spread on the caul. Then take the bone from the shoulder and set it into the meat, then take the other half of the meat and place it over the bone on the other part, so the bone is in the middle, then cover everything with the caul. Then place on a grill of iron and roast until it is done, and serve it. Similarly you can make other parts.*

The trick to this dish is using the caul, a fatty membrane lining from inside the animal, which keeps the stuffing together and also bastes the meat as it is grilled. For the pork belly, Italian pancetta (unsmoked rolled bacon) would work fine. Although the caul is indispensable to the cooking and presentation of this dish as it appears looking like a shoulder joint, the flavor alone can be replicated with ground lamb seasoned as above and grilled, or by re-forming the chopped meat around the bone and baking it like a meat loaf. Lamb is a good substitute in general because the animal called for is not actually a mature sheep, but a "castrone," or young neutered male, in English called a wether.

## Fowl

### ᴈ 19. PEACOCKS ᴈ

*France, 14th c. (Viandier, 102)*

*Peacock, roasted. Kill it like a goose and leave the head and the tail on. Lard it and put on a spit and roast golden and eat with fine salt. And it lasts a good month after it's cooked, and if it gets moldy on top, remove the mold, you'll find it white, good and fine underneath.*

Although not likely to be found on any table today, peacocks were one of the standard favorites in the Middle Ages. They were often skinned, cooked, and then served with the feathers put back on. This was a presentation piece or an *entremets* in French that often appeared between courses. A puzzling feature of this recipe is the idea that peacock flesh can stay good—obviously without refrigeration of any kind. As one manuscript version states, it was even better cold—that is, as leftovers. This idea goes back to ancient times, and there are even stories of people eating peacock flesh years after it was first cooked. This clearly cannot be recommended today.

### ❧ 20. ROAST CHICKEN ❧

*France?, 14th c. (*Tractatus de modo preparandi et condiendi omnia cibaria, *384–5)*

*There are those who in winter time prepare young chickens in this way: first they inflate so that the skin and flesh become separated, then they are placed in the skin of goose legs, then they fill the interior from all sides with these condiments: they take hyssop, parsley and sage, a little parboiled and chopped finely, and you take lean pork flesh and bacon and chicken livers and hard boiled eggs and especially veal; hack that on a board with two knives. Then they add to this mince spices with salt, namely white pepper, long and black, ginger, cinnamon, the which condiments are stuffed inside and outside the chicken and well sewed or tied. They roast it at a distance so that it doesn't rupture and the interior is neither raw not burnt.*

*Roast chicken can be eaten with verjuice or white wine poured on, nor does it need another condiment for it will be flavorful enough.*

It appears that the skin of a goose's leg is used here to give strength as an outer casing while the young chicken roasts inside. Presumably the chicken's own skin is not strong enough. The stuffing also appears to be placed both in the chicken, under its skin, and on the outside of the chicken beneath the goose skin, giving the final dish a football shape. The stuffing includes three kinds of pepper: white, long, and black.

### ❧ 21. STUFFED GOOSE NECK ❧

*France?, 14th c. (*Tractatus de modo preparandi et condiendi omnia cibaria, *386)*

*There are some who prepare the head and neck in this way: first remove the neck bone; then fill the skin like a sausage with these condiments: take blood* with fat and egg yolks and cooked herbs, and they chop up well with a knife on a board, adding spice, with which they fill the neck, and tie the ends and cook in water, after roasting on a grill over the coals, and they eat it.

*I say the same can be done of the neck of swans or cranes.*

For a less grand presentation chicken necks can substitute for the goose, but they will naturally look like small cocktail franks rather than large sausages. This dish is made with blood, but chopped chicken also works, though is obviously different from the original.

## ⇥ 22. CHYKONYS IN BRUETTE (CHICKENS IN BROTH) ⇤

*England, 15th c. (Harleian, 23)*

*Take an Sethe Chykonys, & smyte hem to gobettys; than take Pepir, Gyngere, and Brede y-grounde, and temper it uppe with the self brothe, and with Ale; an coloure it with Safroun, an seethe an serve forth.*

*Take and boil chickens and cut them into mouth-size pieces, then take pepper, ginger, and bread crumbs and moisten it with broth and with ale and color it with saffron and serve it up.*

This is a very simple but typical way of cooking in the fifteenth century. The chicken is first boiled, then cut into bite-size pieces and simmered in a bread-thickened spiced broth. The structure of this recipe is also very medieval—no measurements, cooking times or specific instruction are given. It was assumed that the cook was a professional who knew his way around the kitchen.

## ⇥ 23. ROSE (OF CAPON) ⇤

*Northern England, 15th c. (Liber Cure Cocorum, 13)*

*Take flour of ryse, as white as sylke,*
*And hit welle, with almond mylke;*
*Boyle hit tyl hit be chargyd, thenne*
*Take braune of capon or elle of henne;*
*Loke thou grynd hit wondur smalle,*
*And sithen thou charge hit with alle;*
*Coloure with alkenet, sawnder, or ellys with blode,*
*Fors hit with clowes or macys gode;*
*Seson hit with sugur grete plente,*
*This is a rose, as kokes telle me.*

*Take rice flour as white as silk,*
*And pour in almond milk;*

> *Boil it till it is thick, then*
> *Take flesh of capon or else of hen;*
> *Look you grind it wonderfully small,*
> *And then you add in to it all;*
> *Color with alkanet, sandalwood, or else with blood,*
> *Stuff in cloves and mace good;*
> *Season it with sugar great plenty,*
> *This is a rose, as cooks tell me.*

The final line suggests that the author was not himself a cook, but merely a mediocre poet who learned about this recipe secondhand. In any case, it is a quintessentially medieval dish, a close cousin to the blancmange, which is white. Here the chicken is colored rose with alkanet, which is a purplish-red dye derived from the powdered root of an herb related to borage, or with sandalwood. Colored and spiced foods were a favorite. To make this today, it is best to purchase rice flour or make some by putting raw rice in the blender. Make almond milk by pounding peeled blanched almonds, soaking overnight in water then straining. Add to this boiled chicken breast, which is pounded in a mortar, then colored, spiced and sweetened. Although it sounds like a chicken pudding, the final dish is light and pleasant, with a texture not unlike the interior of chicken nuggets, which are also finely ground and sweetened. Red food dye is probably the easiest substitute, but alkanet can be bought from herbal supply sources, and it grows wild on the East Coast of the United States.

### ⊰ 24. ARMORED CHICKEN ⊱

*Spain—Aragonese-ruled Naples, 15th c. (Rupert of Nola, xiv)*

*Take a chicken and place to roast before the fire and when it is nearly half cooked cover it with lard. Then take egg yolks beaten well and then place the yolks little by little on the chicken. Then take flour and place it on the chicken over the eggs. Turn the chicken the whole time and the crust is even better than the chicken. And this is the way you make armored chicken.*

Although the technique sounds very exotic, as does the name, the net effect of this dish is to create a crunchy crust like one might find on fried chicken. Deep-frying technology was not common, so this application of a crust while turning on a spit is the most practical solution. The directions do not specify whether the lard used is solid strips of salt pork that are tied into slashes in the skin, which is the usual meaning of the verb "to lard," or liquefied lard as we use that term in the United States. For the former, the chicken would need to be removed from the fire while the strips are tied on, so it seems more likely that the author meant to brush with liquefied pork fat, which would of course help create an even crust. The egg yolks can be brushed on slowly afterward, while the chicken turns, and then the flour sprinkled on before the yolks burn. The name of the dish derives from the fact that the crust is golden and hard like armor.

## FISH AND SEAFOOD

### ❧ 25. FRESH SALMON ❧

*France, 14th c. (Viandier, 194)*

*Lard it, and keep the backbone in for roasting, then cut it into pieces and cook in water, wine and salt, and eat it with a janet pepper sauce or cameline. Some put it on the grill to eat, and in a pastry, if you like, powdered with spices and eaten with cameline. If it is salted, it should be cooked in water without salt and eaten with wine and chopped chives.*

Salmon here is subjected to the typical medieval two-part cooking process. Some manuscripts advise to roast first, others to fry. Either way, the bacon is inserted into slits in the sides. It keeps the fish moist and flavors it. Keeping it whole first prevents it from falling apart. The salmon can be filleted and divided into serving portions after roasting and then very gently and briefly poached. The janet is a yellow sauce and can be found in recipe 48. The cameline is based on cinnamon and can be found in the commentary for recipe 11.

### ❧ 26. OYSTERS ❧

*France?, 14th c. (Tractatus de modo preparandi et condiendi omnia cibaria, 389)*

*Cook oyster fish, that is oysters, for a small part of an hour in pure water. Then add cinnamon, ginger, pepper, cumin and crush well with saffron, and moisten with wine or almond milk and a bit of water and let it boil in a pan with onions fried in oil. When it begins to boil, place the boiling water with the oysters. And serve.*

This is one of those common dishes somewhere between a thick soup and a main ingredient in sauce. The addition of almond milk makes this a creamy dish surprisingly like a good chowder. The oysters should be boiled only a few minutes, which seems to be what the author intends by a "modicum" of an hour.

### ❧ 27. GOOD TUNA CASSEROLE ❧

*Spain—Aragonese-ruled Naples, 15th c. (Rupert of Nola, xlvii)*

*First take the tuna and if you like for your master, take the eyes of the tuna and place them in a casserole and likewise take the belly and paunch with almonds, pine nuts and place all together with the eyes in the casserole with a bit of oil and juice of oranges. And after take all the spices and all the herbs like parsley and mint and pound all so that it is well crushed and place this in the casserole with the said spices, and the said almonds being blanched and place in the oven to cook. And a royal sauce you make with garlic and oil.*

This recipe is clearly not related to your mother's tuna noodle casserole, but with the exception of the tuna eyes, it is a very workable and delicious recipe. Tuna steaks either whole or cut into slices mixed with a tablespoon or two of olive oil and a drizzle of sour orange juice and spices and topped with nuts, baked uncovered at 350 degrees for about 30 to 40 minutes will give a good approximation of what this dish tasted like. Sour oranges, or ideally real Seville oranges, are best because the sweet eating orange was not introduced to Europe from China until about the sixteenth century.

### 28. LAMPRAYS BAKE (LAMPREY PIE)

*England, 15th c. (Harleian, 52)*

*Take & make fayre round cofyns of fyne past, & take Freyssche lampreys, & late hem blode iii fyngerys with-in the tayle, and lat hem blede in a vesselle, & late hym deye in the same vesselle in the same blode; than take broun Brede, & kyt it, & stepe it in the Venegre, & draw throw a straynoure; then take the same blode, & pouder of Canel, & cast ther-to tyl it be broun; than caste ther-to pouder Pepir, Salt, & Wyne a lytelle, that it be nogt to strong of venegre. An skald the Lampray, & pare hem clene, & couche hym round on the cofyn, tyl he be helyd; than kyuere hym fayre with a lede, save a lytel hole in the myddelle, & at that hool, blow in the cofynne with thin mowthe a gode blast of Wynde. And sodenly stoppe the hole, that the wynd a-byde with-ynne, to reyse uppe the cofynne, that he falle nowt a-dowune; & whan he is a lytel y-hardid in the oven, pryke the cofyn with a pynne y-stekyd on a roddys ende, for brekyng of the cofynne, & than lat bake, & serve forth colde. And when the lamprey is take owt of the cofynne & etyn, take the Syrippe in the cofynne, & put on a chargere, & caste Wyne ther-to, an pouder Gyngere, & lat boyle in the fyre. Than take fayre Paynemayn y-wette in Wyne, & ley the soppis in the cofynne of the Lamprey, & lay the Syrippe above, & ete it so hot; for it is gode lordys mete.*

*Take and make fair round pastry crusts of fine dough, and take fresh lampreys and let him bleed three fingers from the end of the tail, and let him bleed in a vessel, and let him die in the same vessel in the same blood. Then take brown bread and cut it and soak it in vinegar and draw through a strainer, then take the same blood, powdered cinnamon, and add it in until it's brown. Then add in ground pepper, salt, and a little wine, so the vinegar isn't too strong. Then scald the lamprey, cut off the skin, and lay him in the crust until it is covered. Then cover it with a lid, except for a little hole in the middle, and at that hole, blow into the pie with your mouth, a good blast of air. Then quickly close the hole in the middle so the air stays inside, and keeps up the upper crust so it doesn't fall down. When it is hardened in the oven a little, poke the pie with a pin fastened to the end of a stick, so you can break the pie [later]. Then let it bake and serve it cold. When the lamprey is taken out of the pie and eaten, take the juice in the pie and put it in a pan and add wine, powdered ginger and let it boil on the fire. Then take light bread moistened in wine and lay these sops in the pie of the lamprey and pour the juice above it, and eat it hot, for it is food fit for a Lord.*

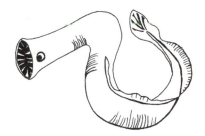

Lamprey eel.

Apart from the fact that it is unlikely anyone will want to eat a lamprey— a nasty, slithering eel-like creature—and certainly not kill it in this gruesome manner, this recipe is among the best examples of how pies were made and eaten in the Middle Ages. They were not sliced with crust and contents together. Rather the pie was a container for the contents, and in this case they are removed and then another side dish is made with bread to soak up the cooking juices. The crust itself would have been thrown away. The interesting trick of blowing in the pie to keep the upper crust from sinking down was to prevent the crust from touching the contents and becoming soggy and perhaps falling apart. In a sense the pie crust is merely an alternative cooking vessel. Lampreys and eels were indeed, as the author states, one of the favorite foods of nobles throughout Europe. In fact many medical authors associated them with gluttony and were fond of telling stories of rulers who died after eating too many. Eels are a decent substitute, assuming lampreys are unavailable, and any fish, whole, would also work well with this technique, remembering that the fish is removed from the pie for serving.

## VEGETABLES

### ✺ 29. FAVA BEANS ✺

*France?, 14th c. (*Tractatus de modo preparandi et condiendi omnia cibaria, *394)*

*New fava beans or peas or grains of new wheat, they are able to make in this way. . . . [Boil] first in water, then they are cooked sufficiently. Next, pound in a mortar pepper, ginger, saffron, cumin and cinnamon, then distemper with almond milk or sheep's and egg yolks, hard or soft, and make it boil with some of the newly cooked favas, always stirring with a spoon. Then remove from the fire and add in other new favas, and serve.*

Just as today, the arrival of fresh fava beans in spring was eagerly anticipated. After shelling, they should be boiled for a few minutes and quickly cooled in ice water. Small favas can be eaten as is while larger ones must also have the skin around each bean removed. The spices, almond milk, and egg mixture make a light sauce for the beans, and only a small amount should be made so as not to completely mask the fresh green flavor of the legume. This fourteenth-century cookbook also contains a recipe for dried favas that are cooked slowly overnight and then the water thrown away before proceeding with the recipe. In later centuries, dried fava beans would be looked down upon as peasant food, but here the author seems to have had little concern about that.

## ⊰ 30. LITTLE LEAVES ⊱

*Italy?, 14th c. (Liber de Coquina, 2–3)*

*To make little leaves, take parsley, fennel, dill and onions, chop them thoroughly with a knife on a board and fry well with oil, and using other little leaves, fry like these except they should be well pounded first . . . and with them add in a little water.*

*You can even add fresh fish, raw without bones, with marjoram and rosemary, parsley and good spices mixed with cloves and pounded well in a mortar with the aforementioned fish. Make from this little tomacella sausages or meatballs like little acorns, and you can put it in with the aforementioned vegetables.*

*And to these vegetables you add pepper agreeably, and if the said vegetables you want to chop, do it with a knife. Moisten however with meat broth and then let it boil. And if you want with the same vegetables some sausages or other salted meat or meatballs. The tomacella mentioned before that was made of fish, you can also make with pork loin, and you add in some spices.*

*For fasting days: Thus you can make the best leaves on fasting days, take parsley, dill, marjoram, fennel, onions, spices and saffron. Pound everything in a mortar. Then cook with oil and serve.*

"Little leaves" in the title refers to herbs including fennel fronds, green onion tops, and other leafy plants rather than tree leaves. The author of this text offers other slight variations not included here, herbs with chicken breast or cooked in almond milk, or pounded and fried quickly alone. It seems as if he was merely brainstorming all the possible variations he had actually cooked. That he offered both Lenten and regular variations provides some evidence that vegetables and fine herbs as here were enjoyed throughout the year. It may seem odd that a dish of fried herbs could be served on its own, but there was not always a rigid distinction

---

### ✣ FOODS FIT FOR VARIOUS PEOPLES AND PROFESSIONS IN 15TH-CENTURY ROME

Johannes of Bockenheim was a German clergyman working in Rome in the early fifteenth century. In a cookbook (*Registrum coquine*), he specifies exactly what kind of person each recipe would be good for: rustics, princes, clerics, even prostitutes. An herb omelet made of greens, cheese, eggs, saffron, and a little sugar is good for copyists and their wives. Copyists were men hired to literally copy out manuscripts before the invention of printing. Interestingly, the recipe is much simpler than another herb omelet that precedes it, and contains fewer expensive spices. Presumably copyists were not paid very well.[2]

---

in the past between herbs and tender greens, and here they are not merely a seasoning.

### ❧ 31. WHITE LEEKS ❧

*Savoy, modern-day border of Italy and France 15th c. (Chiquart, in Flandrin and Lambert*, Fêtes Gourmandes, *69)*

*To make white leeks, have the person who is appointed take the leeks and chop them up very fine and wash them well and place to boil. And then take a good piece of salted pork chine and clean it very well and place to boil with it, and when they are well boiled, remove them to nice clean tables and save the water in which they have boiled. Take a good mortar of blanched almonds, and then take the bouillon in which the said leeks have been boiled and pound the almonds, and if you don't have enough bouillon then use beef broth or mutton—and be careful that it's not too salty. Then place your broth to boil in a nice clean pot. And then take two nice clean knives and chop your leeks, and then pound them in the mortar. And being pounded, add in your bouillon of almonds and the boiling water. And being boiled, when you want to dress it, put your meat in beautiful platters and the leek bouillon put on top.*

By white leeks, Chiquart means the part growing beneath the ground, which is blanched by mounding up earth around it while it grows, which is why leeks usually have dirt inside. The same process can be used for asparagus, indeed any plant deprived of sunlight will not produce chlorophyll and becomes white—including cauliflower. Wash the leeks thoroughly both before and after chopping. The finished dish should be a smooth and thick sauce poured over a hunk of meat. Although a chine, meaning spine, is specified, a cured pork shoulder, small ham, or even hocks would also work.

≈ 32. CABOGES (CABBAGE) ≈

*England, 15th c. (Harleian, 6)*

*Take fayre caboges, an cutte hem, an pike hem clene and clene washe hem,
an parboyle hem in fayre water, an thanne presse hem on a fayre bord; an
than choppe hem, and caste hem in a faire pot with goode freysshe broth, an
with mery-bonys, and let it boyle: thane grate fayre brede and caste ther-to,
an caste ther-to Safron an salt; or ellys take gode grwel y-mad of freys flesshe,
y-draw thorw a straynour, and caste ther-to. An whan thou servyst yt inne,
knocke owt the marw of the bonys, an ley the marwe 2 gobettys or 3 in a
dysshe, as the semyth best, & serve forth.*

*Take fair cabbages and cut them, and pick them clean and wash them. Then
parboil them in fair water and then press them on a fair board. And then chop
them and cast them in a fair pot with good fresh broth and with marrow bones
and let it boil. Then grate fair bread and cast therein, and cast therein saffron
and salt or else take good gruel made of fresh flesh, draw through a strainer and
cast therein. And when you serve it up, knock out the marrow from the bones
and lay two or three mouthfuls in a dish as seems best and serve forth.*

Typically, medieval vegetable recipes call for cooking vegetables well as
well as chopping and straining them into fine purees. This was considered
necessary to make them digestible. Quite often they were thickened with
bread crumbs and combined with meat as well. Here sections of marrow
bones, most likely beef, are included. Like little sections of tubes, the soft
inner marrow can be pushed out of each piece of bone after boiling. The final
dish is extremely rich and meaty.

≈ 33. TANSY ≈

*England, 15th c. (Harleian, 86)*

*Take faire Tansey, and grinde it in a mortar; And take eyren yolkes and white,
And drawe hem thorgh a streynour, and streyne also the Iuse of the Tansey
torgh a streynour: and mesle the egges and the Iuse togidre; And take faire
grece, and cast hit in a pan, and sette over the fyre til hit mylte; and caste
the stuffe thereon, and gader hit togidre with a sawcer or a dissh, as thou wilt
have hit more or lasse; And turne hit in the panne onys or twies, And so serve
it forth hote, yleched.*

*Take fair tansy and grind it in a mortar. Take egg yolks and whites and draw
them through a strainer and strain the juice of the tansy through a strainer
and mix the eggs and the juice together. Then take fair grease and cast it in a
pan and set over the fire till it melts and cast the stuff thereon and gather it
together with a saucer or a dish as you like, more or less, and turn it in the pan
once or twice. And so serve it hot, sliced.*

Tansy is an intriguingly bitter herb that has fern-like leaves and beautiful little yellow flowers. It was used in the past as purgative, though modern herbals warn that it is potentially toxic and should not be eaten during pregnancy. Strangely, it was formerly recommended for pregnant women. There is no indication that this dish was meant as medicine, though physicians said that a tansy is good for the stomach in springtime. The dish is essentially a cut-up green omelet. Any fresh green herb or spinach can be used as a substitute, though the flavor will not be the same. Tansy is easy to grow, though. As another method to obtain the green juice, pound the herb finely then wrap in a cloth then twist and squeeze until the

*Tansy.*

juice seeps through, mix with the egg and fry. It must be thick and firm enough to slice before service, keeping in mind that it would have been eaten with the fingers.

### ❧ 34. TINY LEAVES AND FENNEL ❧

*Italy, 15th c. (Anonimo Toscano, 2)*

*Take spinach, orache, clean well and boil them. Then remove and beat well with a knife. Then take parsley, fennel, anise, with onions and pound and chop with a knife, and fry in good oil. Then take other tiny herbs and fry them together, and add a bit of water and let it boil, and place in pepper and spices, and serve it. Another way, you can add in beaten eggs, fish meat without bones, meat of mutton or pork, or salted meat. Diversify it according to the discretion of the good cook. Or using rosemary, parsley with good fish or pounded meat, country folk make mortadella and comandella and many other things. In this way you can use domestic herbs or wild if you can't get them from the garden.*

What the author of this recipe intends is that any small leafy green or "herb" that happens to be at hand can be used either in a simple sautéed dish, or can be included in a compound dish with fish, meat, or even put into sausages such as mortadella, a kind of bologna, or *commandella*, which also appears to have been a sausage. Orache (*Atriplex hortensis*) is difficult to find in American groceries, but any bland leafy green, even lettuce, can be substituted. The same cooking method also works well with chard, beet greens, or collard greens.

### ❧ 35. COMPOST GOOD AND PERFECT ❧

*Italy, 15th c. (Anonimo Veneziano, 12)*

*If you want to make good compost take sumac or dried grapes and anise, fennel and coriander and dragée candies and a bit of juniper and vinegar and mix everything together and put in enough saffron. Then take turnips or pears and herbs, nice parsnips and boil them together a bit and then throw the sauce over.*

Although the name and how the dish actually looks may not sound very appetizing because the term *compost* today only refers to rotting vegetable matter, we do still have the term *compote*. Here it is the combination of fruit and vegetables that is particularly appealing. To make the dish, peel and cut the vegetables and good firm pears into small dice. Boil them until tender. The sauce includes sumac, which is a sour dried hard red spice from a tree commonly used in the Middle East (not to be confused with poison sumac, which is white). It can still be bought in Middle Eastern grocery stores, usually preground. The other spices should all be dried seeds as well, rather than fresh herbs. The dragée candies are tiny sugar-coated whole spices. One can also obtain excellent, if not as authentic, results, by briefly blanching the root vegetables and then baking with the raw pears seasoned with the spices and then sprinkled with vinegar at the end.

### ≈ 36. EGGPLANT CASSEROLE ≈

*Spain—Aragonese-ruled Naples, 15th c. (Rupert of Nola, xviii)*

*Take eggplants and clean them of the skin and cut each in three or four slices and place them to them to cook in good mutton broth with an equal amount of onions and cook until they are well done. Being cooked remove them from the pot or casserole and press them well with a board. And when they are well flattened add in good Aragonese cheese which is grated and egg yolks and after flatten everything as if it were a stuffing of kid. Then place on fine sauce. To make the sauce place in the casserole ginger, mace, nutmeg, as well as fresh cilantro and parsley all mixed together. Then place the casserole in the oven and when it is cooked sprinkle on sugar and cinnamon and serve it forth.*

*Sumac berries.*

The eggplants in this dish should be boiled only for a few minutes so they stay whole. Flattening them makes the final dish more solid and substantial and the cheese and egg yolks hold it together. In the end the texture is rather like a good eggplant parmigiana, though without the tomatoes, naturally. A Spanish Manchego cheese works superbly here. For the impatient, this is one of the very few dishes that can be cooked in the microwave. Layer peeled slices of 2 large eggplants with sliced onions, spices and grated cheese in a covered casserole and sprinkle with broth (or better olive oil) and cook on high temperature for about 15 minutes. Sprinkle on the sugar and cinnamon and cook again uncovered for about 3 to 5 minutes.

### ⇛ 37. ROYAL FAVA BEANS ⇚

*Spain—Aragonese-ruled Naples, 15th c. (Rupert of Nola, liv)*

*Take the whitest favas which have not been eaten by weevils. Then remove the skins so they are nice and white. And after boil them in clean water that is cold. And when they come to the boil remove them from the fire and pour off the water and drain them well in a manner that no water remains. Then take white almonds and clean and make milk of them but if you have goat's milk it will be better. Then put the favas in the pot to let them cook. Then put in the milk enough so that it will be soup and likewise add fine sugar and put it on the fire. And stir them in the manner of gourds and don't stop at all until they are cooked and test them for salt and all things, plus sugar and when it is well cooked place in pieces of sticks of cinnamon and let it cook well. And when it is cooked and soft enough lift it from the fire, and as you have added in the cinnamon, include a bit of rose water. And after plate it and sprinkle with fine sugar. And with such things you know that any vegetable that smells of smoke, you remove it with a bit of sour yeast in this manner. Take the yeast and put it in a cloth of linen that is white. And when the pot boils add this cloth with yeast in the pot and let it boil the whole time and it removes the smoke. Also if it is too salty take a white cloth of linen and bathe it in cold water and when it boils stir the cloth in the pot and put on the cover and place it on the coals and cover it very well while the cloth is in the pot and on the cover place a great amount of salt. And also under the pot, and then remove the cloth. Than take another cloth bathed in rose water and cover the pot with the cloth and place the cover over the cloth. And thus remove the salt in this manner from soups and the smoke and everything, it is a secret that no one sees at all.*

This dish is what in the Middle Ages would have been called a pottage, or thick soup rather than a "soup" proper, which implies it has bread in it to sop up the liquid. In later centuries dried fava beans would be firmly associated with peasant fare and rarely appear in cookbooks unless they are fresh spring favas. Here, however they are termed "royal," probably because they include spices, sugar, and rosewater, all expensive imported goods. The instructions that follow show that since everything was cooked over fire or coals, the smell of smoke from the fire or burning, could be considered a defect, especially in a light, creamy, and sweet dish such as this. Strangely, today, we actively seek out the aroma of smoke in barbecues and smoked meats, probably because it is not normally in our foods. Furthermore, these directions show that even professional chefs made mistakes such as adding too much salt.

## STARCHES AND PASTA

### ≈ 38. GRUYAU (BARLEY GRUEL) ≈

*France, 14th c. (Viandier, 163)*

*A gruyau of cleaned barley. If it is not cleaned, prepare it by pounding well like wheat in a mortar and then cook it and crush it and let it boil with almond milk, and put in salt and sugar. Some pound and sieve, but it should not be too thick.*

The term *gruyau* seems to be related to gruel. The technique for cleaning wheat involves soaking and then wrapping in a cloth and pounding gently until the hull is separated, but barley available today has already had the hull removed. The presence of almond milk suggests that this may have been a dish for Lent. As specified the grains can be served merely pounded to a coarse consistency or passed through a sieve for a smooth texture. The frumenty made of wheat was served between courses as an *entremets*, but of barley it is a dish for the infirm. Barely and barley water were among the most common foods given to the sick since ancient times.

### ≈ 39. FURMENTE ≈

*Northern England, 15th c. (Liber Cure Cocorum, 7)*

*Take wete, and pyke hit fayre [and clene]*
*And do hit in a mortar shene;*
*Bray hit a lytelle, with water hit spryng*
*Tyl hit hulle, with-oute lesyng.*
*Then wyndo hit wele, need thou mot;*
*Wasshe hit fayre, put hit in a pot;*
*Boyle hit tylle hit breast, then*
*Let hit doun, as I the kenne.*
*Take know mylke, and play hit up*
*To hit be thykkerede to sup.*
*Lye hit up with yolkes of eyren,*
*And kepe hit wele, lest hit berne.*
*Couloure hit with safron and salt hit wele,*
*And servyd hit for the, Syr, at the mele;*
*With sugur candy, thou may hit dowce,*
*If hit be served in grete lordys howce.*
*Take black sugur for mener menne;*
*Be ware the with, for hit wylle brenne.*

*Take wheat and pick it fair [and clean]*
*And put it in a shiny mortar;*
*Pound it a little, sprinkle with water*
*Till it hulls, no lying.*

*Then undo it well, need you must;*
*Wash it fair, put it in pot;*
*Boil it till it bursts, then*
*Lay it aside, as I know.*
*Take now milk, and heat it up*
*Till it be thickened to sop.*
*Add in yolks of egg,*
*And keep it well, lest it burn.*
*Color it with saffron and salt it well,*
*And serve it forth, Sir, at the meal;*
*With sugar candy, you may sweeten it,*
*If it be served in a great Lord's house.*
*Take black sugar for lower men;*
*Be careful with it, for it will burn.*

Frumenty was a kind of porridge made of whole wheat berries normally served with venison in noble households, but clearly ordinary people ate it too, with less expensive and less refined (black) sugar. The procedure is fairly simple and begins by hulling the wheat kernels by moistening and pounding gently in a brass mortar with a little water until the outer coating loosens. The hulls are then washed away and the wheat boiled until it becomes soft. Then it is cooked gently in milk and egg yolks with saffron and covered with sugar candies or dark sugar. Because the author sometimes adds in lines in the interest of a rhyme rather than culinary sense, there are some passages here that are not totally clear. It seems that "with-oute lesyng" means that he is telling you the truth, a common expression in Middle English. The wheat berries one can purchase today require no hulling, instead soak overnight and then boil and proceed with the recipe.

### ❧ 40. FOR FRAUNCHE MELE (BREAD PUDDING) ❧

*Northern England, 15th c. (Liber Cure Cocorum, 36)*

*Take swongene eyren in bassyne clene,*
*And kreme of mylke that is so schene,*
*And myyd bred, thou put there to,*
*And powder of peper er thou more do;*
*Coloure hit with safrone in hast,*
*And kremelyd sewet of schepe on last,*
*And fylle thy bagge that is so gode,*
*And sewe hit fast, Syr, for tho rode;*
*Whenne hit is sothun, thou schalt hit leche,*
*And broyle hyt on gredel, as I the teche*

*Take beaten eggs in a clean basin,*
*And cream of milk that is so shiny,*

*And bread crumb, you put into,*
*And ground pepper before you do more;*
*Color it with saffron quickly,*
*And anoint with sheep fat lastly,*
*And fill the bag that is so good,*
*And sew it tight, sir, by the cross;*
*When it is boiled, you will slice it,*
*And broil it on a griddle, as I teach you.*

This fascinating recipe in the end is similar to grilled slices of polenta that are fashionable today, though obviously based on bread crumbs rather than corn. It is a form of what the English now call a pudding. First, a thick mixture is formed with crustless stale bread beaten or grated into crumbs mixed with cream and eggs and spices. To two eggs add 2 1/2 cups of bread crumbs, 1 cup of cream, 1 tsp ground pepper and a good pinch of saffron powdered. Exact proportions are not important, but the batter should be thick and a little crumbly. Assuming sheep fat is not available, butter will also work—about two tablespoons melted. Furthermore, assuming a bag (meaning a sheep's stomach) is unobtainable, a cloth spread with butter and dusted with flour achieves the same effect. Lay the prepared cloth in a bowl, dusted side up, put the crumb mixture inside and then tie the top tightly with twine, leaving a little room for expansion. It is then ready to be boiled for about 20 minutes until firm. The recipe can be doubled, but it will take longer to boil. Let it cool, remove the cloth, and then slice. These are then grilled either on a stovetop griddle or on a barbecue grill. They can also be fried in butter.

### ⇥ 41. FARRO OF SPELT ⇤

*Italy, 15th c. (Anonimo Toscano, 23)*

*Take faro of spelt clean and cracked, and let it boil a bit, and toss away the water, wash the said faro well and return to cook in goat or sheep's milk, or almond until it is well cooked. Chop some fresh cheese and mix with egg white and place in the boiling faro, and boil a bit. Then add flesh of a young hen or chicken, as with blancmanche, and on top place pork fat; and if you want to make it yellow, color it with saffron and egg yolks, and sprinkle with sugar.*

The texture of this dish is similar to a risotto, though this was probably the original ingredient used before rice became popular in the Middle Ages. The dish is called farro, though today farro and spelt designate the name of the grain itself, an ancient ancestor to modern wheat. Whole farro can be found in Italian specialty shops and can also be soaked overnight before cooking, much like beans.

## ᢒ 42. PARLEM DE FIDEUS (NOODLE SOUP) ᢒ

*Spain—Aragonese-ruled Naples, 15th c. (Rupert of Nola, xx)*

*Take the noodles and clean them of dirt. And when they are nice and clean take a pot that is clean and fill with good chicken broth or mutton that is very fatty and salted and place on the fire and when it begins to boil place the noodles in the broth with a pinch of sugar. And when the noodles are half cooked in the chicken or mutton broth, add in the pot goat's or sheep's milk. If perchance you can't find or don't have any, add that of almonds, for these should never be missing. And leave it so that everything cooks together. And when it is well cooked, lift the pot off the fire and let it rest a bit. And after take plates and sprinkle each with sugar and cinnamon. . . . Many prefer that things which are cooked in broth or meat should not have sugar or milk added. But all this is according to the appetite of the master and each person. And those noodles which are cooked in meat broth deserve good Aragonese cheese which is fine and well grated.*

Fideos are a very thin short type of pasta typical of Catalunya on the east coast of what is today Spain. Unlike Italian pasta, these noodles are today first fried then moistened with broth, much like rice in paella, a practice that hearkens back to the region's Arab past. In this dish, however, they are cooked in a creamy soup, which is also a typical treatment in Italian pasta dishes of the same period. Manchego works for the grated cheese at the end.

## EGGS AND DAIRY

## ᢒ 43. GREEN BROTH OF EGGS AND CHEESE ᢒ

*France, 14th c. (Viandier, 155)*

*Take parsley and a bit of sage and also a bit of saffron in the greens, and bread soaked and broken up in pea puree or boiling water and then ginger mixed with wine and let it boil. Then put cheese in the eggs, when they have been poached in water, and it should be thick and green, and some don't add any bread but put in almond milk.*

Although the order of the directions makes this a little confusing, the final dish should be poached eggs in a thick green sauce with cheese. It is best if the herbs are chopped and the sauce made first and then the eggs are poached, sprinkled with grated cheese and served in a bowl with the sauce underneath. The pea puree the author refers to was a standard thin broth based on dried peas, cooked and sieved. It was used for Lent when meat broths could not be used, as was the almond milk.

## ᕽ 44. HOW TO ROAST CHEESE ᕼ

*France?, 14th c. (Tractatus de modo preparandi et condiendi omnia cibaria, 393)*

*Take a whole cheese, judged to be full fat, on a spit divided and formed in 4 parts and roast before the fire, always turning the spit. And when it is roasted, scrape a knife over a slice of toasted bread, and return to roasting.*

This is the ancestor of a technique still common in Switzerland for serving raclette. Here the melted cheese is turned on a spit but it can also be placed under a broiler and the melted cheese on top scraped off onto toast. The cheese is then replaced to melt another layer.

## ᕽ 45. MALACHES WHYTE (EGG TART) ᕼ

*England, 14th c. (Forme of Cury, 133)*

*Take ayren and wryng hem thurgh a cloth. Take powdour fort, brede igrated, & safroun, & cast thereto a gode quantitie of buttur with a litull salt. Medle all yfere. Make a foyle in a trap & bake it wel therinne, and serve it forth.*

*Take eggs and wring them through a cloth. Take strong powdered spices, grated bread, and saffron and throw in a good quantity of butter with a little salt. Mix it all up. Make a leaf of pastry in a pan and bake it well therein, and serve it.*

Why the author specifies straining the eggs rather than beating them is not clear, but it is a common direction in old cookbooks. The final dish should be a kind of egg tart. For a small 9-inch pan, use six eggs, a teaspoon or less of spices to taste—a mixture of pepper, ginger, cloves or whatever you prefer—about two slices of stale bread and two tablespoons of butter, melted and beaten in with the eggs. The pastry should be very thin and it should be baked until the crust begins to brown and the eggs are firmly set, about a half an hour or a little longer at 350 degrees.

## ᕽ 46. SLICES OF FRESH CHEESE ᕼ

*Spain—Aragonese-ruled Naples, 15th c. (Rupert of Nola, xxxi)*

*Take fresh cheese and cut it, each as big as a finger and make a dough that is well risen and made of beautiful flour and is fully mixed. Next take some egg yolks and mix it with the dough and the slices of cheese below and above. Then let them fry in a pan with fat that is good and turn them often so it doesn't burn. But if you make it boil in grease like doughnuts then it will be much better. And when they are cooked put on top sugar and eat them hot for any other way it is not at all a good dish.*

Although Rupert uses the term *pasta* in the original Catalan—meaning pastry dough in this recipe—it seems that his comparison with fried doughnuts suggests that this is cheese in a thick, yeasty batter. Cheese encased in risen dough would also work nicely—like a little calzone—but one wonders how the eggs could be mixed in with risen dough. Perhaps what he means is that the interior of each piece of dough is brushed with egg yolks and then each piece of cheese is encased in dough. Either way, a young mild but firm white cheese would work best, such as a goat's milk garrotxa from Catalunya.

### ⇨ 47. STUFFED EGGS ⇦

*Italy, 15th c. (Anonimo Veneziano, 26)*

*If you want to make stuffed eggs, take the eggs and place them to boil until they are completely hard and when they are cooked take them out and put them in cold water and shell them and cut them in half and pull out the yolks and take lean cheese as best you can find that is very sweet and herbs that you have cleaned well and washed and pounded in a mortar. When they are well beaten, take the egg yolks, the cheese and the spices and place in the mortar with the good herbs and pound well together into a paste, and moisten with raw egg or it will not be good, and place in a pan over the fire, and take the whites of egg that you have and fill with the mixture and let it cook. What they are cooked remove and powder above with sugar and bring hot to the table. And if you want to make them tasty, take, etc.*

The directions here have probably been muddled by miscopying. Why one would cook the mixture before stuffing is a mystery. The recipe works fine if one merely stuffs the eggs with the mixture and cooks it gently in a pan cut side down until the filling has firmed up. The last line also appears to be cut off and may mean that it can be further seasoned if one likes, perhaps with spices. In any case, these make a pleasant change from devilled eggs common today, which are served cold.

## SAUCES

### ⇨ 48. A JAUNETTE SAUCE FOR FISH ⇦

*France, 14th c. (Viandier, 156)*

*A yellow sauce for fried fish. Fry in oil without flour. Pound almonds, moisten mostly with wine, and verjuice, and strain it and let it boil. Then pound ginger, cloves, grains of paradise, and a bit of saffron, and moisten with your bouillon, and add it in to boil well, and add sugar, it should be thick.*

Although some manuscripts interpreted the French phrase *"poisson froit"* to mean cold fish, it seems to make more sense if the latter word is the past tense of "to fry." Hence, it specifies not flouring the fish before frying. The sauce should include enough saffron to make it bright yellow—a good pinch at least. A handful of peeled and pounded almonds and a cup of wine should make enough sauce for a few servings. A firm but light fish such as halibut works well, but almost any fish is fine.

### ⇥ 49. MUSTARD ⇤

*France?, 14th c. (*Tractatus de modo preparandi et condiendi omnia cibaria, *395)*

*Mustard you can make with grains either of mustard or of arugula. And you can season it along with honey or boiled grape must. Otherwise, even with cooked egg yolks and sugar. If you make it for fish moisten with vinegar; for meat with verjuice. And it is better.*

*A mustard confection: take anise and a little more of cumin, and crush in a mortar. Then add more of cinnamon than of sugar, moistened with vinegar, and add bread crumb. Crush pepper in a mortar with toasted bread and moisten with meat broth and wine or vinegar. Then in a little pot or pan let it boil and stir well.*

The earliest forms of mustard were made with both mustard seed and sapa or boiled down grape must. It is actually from the latter ingredient that we get the name for both the condiment and the plant. Clearly there were many different forms, often spicy, sweet and sour. There were also variations using fruit.

### ⇥ 50. PUR VERDE SAWCE (GREEN SAUCE) ⇤

*Northern England, 15th c. (*Liber Cure Cocorum, *27)*

*Take persole, peletre an oyns, and grynde,*
*Take white bred myude by kynde*
*Temper alle up with venegur or wyne,*
*Force hit with powder of peper fine.*

*Take parsley and an ounce of pellitory and grind*
*Take white bread crumb by kind*
*Moisten all with vinegar or wine,*
*Stuff it with powder of pepper fine.*

This sauce is a standard throughout medieval cookery and an ancestor of a modern pesto. It can be used with virtually any kind of meat. Bread was a universal thickening agent, and the combination of herbs, pepper, and sour vinegar is a typically medieval combination. The pellitory mentioned is an herb (*Anacyclus pyrethrum*) similar to chamomile with daisy-like flowers and fern-like leaves. It is bitter and oil extracted from the plant was once used to treat toothaches. Any green herb will serve as a substitute though, and few recipes in other cookbooks specify this particular herb.

### ❧ 51. GOOD SAUCE FOR CHICKENS ☙

*Italy, 15th c. (Anonimo Veneziano, 5)*

*To Make a good sauce for chickens, take pomegranate and make wine by hand, and place in this wine good sweet spices, and if it seems too strong, add pounded anise, or rosewater. Others use wine of sour pomegranates and wine of good sweet grapes, and place these two wines together with enough sweet spices. If you don't have grapes put in a bit of honey and let it boil, the spices should be raw; you don't want to let it stand so it spoils.*

This is one of many recipes that shows direct influence of Middle Eastern cuisine on that of Europe. The Venetians would have had firsthand knowledge of these cultures through the spice trade. Reduced pomegranate syrup was and still is a typical flavoring of the eastern Mediterranean, and although this recipe advises using "wine"—actually juice—the combination of a sweet and sour fruit sauce with spices on meat is typical of both cuisines in the Middle Ages.

### ❧ 52. CIVET OR BLACK SAUCE FOR BOAR ☙

*Italy, 15th c. (Anonimo Veneziano, 8)*

*If you want to make a black sauce for wild pig, take meat that has been well cooked and well beaten and well pounded in a mortar. Take the crumb of bread well toasted until it's black and soak it well in vinegar until well softened, well sieved and mixed with the pounded meat. Add long pepper, grains of paradise, ginger and pound these three things in a spice mortar, and place in the sauce with vinegar, lean meat broth and let this sauce boil in a vessel. This sauce should be black, powerfully spicy and sour with vinegar.*

The directions here suggest that medieval palates did indeed prefer very strong combinations of opposing flavors, here bitter, sour, and spicy. This was considered the appropriate condiment for strong-flavored, though of course never rotten-smelling, boar. It also includes some of the more exotic spices in the medieval larder, which can still be purchased today with a little effort. Long pepper is a relative of black pepper that looks like a little black stick. Grains of paradise or in Venetian dialect here, *melegette*, come from the east coast of Africa and are a very hot little pepper like seed. They would in the course of the centuries be replaced with chili peppers or regular black pepper.

## FRUIT

### ⊰ 53. FRIED APPLES ⊱

*France?, 14th c. (*Tractatus de modo preparandi et condiendi omnia cibaria*, 395)*

*Apple tree in garden.*

> *Place apples cut thinly in meat broth and let it boil a bit, and then remove the peel. And if you want, pound spices and saffron and a bit of flour to fry, and add whatever fat you like or butter.*

The combination of apples with meat broth may seem odd, but these are essentially a side dish to accompany meats. The spices and flour should be lightly sprinkled on the apples, which have been cooked very briefly, and then quickly fried until golden brown. Use a firm and tart apple such as McIntosh or Granny Smith.

### ⊰ 54. ON LOMBARD COMPOST ⊱

*Italy?, 14th c. (*Liber de Coquina*, 419)*

> *To the Lombard Compost take finely chopped saffron, anise seeds and fennel. Take to cook in must and cook until reduced by half. With this must moisten mustard.*

> *Then take little turnips and parsnips, figs, apples divided into fours, and pears divided in half, whole carrots, radishes, parsley, white fennel, and place to cook the above figs, apples, pears and radishes in water. When they are cooked, compose them nicely in a clean vase, putting over them the moistened mustard and seeds above mentioned.*

> *If you wish you can add honey. And you can make it with sumac and canella moistened. And with the said must, to redden, add mulberries which are found way up in trees. And you can make it with raspberries that you find in the fields. And you can balance it with sugar and vinegar.*

The mustard the author speaks of is prepared with mustard seeds pounded in reduced grape must. The resulting relish, the descendant of which is still made in Cremona, is both sweet, sour, and spicy. Sumac is a hard, red, berry-like seed that when crushed is used to give a bright sour flavor to dishes or is sprinkled on flat bread. It can be found in Middle Eastern grocery stores and should not be confused with poison sumac, which is white. Compare this recipe with that of Lancelot (Recipe 156), where mustard had completely changed, as of course it has again.

## ❧ 55. RYSSHEWS OF FRUYT ❧

*England, 15th c. (Forme of Cury, 141)*

*Take fyges and raisouns; pyke hem and waisshe hem in wyne. Grynde hem
with apples and peeres ypared and ypiked clene. Do thereto gode powdours
and hole spices; make balles thereof, frye in oil, and serve hem forth.*

*Take figs and raisins, pick them clean, and wash them in wine. Grind them
with apples and pears, peeled and picked clean. Add in spice powder and
whole spices, make balls of this and fry in oil. Serve them.*

Without any binding agent, it seems that these fruit balls (Rysshews)
would have been sautéed in a shallow pan rather than deep-fried like fritters.
They would fly apart in a good deal of oil. In a frying pan, though, the sticki-
ness of the dried fruit keeps them together if they are very well pounded
into a smooth paste. The author leaves it up to the reader to add whatever
she likes, so any combination of cinnamon, cloves, nutmeg, or more exotic
spices will serve. More perplexing is the use of whole spices in many medieval recipes. It can only be assumed that no one minded chomping down on
a whole clove or sliver of cinnamon, unless these were candied, which is a
possibility, though unspecified.

## ❧ 56. STRAWBERYE ❧

*England, 15th c. (Harleian, 29)*

*Take Strawberys, & waysshe hem in tyme of yere in gode red wyne; than
strayne thorwe a clothe, & do hem in a potte with gode Almaunde mylke,
a-lay it with Amydoun other with the flore of Rys, & make it chargeaunt and
lat it boyle, and do ther-in Roysonys of coraunce, Safroun, Pepir, Sugre grete
plente, pouder Gyngere, Canel, Galyngale; poynte it with Vynegre, & a lytil
white grece put ther-to; color it with Alkenade, & droppe it a-bowte, plante it
with the graynys of Pome-garnad, & than serve it forth.*

*Take strawberries in season and soak them in good red wine. Then strain
through a cloth and cook them in a pot with almond milk, add in wheat
starch or rice starch and let it boil until thick. And add in currants, saffron,
pepper, a great deal of sugar, ground ginger, cinnamon, galingale. Perk it up
with vinegar and a little lard added in. Color it with alkanet sprinkled about
and stick in pomegranate seeds and then serve it.*

This dish is a kind of spicy thick strawberry pudding and, although the
ingredients sound completely bizarre together, the flavors meld nicely.
Galingale is a spicy relative of ginger that can be bought in Southeast
Asian shops. Use dried rather than fresh. Alkanet, a red dye made from the
root of a European herb (*Alkanna tinctoria*), is probably the only ingredient

that will be difficult to find; it is only used here as a coloring and can be omitted.

### ⊰ 57. GOOD CODONYAT (QUINCE) ⊱

*Spain—Aragonese-ruled Naples, 15th c. (Rupert of Nola, xxxvi)*

*Take as many quinces as you have guests, in the quantity that you wish to make, and quarter them and remove the core and then pare away the peel and when they are well cleaned soak in tepid water. Next remove from this water and place them to boil in cold water and when they begin to be soft, remove them, they will be cooked. Being removed from the cauldron, pound them well in a mortar. Then moisten them with a bit of their water and pass through a sieve. Next take seven pounds of almonds and wash them without peeling in cold water, or tepid which is better, and pound them well in a mortar and when they are well pounded pass through a sieve moistened with tepid water. If it is a meat day moisten with meat broth and add in milk to the quinces. Next add in all manner of fine spices such as good ginger and good cinnamon and saffron, grains of paradise and nutmeg, and mace. And if it is a meat day add in egg yolks for each plate. And if it is a fish day don't. When it becomes well thickened put it in plates and sprinkle on sugar and cinnamon.*

This is a thick, porridge-like dish made of quince. More typically the term *codonyat* refers to a sweet quince paste, called *membrillo* in Spain. A good proportion of Rupert's recipes include almonds, sugar, and exotic spices, and this clearly reflects the taste preference of his royal patrons.

## SWEETS

### ⊰ 58. CREPES LARGE AND SMALL ⊱

*France, 14th c. (Viandier, 256)*

*For the large ones use a syrup pot or brass basin and for the small use an iron pan. Make them with egg yolks and flour beaten together, have a wooden bowl and hot fat, and place the batter in the aforementioned bowl, it should not be too thick. Dip your hand into the pan above the hot fat and keep them from browning too much. For little crepes you can beat egg whites and yolks in with the flour, so that they will be a little thicker than for big crepes. You need a little fire but enough so the fire is hot, and take a wooden bowl pierced at the bottom and put in the batter and then when everything is ready, let it pour out, and make them like a little buckle or bigger, and across the buckle a kind of fastener also of dough; and let it cook in the fat until they are puffy.*

These are clearly the direct ancestor of what we call today funnel cakes and not at all what is today called a crepe in France. For the larger version, the author appears to mean dip your hand into the bowl containing the batter, rather than into the pan itself. The idea is that the batter will dribble from your hand into the fat, creating a pattern. The second option sounds much safer, and is easier to make using a funnel, holding in the batter with a finger until ready to form. Vegetable oil is also a more practical modern ingredient; by fat the author probably had rendered lard in mind. Taillevent, or whoever the original author was, liked the shape of a buckle—the kind used on shoes or belts, a circle with a cross bar and fastening pin—sort of like a little wheel in the end. Any shape is appropriate though, including letters. Although not specified, these are best heavily sprinkled with sugar right after frying.

#### ⊰ 59. FYGEY ⊱

*England, 14th c. (Forme of Cury, 118)*

*Take almaundes blaunched; grynde hem and drawe hem up with water and wyne, quarter fyges, hole raisons. Cast thereto powdour ginger and hony clarified; seeth it wel & salt it, & serve forth.*

*Take blanched almonds, grind them, remove and mix with water, wine, quartered figs, whole raisins. Add in powdered ginger, clarified honey, boil it well and salt it, and serve.*

This is an interesting variation of figgy pudding based on almonds and can be served at Christmas—as in the song "We Wish You a Merry Christmas." For two servings, a quarter pound of almonds and a cup each of water and white wine will suffice, with a handful of raisins and a few quartered dried figs. Ginger and honey can be added to taste. The final dish should be thick like a modern-day pudding.

#### ⊰ 60. TO CANDY GREEN ALMONDS, UNRIPE PEACHES AND GREEN WALNUTS, BEING LITTLE YOUNG ONES, NEITHER TOO HARD OR SOFT, ETC. ⊱

*Italy, 15th c. (Anonimo Veneziano, 67)*

*Take the said almonds clean and perforate them, the walnuts with six holes, the peaches with six, the almonds with four. They should be soaked in water and every day the water changed many times until they are sweet, then boil them in water; the walnuts boil half an hour, the peaches and almonds when they begin to soften boil half a quarter of an hour, then put them to dry in the shade and in the wind in a basket or on a rack for three days, the peaches and almonds for two. Then fill the holes with cloves, cinnamon and ginger. Next boil them in honey for the space of 6 paternosters, then remove from the honey and boil in another honey until the honey is cooked. Then over the honey put fine spices and put in a jar in the sun for the space of fifteen days well sealed. The peaches should be made in the same way except that they want to be boiled in the first honey until they are cooked, they don't need to be changed. Keep in mind that the almonds should not be used past mid April in hot places, because their shell will be too hard.*

Young fuzzy green almonds and immature peaches look almost identical early in the spring. Both, along with walnuts, have been eaten at this stage but require either pickling, or as in this recipe, candying. The soaking will take many days to completely remove bitterness, especially in the case of walnuts—which at this point look like little green balls. The shell is soft at this point and embedded in the green flesh. After boiling and drying, the holes should probably be filled with ground spices. To recite six paternosters (the Lord's Prayer) takes about three minutes.

### ⇥ 61. TO MAKE NUN'S BOZOLATI ⇤

*Italy, 15th c. (Anonimo Veneziano, 68)*

*Take eggs beaten very well and a bit of salt, as many eggs as you want with the fine flour that you want to make the aforementioned. Make the dough with the beaten eggs without any water. If you want honey, for every ten eggs you want a good kitchen spoon of honey, if you want them with sugar for every 10 eggs you want an ounce of sugar. You want it to be soaked and formed quickly and have in mind that they must be cooked at once, so that they don't catch a breeze nor the sun, which will quickly spoil them. They should be cooked in a testa that doesn't burn the bozolati. Thus when you go to cook them, one by one, make sure that the earthenware has not been greased, clean it well if it was greased.*

The name of these confections appears to be related to the bozzolo, or silk-worm's cocoon, and may refer to the fact that nuns pulled silk from cocoons and these have a similar shape and a silky texture inside. The name might also be a little ribald. Cake flour works best to achieve this texture and the batter should be somewhere between a pancake batter and a biscuit dough. Little cocoon shapes can be formed with two spoons. They are cooked over the coals in an earthenware vessel, the testa, which in this case should not be greased, presumably to prevent scorching. A nonstick pan works fine as well. The egg yolk and flour mixture result in a very soft and rich kind of biscuit.

### ⇥ 62. FRYTOURS (FRITTERS) ⇤

*England, 15th c. (Harleian, 73)*

*Take yolkes of egges, drawe hem thorgh a streynour, caste there-to faire floure, berme and ale; stere it*

*Woman with a testa.*

*togidre til hit be thik. Take pared appelles, cut hem thyn like obleies, ley hem in the batur, then put hem into a ffrying pan, and fry hem in faire grece or buttur til thei ben browne yelowe; then put hem in dishes, and strawe Sugur in hem ynogh, And serve hem forthe.*

*Take egg yolks, draw them through a strainer, cast on fine flour, yeast, and ale, and stir it together until it is thick. Take sliced apples, cut them like wafers, lay them in the batter, then put them into a frying pan and fry them in good grease or butter until they are golden brown, then put them in dishes and sprinkle on them enough sugar. And serve them forth.*

This recipe is indicative of a common cooking technique adapted to English ingredients, which incidentally works better than other continental versions, some of which include milk or wine, no yeast, or a different cooking fat. The apples should be peeled and cored and cut horizontally into wafer shapes, which is what "obleies" refers to. Commercial yeast either in cake from or powdered can be used for berme, and the best results are achieved if the batter is allowed to rest to let the yeast bloom. A cast-iron skillet with at least two inches of cooking oil or melted butter works best. The cooking oil should be hot and is ready when a small spoonful of batter floats to the surface and sizzles. It is too hot if it browns immediately. If using butter it should be heated below the smoking point. Cook about four or five fritters fit in a pan at once, depending on the size of the apple.

### ᘓ 63. GARBIES A LA CATALANA ᘔ

*Spain—Aragonese-ruled Naples, 15th c. (Rupert of Nola, xxxiv–xxxv)*

*Take borage and wheatgrass and clean them and after let them boil in salted water and when cooked drain off the water in which they were cooked and place between two cutting boards so that you can press out all the water. Next take good fresh cheese and all the good fine spices. Next take a bit of fine wheat flour. Then take fresh lard that has not been salted. Make a dough with this flour and the lard and a bit of tepid water. Then take the borage and wheatgrass and the cheese and spices and chop everything together well. Next take many egg yolks that have been hard boiled and return to chopping everything together. Next make the dough very thin and take the fresh cheese and mix it with the other chopped things. Then make with this dough a disk like your hand and place the mixture in the disk and cover gently. Then take a pan of tinned copper and heat the fresh lard or butter and when it is hot, place the coquettes in and cook. Then place in a plate and put on rosewater and honey or if you want eat them with sugar and cinnamon.*

Although the directions are not entirely clear since they specify to chop the cheese with the green ingredients and then they advise adding cheese in a few lines down, it will really not make a difference when you add it. By fresh cheese the author means something soft like cottage cheese or farmer cheese. It also will not matter if each individual disk is folded over or covered with another disk. You will have either circles, like little ravioli, or half moons. A shallow layer of fat will be enough to fry these. The author calls them coquettes or little cakes.

## DRINKS

### ◄ 64. TO DEGREASE ALL WINES ►

*France, 14th c. (*Viandier, 235)

*Take a bowl of seeds from red wine only, dried and pounded, and a full bowl of the grease of the same kind and color of wine and a denier of bread yeast and half a pound of alum and two knobs of ginger and a bit of burnt wine lees, all these things well crushed and beaten, place in the vessel then stir well with a short stick split at the end into fours, until the scum rises, and the stick should go only a foot into the vessel; then you can decant it.*

What exactly grease is in a barrel of spoiled wine might be is uncertain, but it seems to be a cloudy thickness that is removed with the ingredients and procedure above. The recipe shows that wine was expensive enough that one would resort to remedies, even if it was already spoiled. Other faults included a musty smell, bitterness, a woody flavor, and general cloudiness, all of which could apparently be corrected to satisfy medieval drinkers.

### ◄ 65. WINE COMMENTS ►

*France?, 14th c. (*Tractatus de modo preparandi et condiendi omnia cibaria, 381)

*Our talk takes its start with wine, since this is the universally preferred drink and among other drinks so much better and more dignified. The spirit and body it invigorates, digests food, corrects bad complexion, drives away sadness and cares, and makes man cheerful and jolly. I say this if it is good and not corrupt, and drunk in moderation. Corrupt wine causes the opposite, it impedes digestion, corrupts foods, generates bad blood, and makes men sad, sluggish and ponderous.*

*As elsewhere described, the best and most praise-worthy is a matter to some extent of conserving its goodness, so it does not corrupt, or equally if already corrupt, bringing it back to its pristine state. And thus of wine, since it is a more worthy drink than others, labor ever more diligently in this regard so that its goodness is conserved, and even if on account of negligence it becomes corrupt, you can apply remedies so that it is brought back to its original state. First its conservation must be shown.*

*So that wine does not corrupt, take good reddish honey, and cook it, skimming it a bit till it firms, then in a bit of good wine infuse Italian crocus, then this mixture place in a barrel of wine, it preserves wine and gives it color and good flavor.*

Along with saffron ("crocus"), the author also suggests grains of musk, bay leaves, and oregano, as well as spices to correct various faults in wine. Ostensibly these would also flavor the wine, and it may be that the origin of these concoctions is partly medicinal but also an attempt to mask the flavor of wine that had gone bad. The very fact that the author starts the cookbook with these remedies suggests this was a major concern. One wine recipe, and there are twenty in all, describes how to make "claret" with 7 ounces of cinnamon, 6 of ginger, galangal leaves, spikenard, 3 ounces of cloves, 3 of long pepper, and honey. The recipe following it uses about forty spices and medicinal drugs. To make a concoction such as these, one can use either red or white wine plus any combination of spices, gently heated and then soaked overnight or for several days and sweetened to taste with honey. It is served at room temperature.

### ❧ 66. VIN COCTO (COOKED WINE) ❧

*Italy, 15th c. (Anonimo Veneziano, 64)*

*To make cooked wine, take dark red wine, the finest you can get and good honey; Place them to boil together with cinnamon flowers, and boil until reduced to one third and for every four cups of wine there should be one full of honey.*

*Vin cocto* was not used as a beverage, but rather a cooking ingredient, to lend sweetness and depth to a dish. It is essentially a reduced wine syrup. Similar to this is *mosto cotto* or cooked grape must, i.e., juice, which was also used. *Defrutum* was another version, and some authors differentiated these by specifying how far they should be reduced, by a third or a quarter. *Passum* was another relative, made with raisins, so the flavor would be even sweeter and richer.

# 3

## 🕊 THE RENAISSANCE

The recipes in this section are taken entirely from printed cookbooks and thus not only served a much broader readership but probably reached more than only the wealthiest of readers. Precise measurements and concise instructions became more common as well, and this seems to suggest that these works were written for less seasoned professionals. Martino of Como's work (*Libro de arte coquinaria*; Book on the Art of Cookery) was actually the first cookbook in print around 1470, although it was hidden within another work: *De honesta voluptate* (On Honest Pleasure) of Bartolomeo Sacchi, called Platina. By the sixteenth century, other works appeared. In France there was a handful of similar works under various titles; the one used here (*Livre fort excellent de cuisine* of 1555) contained the most new recipes, though it and those like it have often been confused with printed and expanded editions of the Viandier. About the same time entirely new and novel works were printed in Ferrara, particularly Christoforo di Messisbugo's *Banchetti* (Banquets), which both records feasts at the Este court and gives recipes; and *La Singolare Dottrina* (The Singular Doctrine), by Domenico Romoli, which comes from Florence. In England, new cookbooks appeared and in Spain, Rupert of Nola's work was printed in both Catalan and Spanish.

## COLD FOOD

### ❧ 67. TO MAKE PROSCIUTTO ❧

*Italy, 1549 (Messisbugo, 103ᵛ)*

*Take the little pork thighs from 8–10 pounds and place in salt. Every 2 days rub them well with your hands so they are well salted, draw off any brine from it, and let it remain in salt for 23 days. Then take a pot of white wine or red and boil it. Then take the hams, one by one and dip in the boiling wine, exchange them, switching thus three or four times and place them side by side and then return to the beginning to do the same. This you do six times for each. Next place them stretched across a table and take a pound of well pounded coriander, and sprinkle the hams, and then place them to press between two boards, and when they have remained there for a time thus, take a pound of crushed coriander, a pound of fennel, and three ounces powdered cloves, and cover the side. Then return on the other side to press for two more days. Then remove from the press and set them to dry in a hot place, but not where there is too much flame, and it will be absolutely perfect.*

This recipe is a clear reminder that a food eaten long ago is not necessarily the same as a product of the same name today. This recipe is much more of a spiced and smoked ham and the exterior would probably be partially cooked as well from the boiling wine. It is a distant ancestor to the raw prosciutto common today in Italy. The hot place Messisbugo mentions is most likely in the chimney or near but not directly over flames, so the meat is cured and then dried slowly, but not cooked in the drying process. Quite often these hams, and even salami, would be cooked in wine and spices and served cold before a banquet in the first course.

## SOUPS

### ❧ 68. HEMP SEED SOUP ❧

*Italy, 1470 (Martino, 32)*

*To make 12 servings, take a pound of hemp seeds. Clean them and let them boil in a pot until they begin to open, and then add a pound of white almonds, well pounded, and add them to the seeds. Pound it well and add a crustless bread. Distemper this with meat broth or thin chicken broth and pass through a sieve. Set it to boil in a pot over the coals far from the fire, stirring many times with a spoon. Then add half a pound of sugar and half an ounce of ginger, and a bit of saffron with rosewater. Serve it with sweet spices on top.*

Hemp was not a typical ingredient in food and was probably more often consumed by the poor than by wealthy people. It would have been relatively easy to find though because hemp was used to make ropes and was widely grown. When this recipe was first printed in a book called *De honesta voluptate* (On Honest Pleasure), the author, Platina, translated Martino's Italian into Latin. Thus *minestra di seme di canepa* became *Cibarium Cannabinum* or cannabis soup. Although related to the drug, it does not have the same properties, though interestingly Platina adds the following comments to the recipe: "This I think is similar to the Sienese baricocoli; however from many regular things irregular foods are made; for this is difficult to digest and causes nausea and stomach aches."[1] Perhaps Platina's advice to avoid this soup should be heeded.

### ⧉ 69. GARLIC SOUP ⧉

*France, 1555 (*Livre fort excellent de cuisine, *ix)*

*For a soup of garlic, take white wine and place in some beef marrow which has been well boiled and some beautiful garlic. Take the garlic and peel it and place it to boil with it. Take a partridge or two roasted and quartered. For the spices, ginger, cloves, a great deal of sugar, finely chopped rosemary and let everything boil together well. Then arrange the lovely roast [birds], place them in the bottom of the plate and serve with cinnamon or ginger.*

The author appears to become carried away with the beauty of the ingredients here, though they are very simple. For the marrow, soup bones or veal shanks are best. Boil them and remove the marrow from bone. The garlic cloves should remain whole. A much simpler, though less authentic version can be made with leftover chicken and whole garlic cloves boiled in white wine with spices.

### ⧉ 70. DIGESTIVE POTTAGE ⧉

*France, 1555 (*Livre fort excellent de cuisine, *lxvi)*

*To make a digestive pottage take a capon, a leg of veal and a half neck of mutton and let everything boil together with a little salt. Make it boil vigorously. When is well cooked take the bouillon and pass it through a sieve and place in an earthenware pot. Then take whole cloves and cinnamon in a white cloth and throw it in the said pot with a little rosewater just as you see is needed by reason. Then take bread crumb removed from the crust, egg yolks, a bit of saffron and verjuice and white powder, sugar, white wine, cinnamon, and throw everything together with the said bouillon and remove it so that it does not smell like smoke, and it is best when you work in the evening.*

From the author's suggestions this recipe is intended for the light evening meal or supper, a word which actually comes from the word *sop* or *soup*.

A pottage is a thick soup. It is intended to aid digestion, which refers not only to the action in the stomach, but the absorption of nutrients throughout the body. Being restorative, from which the word "restaurant" also derives, soups like this enabled a person to work late. Verjuice is unripe grape juice, called for in so many recipes.

### ⇥ 71. ITALIAN POTTAGE ⇤

*Italy, 1549 (Messisbugo, 92)*

*Take fat meat cut in little pieces, neither large nor small, and fry in melted lamb fat until they become colored. Then take a little broth and then some cleaned dried chestnuts, well washed, and place to cook with the meat, and after it is sautéed in this broth put together a bit of every sort of spice, but a little more cinnamon and crushed raw coriander, a half a pound of honey and let it then cook as you please and becomes colored, place in the pot together with the other things and leave to cook well, and when it is served place sugar and cinnamon over.*

Although not very clear given the lack of punctuation, the honey and spices are left to brown and then are added to the meat and chestnuts. Whatever the quantity of meat the final result will be very sweet. The ingredients here also suggest that this is a rather rustic dish; honey is not often used by Messisbugo, nor are dried chestnuts.

### ⇥ 72. TO MAKE A WHITE BROATHE ⇤

*England, 1540s or 50s (A Proper Newe Booke of Cokerye, Bii^v)*

*Take a necke of mutton and fayre water, and sette it upon the fyre and scome it cleane, and lette it boyle halfe awaye, then take forthe of the broathe two ladlefull, and put them in a platter, then chop two handefuls of parsely not to small, and let it boile with the mutton, then take twelve egges, and the sayde two ladle fuls of broathe and vergis, so that it be tarte of the verjis, and streyne them all together then season your broathe with salte, and a little before you goo to diner, put al these to your mutton, and stere it well for quailing, and serve it forth with soppes.*

The final consistency of this soup is slightly thick, the flavor sour, and the color light and milky from the eggs. It is much like the Greek egg-lemon soup. This is achieved by stirring the eggs and a little broth together with verjuice and adding them at the last minute over very gentle heat while stirring to prevent them from quailing—that is, curdling. This now-archaic verb in English seems related to the Spanish quajare—to curdle. The meat is served with the broth on a slice of bread in a bowl.

## MEAT

### 73. TO MAKE ROLLS OF MEAT FROM VEAL OR OTHER GOOD MEAT

*Italy, 1470 (Martino, 12)*

Barbeque.

*First take the lean meat from the rump and cut in long, thin slices and beat well on a chopping block or table with the side of the knife, and take salt and pounded fennel and place over the said slices of meat. Then take parsley, marjoram and good lardo and beat these things together with a bit of good spices, and spread these things well on the said slices. Then roll them up and stick on the spit to cook. But do not leave too long to dry on the fire.*

Rump meat cooks quickly and must be very tender, so a cutlet from the loin or leg (scallopine) works best. Flatten the slices gently by smacking with the flat side of the knife blade; in another recipe for veal cutlets, Martino specifies not to pound too thin. A flat, heavy disk of metal with a handle, in Italian, *batticarne*, is ideal, but not a meat tenderizer with a rough surface, which tears the meat. A shish kebab skewer with three or four of these rolls cooked on the grill is the easiest method today. Martino would have placed the spit on a jack in front of the fire. Platina in his Latin translation adds that these are very nourishing, make the body solid and leave little residue—meaning indigestible parts.[2] Lardo is cured unsmoked belly fat rather than rendered lard.

### 74. HARE WITH PAPPARDELLE (NOODLES)

*Italy, 1560 (Romoli, 151)*

*You must have a fat hare that has not been shot, but freshly caught. Make a little cut so that you can carefully remove the bowels and tripe, placing inside two bunches of sage, rosemary and bay leaves, and let it hang until it becomes high. Then skin it, singe it, and remove the liver, lungs, all the blood and place them in a clean vessel. Cut all the interior parts out of the hare, washing with water and cook them with the heart and liver in the same vessel so that it will be bloodier. Wash with this a bit of pugniticcio of domestic pork, which is the part where the pig was wounded. Take a piece of good fat prosciutto, and lean meat without the bone and let it boil with everything else, skimming once or twice when the scum is thick. Make it so the broth is black and full of blood. If it's not enough, add some pork [blood]. When it's skimmed, put in a good quantity of crushed pepper. When it's done put all the broth in a tin-lined casserole. When it begins to boil place in your pasta sheets, being light, delicate and soft. Of this prepare a plate, eating the meat with a pepper sauce.*

Although this dish may sound revolting, it is actually quite delicious and can still be found on menus in Italy. It can easily be prepared without the blood, and substituting domestic rabbit for the hare, though the taste will be much more delicate. Stewing the rabbit meat with giblets and some broth approaches the original. The pappardelle are merely wide noodles. Exactly what pugniticcio was is unspecified, though it may have been a cured pork neck because this is where pigs were bled.

## FOWL

### ❧ 75. SOFFRITO OF MEAT, OR OF PIGEONS, OR OF CHICKENS OR OF KID ❧

*Italy, 1470 (Martino, 8)*

*First clean very well and cut in quarters, or rather in little pieces, and place in a pot to fry with good lardo turning often times with a spoon. And when the meat is almost cooked throw away the greater part of the fat in the pot. Then take good verjuice, two egg yolks, a tiny bit of good broth and good spices, and mix these things together with enough saffron so that it will be yellow and place in the said pot together with the meat and let it boil again a little until everything seems to you cooked. Then take a tiny bit of parsley beaten fine and place together with the said soffrito in a plate and serve to the table. And this kind of soffrito can be sweet or sour following common taste or of the patron.*

Technically this is a kind of fricassee, a fried meat that then has a sauce added. The term "soffrito" means exactly the same thing—a fried dish. The technique is most likely of Spanish or Catalan origin. The sauce should be just enough to moisten and cover the chicken or other meat—and the yolks should make it smooth and thick. A little sugar does work well also, as Martino suggests. Though he uses the term *patrone*, this implies master, not patron as in a restaurant.

### ❧ 76. ROASTED CAPON ❧

*France, 1555 (Livre fort excellent de cuisine, ii^v)*

*For a roasted capon with orange in a red sauce, take red wine and beef bouillon which is fat. Take next spices—cinnamon and a bit of fine spices, a great deal of sugar. Peel your oranges and cut them into rounds and place them to boil with a bit of rosemary added with them. And barely let it boil. To serve place some sugar on top.*

Although the combination of a great deal of sugar with a poultry dish strikes us as odd today, sugar was one of the most esteemed of flavorings and shows up in many unexpected places and is not in the least disagreeable in this context. The fine spices the author refers are elsewhere in that cookbook described as a combination of ginger, pepper, cinnamon, nutmeg, cloves, and grains of paradise, which is a typical medieval mixture. A cook would have this mixture, as well as the bouillon, on hand for many different dishes. Although it is not specified, foods were commonly subjected to two different cooking procedures, so it is likely that the capon is simmered in the sauce before serving.

### 77. DODINE BLANCHE (DUCK IN WHITE SAUCE)

*France, 1555 (Livre fort excellent de cuisine, I*ᵛ*)*

*To make dodine blanche take cow's milk, cooked egg yolks, white powder, onions well fried in rounds. Pass all through a sieve and cook it in a pan, and do not forget to sugar and salt to taste. Add the drippings from your duck.*

This recipe assumes that you have already roasted a duck before the fire and collected the drippings in a pan. The same can be done by roasting a duck in the oven and pouring off the drippings. The fat would not have been skimmed off and discarded. The quantity of milk for the sauce is not specified, but about 2 cups will yield a full gravy boat. If you don't have a sturdy sieve, add one fried onion to the milk, plus the white powder, which is dried ginger, and a pinch of starch (corn starch will work), plus two cooked egg yolks and put in a blender. Then cook this mixture in a saucepan and add the drippings. Serve with the duck.

### 78. PHEASANT, CAPON OR PIGEON, BREAST OF VEAL OR OTHER MEAT STEWED IN A POT, IN THE OVEN

*Italy, 1549 (Messisbugo, 93)*

*Take a pheasant or other, dressed and made up again and place it in a pan with a bit of prosciutto or salted meat cut in slices and marjoram, nutmeg and orange juice, a bit of broth and ground pepper and a bit of saffron. Then have made a covering of pastry, placed in position over the pot, place it in an oven and thus stew in a pot, until what is inside is cooked, then serve it. It should be eaten hot, for it is the most divine dish.*

This is basically a pot pie containing a whole bird, presumably *rifatto*—to be remade means that it is repositioned in shape after being cleaned. Also the typesetter seems to have set *tuffata in pignatta* (plunged in a pot), when it seems likely that the author meant *stuffata* (stewed in a pot). What distinguishes it from earlier similar recipes is the combination of a single salty element, single herb, merely a few spices, and a single acid together in

*Sea bass.*

a way that they balance each other without the crowding of flavors. The crust would have provided an unctuous and sweet element as well. Pheasant was also among the most esteemed foods on noble tables.

## FISH

### ᴥ 79. A LARGE SEA BASS ᴥ

*Italy, 1470 (Martino, 80)*

*Let it simmer . . . , when it is less than four or five pounds fry it in good oil or roast it over a grill, remembering as has been said, that it should not be scaled or opened. For it you should make a marinade with vinegar and oil and a lot of salt and with a sprig of bay leaves or rosemary, bathe the fish with this marinade many times, turning it often on the grill, letting it cook very well slowly, until it is well cooked. And note that every fish above all must be well cooked well, because its nature is humid and not being well cooked it is unhealthy.*

This recipe works best with a sea bass that has indeed been cleaned, but as Martino mentions is not scaled or split. A modern barbecue grill is ideal for this simple preparation. The comments at the end reveal that Martino was health-conscious. It was thought that because fish are excessively moist, they would increase the phlegmatic humors in people who eat them and thus need to be corrected, sometimes with hot spices or with acidic ingredients believed to aid digestion, but also with thorough cooking. Renaissance diners would thus have never even thought of eating raw fish.

### ᴥ 80. PIKE IN ENGLISH SAUCE ᴥ

*France, 1555 (Livre fort excellent de cuisine, viii)*

*To make a pike in English Sauce, take your pike slashed and place it in an earthenware pan. Take good red wine and vinegar and some beer, add a good amount of rosemary and place it to cook with good butter, cinnamon for spices and nutmeg and stew well on the coals in this court bouillon.*

This extremely simple recipe seems to be associated with England because of the addition of beer. The combination of wine and beer, not to mention vinegar, appears odd to say the least, but was not an unheard of mix. The fish should be cleaned but left whole, and slashed three or four times diagonally to allow the flavors to seep in. It is essentially poached on a very low flame. The earthenware vessel called for here was probably meant to prevent the vinegar from picking up the flavor of a cast-iron pot.

### ᪣ 81. CARP FRITTERS ᪥

*France, 1555 (Livre fort excellent de cuisine, xiv)*

*You can also take the heads of the said carps and boil them and let them cool. Then take eggs and beat them with a bit of white powder and saffron and fine salt and soak the carp heads in it. Let them fry in good butter and they will look like they are fritters. You can sugar them if you wish.*

*Dish of carp heads.*

In *Livre fort excellent*, this recipe follows a *paste en pot* of carp recipe, which is made of the flesh chopped up with onion, pea puree and spices as well as chestnuts if desired. It is a kind of paste or pâté cooked in a pot. Because this recipe follows, it appears that it was intended as an economical way to use all parts of the fish, and we can assume that several were used since the directions specify many heads. It also appears that this is a mock dish, meant to look like whatever kind of fritters, or *bignetz*, diners would have been more accustomed to. Strangely, the recipe does not call for flour, and although egg alone does work, it does not create a crispy, fritter-like texture. It may have been inadvertently left out of the recipe or may have been included in the white powder along with sugar and ginger.

### ᪣ 82. CAVIAR TO EAT FRESH AND TO KEEP ᪥

*Italy, 1549 (Messisbugo, 110ᵛ–111)*

*Take the eggs of the Sturgeon, and the blacker they are the better, and spread them out on a table with the side of a knife, cleaning them well of membranes and gristle, and for every 25 pounds of eggs, place 12 and a half ounces of salt, which is an ounce and a half per pound of egg. Then place it in a vessel with the salt, and leave it for a night, then take a new clean board three feet long and a foot wide with the edge of wood nailed around, high as three fingers. Then take the said eggs, and place them on the board, and put them in an oven that is honestly hot for the space of two pater nosters, then take it out, and mix it well with a wooden spatula, and replace it one more time leaving it as is said above. And do this until it is cooked, and this will be when the eggs do not burst between the teeth, and this will be around the third time, and you must be careful with this cooking because to conserve it a year or two do it in this manner. Put it in a vase of stone well glazed with a bit of oil over, in a cool place, and when it's very hot, every twenty days you must lift the covering that's over it and add a little oil. When it is not hot, it will be enough to check it every two months.*

*Those who want to eat it fresh, which is the best, you place only a third of an ounce of salt per pound of eggs, one and a half of ground pepper for every weight of eggs. But do not put pepper in the one to keep because it makes it rancid. Place in pounded nonetheless, put in half an ounce per weight, and add with the salt when you salt the eggs.*

Apart from this intriguing method of gently cooking the caviar on a nail-studded plank, this preservation method was invented as a way to store one of the most precious foods available. Though it may seem strange that it was cooked at all, it was quite common, though Messisbugo prefers it fresh. It takes exactly one minute to say two paternosters (Lord's Prayer) in Latin at a reverent pace.

### ⇥ 83. SINGULAR WAY TO COOK AND GARNISH SHRIMP ⇤

*Italy, 1560 (Romoli, 196ᵛ)*

*After the shrimp are boiled, clean only the tail, leaving it thus clean attached to the body, and place to fry in a pan with fresh butter and after place on it vinegar, verjuice or orange juice with a bit of fine cinnamon. Give it two turns in the pan with some gooseberries or unripe grapes, or with whole sour cherries. When it is time, remove the pan, leaving it, before eating it, to remain a while cooking.*

Romoli is clearly using whole shrimp with the heads on, but the recipe can be made with the tails only. Be sure to leave the shell on for the initial boiling, then clean and add the other ingredients. Modern diners will find it unusual to combine shell fish with cinnamon and cherries, but the sourness will actually complement the fish flavor nicely.

## VEGETABLES

### ⇥ 84. HOW TO COOK MUSHROOMS ⇤

*Italy, 1470 (Martino, 31)*

*Clean the mushrooms very well, and let them boil in water with two or three heads of garlic and with fresh bread crumbs. And this is done because by nature they are venomous. Then remove them and let the water drain in a way that they are dry, and then fry in good oil or in lardo. And when they are cooked, place over some spices.*

The garlic, as Martino notes, is not for flavor but serves as an antidote for the mushroom's poison. All mushrooms were considered more or less poisonous, as a rule, not merely some species. The crumbs called for here, or *mollicha*, were a typical thickening agent derived from the soft white interior of a bread with the crusts removed. Again, this was to absorb the poison. Incidentally, the procedure practically ruins any good mushroom. Platina also notes that pears cooked with mushrooms removes the poison if any is present, lore which is also recorded in the *Regimen* of Salerno, the most popular health manual of the Middle Ages.[3] Platina only briefly paraphrases Martino's directions and insists that however you cook mushrooms, though they may please the palate, they are difficult to digest and generate pernicious humors.[4]

*Growing fava beans.*

### ~ 85. TART OF LUPINS, FAVA BEANS, FAGIOLI BEANS, ASPARAGUS OR ONIONS, ARTICHOKES OR ANOTHER THING ~

*Italy, 1549 (Messisbugo, 64ᵛ)*

*Take one of the above mentioned things and cook it in broth for meat days, or in water with butter for lean days, then pass through a sieve and place it in a vessel with a half pound of hard cheese grated, and a pound of fresh butter and 8 ounces of sugar, one ounce of cinnamon pounded fine and a quarter ounce of pounded pepper, a pinch of pounded ginger and three beaten eggs and incorporate everything together. Then fill your pastry shell and make the tart placing over it 4 ounces of fresh butter and place it to cook. When it is almost cooked place over it 4 ounces of sugar and let it finish cooking. In place of butter, what goes in the mixture on meat days will be better: two pounds of beef fat or veal which is placed to boil with the lupins, or other thing, and the same goes in those made of fruit, of which is spoken above.*

The black lupin is a wild leguminous plant that physicians considered dangerous to eat and best left to the poor. Among Messisbugo's patrons, there was no social stigma against eating them though, at least not in this elegant form. The fagioli could possibly have been new world beans whose genus is now designated *Phaseolus*, but more likely they are black-eyed peas, which were also called "fasoli" then. The vessel he specifies is called a vaso—but obviously our conception of a vase for flowers will not work, but rather an urn-shaped pot with a wide lip, pronounced foot, and handles. Using a regular mixing bowl is fine.

### ~ 86. A TARTE TO PROVOKE COURAGE EITHER IN A MAN OR WOMAN ~

*England, 1588 (The Good Huswifes Handmaide for the Kitchen, 39)*

*Take a good quart of wine, and boyle therein two Burre rootes scraped cleane, two good Quinces, and a Potaton roote well pared and an ounce of Dates and when all these are boyled verie tender, let them be drawne through a strainer wine and al, and then put in the yolks of eight Egs, and the braines of three or foure cocke Sparrowes, and straine them into the other, and a litle Rosewater, and seeth them all with Sugar, Synamon and Ginger, and cloves and Mace, and put in a litle Sweet Butter, and set it upon a chafingdish of coales betweene two platters, and so let it boyle till it be something big.*

Presumably the author intends that this dish be used to promote courage of the amorous kind. Roots in general were considered by physicians as useful aphrodisiacs. Shakespeare, a contemporary of the cookbook author, had Falstaff in *The Merry Wives of Windsor* say, "Let the sky rain potatoes," as a prelude to amorous adventure. The potatoes used at this time were probably sweet potatoes. Obviously sparrow brains is not something one would want to cook today, but otherwise the Burre roots—or burdock, which can be bought in Japanese grocery stores where it is called gobo—and sweet potatoes (and this is a fairly early recipe for them) baked with spices and eggs in a sweet tart makes a very interesting dish. The last lines suggest that the eggs make it puff up like a soufflé.

---

### ✦ ENGLISH FEAST MENU, C. 1500

The contents of English feasts changed little from the latter Middle Ages into the sixteenth century. In a book on carving printed by Wynkyn de Worde, menus were included for different times of year. The following was what should be served from the Feast of St. John the Baptist (June 24) to Michaelmas (September 29). The first course included a pottage, greens, gruel, frumenty (wheat) with venison mortrus (sauce pounded in a mortar), legs of pork with green sauce, roasted capon, and swan with chawdron (a spiced sauce of giblets). In the second course were pottage with roasted mutton, veal, pork, chickens or glazed pigeons, herons, fritters, or other bakemeats (pies).[5]

---

## STARCHES

### ❧ 87. RICE WITH ALMOND MILK ❧

*Italy, 1470 (Martino, 35)*

*To make ten servings, take a pound of almonds and clean well so they are white. Then take half a pound of rice and wash it two or three times with tepid water and place on the fire with clear water and let it cook well. Then remove them and set to dry. Then pound the said almonds well, moistening and sprinkling on top often with a bit of cool water, so they don't get oily; then temper with cool water and pass through a sieve and place this milk to boil in a pot adding half a pound of fine sugar. And when it begins to boil place in the rice and put the pot over the coals far from the fire, stirring often with a spoon so it doesn't burn up, and let it boil for half an hour. Similarly, you can cook this rice with goat's milk or other milk. And because such minestre easily burn, if they have, the way to rid it is this: remove the minestra from the pot, be careful not to touch the bottom, and place it in another clean pot. Then take a white cloth and fold it three or four times And bathe it in cool water. Then squeeze out the water and place the cloth thus doubled over the pot of minestra, and let it stand for a quarter hour, then bathe another time and replace over the pot if it is necessary, and in this way the smoke will be removed. I haven't found a better remedy to remove smoke. The same works with faro.*

Beginning in the fifteenth century, rice was grown extensively in Italy, especially in the north. This is the ancestor of a modern risotto, though the cooking technique is entirely different and the final dish is quite sweet. Since it is called a minestra, which means a kind of thick soup, it should probably be slightly liquid rather than firm. This recipe also provides a good reminder that even professional chefs could ruin food sitting on the fire. Martino's directions for saving a burnt dish echo Rupert of Nola's (see recipe #37, Royal Fava Beans), in the section on vegetables, though it is actually much simpler. There are other indications in his cookbook that he learned a great deal from the Catalan cookbook author and several recipes labeled as Catalan come directly from Rupert.

### 88. TO MAKE TEN PLATES OF "MACCHERONI"

*Italy, 1549 (Messisbugo, 52)*

*Take 5 pounds of white flour, and two white breads grated. Mix it well with the flour. Then have some boiling water ready. Mix in three eggs and make a dough that is not too tough nor too soft. Let it rest a bit, then cut it into pieces about the size of a chestnut. Make your macaroni on the back of a grater. Cook them in the boiling water until done. Add a bit of salt, and take 2½ pounds of grated hard cheese with an ounce and a half of crushed pepper. Mix it together. When you want to serve it, place the cheese below and above, plus a pound and a half of fresh melted butter on top. Then cover with the other plates and put them in a hot oven until you're ready to send it to the table and set them down. If you put a bit of sugar and cinnamon over it, it will be better.*

These are clearly dumplings, more closely related to modern gnocchi than hollow tubes of pasta, and this was probably the original form of macaroni, which by this time meant something quite different in various parts of Italy. The procedure for forming them involves pressing and rolling the lumps of dough along the sharp side of a cheese grater creating a pointed surface that absorbs the butter and cheese. Baking between two plates was also a common procedure, the upper plate being inverted and then in this case, several other plates being heated and used for service as well. A covered casserole also works. As for the quantity called for, apart from the fact that a standard pound troy weight was 12 ounces rather than 16, this still is enough for more than a dozen servings. The exact proportions of each ingredient really don't matter, but 2 cups of flour to 1 of crumbs, enough boiling water to form a stiff dough and one egg yield a good dumpling that will hold together.

### ✺ 89. TO MAKE RAVIOLI FOR MEAT AND LEAN DAYS, FOR 10 PLATES ✺

*Italy, 1549 (Messisbugo, 57)*

*Take beet greens well washed and chopped, and place in a vessel with 6 pounds of good grated cheese and 2 pounds of fresh butter and 20 eggs, and one ounce of pepper, a half ounce of ginger, an ounce of cinnamon, and two grated breads passed through a sieve, and a half pound of raisins, and knead everything together. Then have half a pound of white flour spread on a table, and with this mixture make your ravioli as large or small as you wish. Then let them cook in water, on lean days with butter and a little saffron in the water, and let them cook quickly so they don't break. Then serve them with good cheese grated over, and for meat days cook them in good broth with saffron, and raisins in the dough, and when they are cooked take cheese, sugar and cinnamon mixed together, and when you wish to serve sprinkle cheese below and above, and when you want to vary it you can make them without beets but with a bit of povina cheese.*

This pasta is also closer to a kind of gnocchi because there is no actual sheet of dough enclosing the filling. The mixture is merely rolled in the flour spread on the table. The *povina* was a buffalo cheese, probably similar to mozzarella. Any green will work in this recipe, and in fact the word *bieta* was used generically for any green leafy rabe, chard, or similar plant. The 10 plates that Messisbugo speaks of must have been enormous, and clearly each is meant to serve an entire table. It is also clear that when potatoes were introduced to Italy, they merely replaced the bread crumbs in recipes like this, much as corn replaced native grains in polenta. Like many of Messisbugo's recipes, variants are given for days when the church permitted meat and for Lent or Advent when meat was forbidden, but apparently butter was not.

### ✺ 90. TO MAKE PANCAKES ✺

*England, 1588 (The Good Huswifes Handmaide for the Kitchen, 59)*

*Take new thicke Creame a pinte, four or five yolks of Egs, a good handful of flower, and two or three spoonfuls of Ale, strain them altogether into a faire platter, and season it with a good handful of Sugar, a spoonful of Synamon, and a litle Ginger: then take a frying pan, and with a ladle out to the further side of your pan some of your stuffe, and hold the pan aslope, so that your stuffe may run abroad over all your pan, as thin as may be: then set it to the fyre, and let the fyre be verie soft, and when the one side is baked, then turne the other, and bake them as dry as ye can without burning.*

Unlike modern pancakes, the batter for these is very thin and when fried becomes crisp. They are more like crispy sweet crepes than the fluffy risen pancakes of today.

> Pancakes were traditionally eaten on Shrove Tuesday, the day right before Lent when people had to use up forbidden foods such as eggs, butter, and other dairy products. The word "Shrove" comes from the verb "to shrive," meaning to confess one's sins and be absolved. In England there is also a traditional pancake race held on this day, going back to 1445 in the town of Olney in Buckinghamshire. The legend goes that a woman was cooking pancakes when she heard the church bell ring and ran to church with the hot pan in her hand, still wearing an apron. The race reenacts this.

### ⊰ 91. FRIED FRESH BUTTER ⊱

*France, 1555 (Livre fort excellent de cuisine, xxiv)*

*Take a stale white bread and make very fine crumbs, take 2 ounces of starch, 2 ounces of sugar and a bit of cinnamon and pound as much fresh butter as these drugs or more, then form into a kind of loaf of butter. And soak with flour, egg yolks, a little rosewater, sugar, salt, without adding water, then soak everything together with this batter like for wafers. And when it is soaked melt a bit of fresh butter and place in your pan as if you want to make maleffrain then place your loaf of butter in your pan on the said crust and envelop it with grease. And turn it from one side to the other and make it cook. Serve hot with sugar on top.*

This recipe is similar to one found in a fifteenth-century version of the *Viandier* but differs in some respects and is a little harder to follow. It seems as if the author intends that the entire loaf of crumbs and butter be soaked in the batter, which will form a kind of crust on the outside keeping the contents within. There were also similar recipes that roasted the butter on a spit. The word *maleffrain* does not appear in historic French dictionaries and may be either a typesetter's error or a slang word for some kind of fritter. Interestingly, the author calls the spices "drugs," which is also how they were used.

## Eggs and Dairy

### ⊰ 92. EGGS ON THE GRILL ⊱

*Italy, 1470 (Martino, 76)*

*Beat two fresh eggs very well and heat and empty pan enough so that it is very hot and toss in these beaten eggs. Let it go around the whole pan the way you make a frittata very thin like paper. When it seems to you well cooked fold in the four sides so that it is square like a little frame. And place this on the grill, breaking onto it as many fresh eggs as it seems to you it can hold above, heat it below and above gently the way you do a tart, sprinkling over sugar and cinnamon. When it seems to you that the said eggs are firm, lifting them from the grill, you will bring them to the table, thus they will be in their little frame.*

This can be done on a very moderate barbecue grill with the lid covered. If the eggs are broken very carefully directly onto the frittata, they will not slide off. Clearly Martino is trying to invent as many fantastic new ways to serve eggs as possible. In one of the Martino manuscripts it even describes how to cook eggs on a piece of paper as a kind of trick. Parchment paper, rolled and crimped along the entire edge so that it can hold a little oil, is place on hot coals or above a candle, but not too close. In this an egg is gently cooked.[6] Strange as it may seem, water can also be boiled in a paper bag. The bag must be folded into a container without any glued seams below, so a regular paper bag will not work. But if the water does not leak out, it can be held directly over a flame. The water prevents it from catching on fire.

### ⇥ 93. TO MAKE EGGES IN MONESHYNE ⇤

*England, 1540s or 50s (A Proper Newe Booke of Cokerye, Biv)*

*Take a dyshe of rosewater and a dyshe full of suger, and sette them upon a chafyngdysh, and let them boyle, than take the yolkes of viii or viiii egges newe layde and putte them thereto, every one from other, and lette them harden a little, and so after this maner serve them forthe, and case a lyttle synamon and suger upon them.*

The sugar and rosewater are the cooking medium into which the egg yolks are carefully and lightly poached while keeping them separate. They are reminiscent of a full moon, hence the word *Moneshyne* in the recipe name. A century later, cookbook author Robert May has several recipes of the same name that are what we would call "sunny side up" fried eggs, which he serves with fried onion rounds. But he also has a variant of this recipe scarcely changed except that it is clarified somewhat. A syrup of rosewater, sugar, and sack (sherry) or white wine is brought to the boil and the egg yolks are dropped in with some ambergris, turned, kept separate, and cooked until hard.[7]

### ⇥ 94. JASPER OF MILK ⇤

*France, 1555 (Livre fort excellent de cuisine, xxiv)*

*Take good fat milk and as much egg whites passed through a sieve, a bit of parsley chopped, a bit of white powder, seasoned with salt. Then take everything together and let it boil. And when it is cooked and you turn it out onto a napkin to press until it is cold, from one day to another is cold enough. Then cut in little slices and fry in butter. Serve hot with sugar on top and bring to the table and it looks like jasper.*

Jasper is a green and white mottled stone, thus this dish is a kind of surprise or subtlety. The white powder the author mentions is sugar and ginger.

### ⇥ 95. FRITTATA SIMPLE, GREEN, FILLED AND DIFFICULT ⇤

*Italy, 1549 (Messisbugo, 110)*

*Take ten eggs, because this is typical, and beat them very well with a little salt, and when they are well beaten, add in a little water, then put in a pan six ounces of fresh butter and when it is melted throw in the egg and cook your frittata, the water will make it soft, then put on top pounded cinnamon so it will be prepared. If you want it green put mint, parsley and other oily herbs in pounded finely with a knife, following the way mentioned above to cook it. If you want it filled you put in fat grated cheese or povina, and raisins inside, and pine nuts, and onions finely chopped, and fresh fennel, and use sometimes one thing or another. And if you want it fussy, follow the directions given first, add prosciutto finely chopped or three or four ounces of mortadella, following the directions for cooking the others, and on top of all of them a lot of pounded cinnamon goes well.*

The variations offered here clearly let the cook add whatever is at hand. A frittata is unlike an omelet in that it is cooked in one layer and is not stirred or folded in half. The texture is thus more firm. One can, if feeling adventurous, slide the fritatta onto a plate when nearly done and then put the pan on top and flip the two so that the other side can be browned. There is no indication that this was done in the past though. For the cheese, a hard grating cheese or a soft mozzarella work well, as will practically any cheese.

## SAUCES

### ⇥ 96. CAMELINE SAUCE ⇤

*Italy, 1470 (Martino, 43)*

*Have some raisins pounded very well. Have two or three slices of bread toasted, then soaked in red wine, more or less depending on the quantity that you want to make. Pound together the aforementioned things. Then take a bit of red wine, some sapa and verjuice, and whoever doesn't like verjuice can make it with vinegar, making it sweet our sour according to what pleases you. Pass all this composition through a sieve, adding then enough good cinnamon, a bit of cloves and nutmeg pounded.*

This was a standard sauce through the Middle Ages, used with many types of meat. Its name has generated a good deal of discussion. It was often assumed cameline had some connection to canella (another name for cinnamon or cassia) because that spice was often included, but not always. It has also been suggested that the sauce is brownish like a camel. Perhaps it was meant to resemble the cameline flower, golden in color, though the sauce is definitely dark brown. Unlike sauces based on herbs, such as a pesto, this can actually be made as well in a blender as by pounding it, and sieving is unnecessary if you are using seedless raisins and ground spices.

### ◄ 97. WHITE AGLIATA (GARLIC SAUCE) ►

*Italy, 1470 (Martino, 48)*

*Take almonds cleaned very well and pound them, and when they are half pounded place in the quantity of garlic that you want, and pound it together sprinkling on some cold water so it doesn't become greasy. Then take the interior of white bread and let it soften in light meat broth or of fish depending on the season, and this agliata can be served and adapted for all seasons, both meat and fast days as you wish.*

The agliata was also a common sauce for centuries before Martino was writing. It takes its name from garlic, or *aglio* in Italian. It absolutely must be made in a mortar. A cup of peeled blanched almonds, one garlic clove, and a slice of crustless white bread soaked in broth will made enough sauce for two.

### ◄ 98. HELL SAUCE ►

*France, 1555 (Livre fort excellent de cuisine, xxxiii^v)*

*Let your pigs feet boil until well cooked in good bouillon. And when they are well cooked, take them and place them to roast on a grill. Then chop them into large morsels in a plate with green sauce over them. When your feet are cooking golden on the grill, take onions chopped fine and place them in a plate and stew them with verjuice. And when they are stewed enough, add a bit of mustard, then take your pig's feet divided in pieces and place it on a completely hot plate with live coals on top, and then put your tart sauce on top and serve it at once to the table.*

*Pot and utensils.*

This is not exactly a sauce, but a kind of joke. One wonders how it could have been edible, or what effect it was meant to have. Presumably the meat and sauce would be brought to the table sizzling on the platter, creating a dramatic effect bubbling with molten lava flows like hell. The server would most likely have been very dexterous in removing the edible portions from the hot coals.

### ⇄ 99. SAUCE FOR ROAST BEEF ⇆

*France, 1555 (Livre fort excellent de cuisine, xlix[v] )*

*Let your beef roast, stuck with cloves, and when it is half cooked, douse your beef with vinegar and place your pan beneath to save the vinegar. And place in fine spices and crushed pepper and a bit of toasted bread if you like, and put in a bit of sage to strengthen the flavor, and let it boil. If the vinegar is too strong, add a bit of verjuice or good bouillon seasoned with salt. Serve hot over the beef.*

The sixteenth-century author of this recipe is beginning to use drippings and broths as a base for sauce, even though there is still much in common with earlier sauces. If a spit and drip pan are unavailable, the vinegar can be poured a little at a time over a roast beef, ideally on a rack in a pan set in the oven. After removing the beef, make the sauce directly in the roasting pan. The fine spices would be cinnamon, cloves, nutmeg, and ginger. The sauce can be strained as well, though it is not necessary, and the author does not say to do so.

### ⇄ 100. TO MAKE THE SAUCE CALLED CORDIAL TO PLACE OVER COOKED FISH ⇆

*Italy, 1560 (Romoli, 196)*

*Placing the fish on a grill to cook or over the coals or roasted in some other way, it will be unique if on top you place the following sauce, called cordial, if made in the following manner. Into verjuice and sapa in equal measure, beat two egg yolks with saffron, and place over the fire until it thickens. Then place over the fish you have cooked, with sugar and cinnamon if you want it sweet.*

This is an absolutely simple sauce, but typical of the period. Many sixteenth-century sauces were thickened with egg yolk, not cooked so the yolk itself cooks, but lightly heated while stirring so it merely thickens. In fact this resembles a modern zabaglione—an egg yolk–thickened, wine-based dessert. The combination of unripe grape juice and cooked concentrated grape juice might seem a waste of energy, but neither actually contains alcohol, and the tart, bitter flavor of one balances nicely with the dense, molasses-like flavor and texture of the other. Sweetened and spiced it is an ideal sauce for grilled salmon or tuna. The name itself is rather odd as cordials were usually medicines taken to calm the heart, many of which today are sipped as after-dinner drinks.

### ⇥ 101. A PYKE SAUCE FOR PYKE, BREME, PERCHE, ROCHE, CARPE, ELES, FLOYKES, AND AL MANER OF BROUKE FYSHE ⇤

*England, 1540s or 50s (A Proper Newe Booke of Cokerye, Av$^{iv}$)*

*Take a posye of Rosemary and time, and bynde them together, and put in also a quantitye of perselye not bounde, and put into the caudron of water, salte and yeste, and the herbes, and lette them boyle a pretye whyle, then putte in the fysche, and a good quantitye of butter, and let them boyle a good season, and you shall have a good Pyke sauce. For all these fysches above written, yf they muste bee broiled, take sauce for them, butter, peepper, and vyneger, and boyle it upon a chafyngdyshe, and then laye the broiled fyshe upon the dysche, but for eeles and freshe Salmon nothing but Pepper and vyneger over boyled. And also yf you wyll frye them, you muste take a good quantitie of persely, after the fyshe is fryed, put in the persely into the fryinge panne, and let it frye in the butter, and take it up and put it on the fryed fyshe, and frye place, whytinge and such other fyshe, except Eles, freshe Salmon, Conger, which be never fryed but baken, boyled, roosted, or sodden.*

These are essentially nothing more than herbed butter sauces. What is remarkable about these is the absence of spices and for the most part sour ingredients. This indicated that either these recipes were meant for households that would not want to spend lavishly on such items, or a recognition that they would overpower the delicate flavor of freshwater fish.

## FRUIT

### ⇥ 102. CHERRY AND ROSE TART ⇤

*Italy, 1470 (Martino, 56)*

*Get the darkest cherries you can find and take out the pits, pound very well in a mortar and get some red roses very well chopped with a knife, with a bit of fresh cheese and a bit of good old cheese, adding spices such as cinnamon, ginger and a little pepper and some sugar, and mix very well all these things, adding even three or four eggs according to the quantity you want to make, and with a crust beneath put it to cook at your leisure in a pan. And when it is cooked put on top sugar and some rosewater.*

The combination of cheese and fruit in a tart, almost unheard of today except perhaps in a danish, was a common combination in the Renaissance. Along with roses it becomes even a little odder. It is best to use only the red part of each rose petal as the white bases can be a little bitter, and do not use roses that have been treated with chemicals. For the cheeses, cottage cheese and parmigiano will work, but so will any soft and hard cheese. The final tart should be a lurid pink in color.

## ᴥ 103. CHESTNUTS ᴥ

*France, 1555 (*Livre fort excellent de cuisine, *lvii)*

*Take chestnuts and pierce them and cook them a bit between two coals until they can be peeled, then put them into a pastry after they have been peeled and season like quinces mentioned above except that they need a little hypocras when they are nearly cooked for two or three dozen. They need two ounces of sweet duke's powder. Sweet cloves.*

Chestnuts have been included here because they are cooked in a way conventionally reserved for fruit. The author has resorted to shorthand notation, but the spices used in the preceding quince recipe are sugar, cinnamon, cloves; it also calls for butter or beef marrow. The chestnuts can be roasted in a perforated pan over the fire for about ten minutes, which adds to the flavor, or in an oven. Cutting a little x into the end makes peeling easier. Hypocras is a spiced wine. The duke's powder is a spice mixture of cinnamon, ginger, and cloves that would have been premixed and was used in a variety of dishes. The exact combination of spices is really a matter of taste, as this recipe calls for a wide variety and several are used more than once.

## ᴥ 104. TO MAKE A COMPOTE OF MELON PEELS OR PEELS OF GOURD, OR TURNIPS, OR WHOLE UNRIPE PEACHES IN A CONSERVE FOR LENT ᴥ

*Italy, 1549 (Messisbugo, 106ᵛ–107)*

*Take the quantity of the abovementioned things [in the recipe title] that you want, and clean and place to soak in vinegar with salt for fifteen or twenty days. Then remove from the vinegar and place them in a vessel with water and give a good boil, then remove and place in another vessel with fresh water, and leave them until they are cooled. Then remove them from this water and lay them on a board placing next another board on top weighted so they are pressed, and leave like this pressed down for a day. Next take a vessel and put it in with enough sapa so that the contents will be covered and give it a good boil in this sapa, in a way however that it will not fall apart. Put it in a convenient-sized urn and pour over the sapa in which it has boiled and leave it thus for twenty days. Then take another urn and remove it from the first urn and add in honey, sapa, cinnamon, pepper, ginger, and saffron according to the quantity that you want to make, and sprigs of rosemary and sage and let it boil again another time with these things, and turn into the urn with the liquid and it will be done. If you don't want to burden yourself with the expense, boil the last time in honey alone. Note that the peaches don't need to be pressed.*

This ancestor of modern-day pickled watermelon rinds is still made in Italy and Spain and is worth hunting down if you don't have the time to make it yourself. The sapa is boiled-down grape juice and is very thick and dark, like maple syrup in consistency. The final product is spicy, bitter, sweet, and sour all at the same time, a combination that was appreciated in the past. If using melons, the very outer peel must be removed, it is only the hard rind that is needed, and the same goes for gourd. A hard New World squash would also work, though probably would not take pressing without falling apart. Turnips also must be peeled and cut into cubes; they also make very interesting conserves.

---

### ✦ COOKS MUST NOT BE GLUTTONS

Throughout the culinary literature there are references to cooks both eating and drinking too much. In his *Ars magirica* (Art of Cooking), Swiss author Iodoco Willich insisted that above all, to serve his master well, a cook must not be gluttonous, indulging his appetite whenever it strikes. Rather he should be "artful, experienced, laborious, ambitious, clean, and must excel in taste, but never gluttonous or voracious."[8] He also described all the various equipment a cook must have: tripods, pots, pans, grates, plates, and even a *bain marie*, which is a kind of water bath or double boiler used by pharmacists that by the sixteenth century was working its way into kitchens.[9]

---

### ⊰ 105. TO MAKE A TART OF PRUNES ⊱

*England, 1540s or 50s (A Proper Newe Booke of Cokerye, 68)*

*Take prunes and set them upon a chafer with a little red wyne, and putte therto a manchet, and let them boyle together, then drawe them throwe a streyner with the yolkes of foure egges and season it up with suger and so bake it.*

It appears that the final texture of this tart should be smooth, and so cutting up the prunes before boiling with the manchet—a small white bread—will later make it easier to pass through a strainer. Although the recipe does not call for a crust, a few pages earlier in the book there is a recipe for "short paest for tarte" that is made with water, butter, a little saffron, and two egg yolks. It is rolled out very thin. A tart, made without a top crust, can be sliced and served, unlike many pies of this period.

SWEETS

### ⊰ 106. TO MAKE MOSTACCIOLI OF SUGAR ⊱

*Italy, 1549 (Messisbugo, 40ᵛ)*

*Take 3 pounds of candied citron peel cut up minutely, 5 pounds of strained honey, five eighths of pepper, a scruple of saffron, three quarters of an ounce of cinnamon, three grains of musk, flour enough to make a dough of this syrup.*

*Then make your mostaccioli large or small as you please. But to cook them like pan pepato make each between 4 and 6 ounces each, not bigger.*

The precise measurements for these cookies are terms used by apothecaries. A pound actually contained 12 ounces. There are 8 drams in an ounce, 3 scruples per dram, and 20 grains per scruple. Few people today own a scale with such weights, and this recipe makes an enormous batch, so the following measurements have been reduced to one-fourth in quantity. Use 9 ounces of candied citron, 15 ounces of honey (about 1¼ cup), 1¾ ounces of pepper, a tiny pinch of saffron and a big pinch of cinnamon. If you can find musk, the proportion would be infinitesimal. Bake the mixture in any shape, in a moderate over about 300 degrees until crispy or in small round cakes. Pan pepato is a flat round cake of dried fruits and spices, a close relative of *pan forte* of Siena. These cookies are also used frequently in other recipes, ground up as a thickener, stuffing, and flavoring. The name *mostaccioli* comes from the word *must*, meaning grape juice, with which they were probably originally made.

### 107. TO MAKE 10 PUFF-PASTRY PIZZAS

*Italy, 1549 (Messisbugo, 43ᵛ)*

*Pull the soft interior out of four white breads and soak it in tepid water. Take 3 pounds of the finest wheat flour, ten egg yolks and a pound of fresh butter, three ounces of rose water and seven ounces of sugar. Mix everything together with the bread, making a dough. Roll it out into a sheet as you would a lasagna dough, and make it as light as you can. Then take a pound and a half of fresh butter, heated, and pour it over the sheet. Let it cool. Then roll a spiral pastry cutter the length of the sheet and cut it into ten pieces. Next make your puff pizzas. Have a pan ready with 4 pounds of fresh butter, and fry your puff pizzas in it. When they are fried, sprinkle a half pound of sugar over them.*

The word "pizza" is used, though clearly it had a very different meaning in the past and in northern Italy. In fact, any little cake or pastry might be called a pizza. What is surprising is that both in boiled pasta and fried pastry, bread is used along with flour. This may have originated as a way to use up bread that had begun to go stale, though in wealthier households they would probably have used fresh bread as is indicated here by the fact that it is still soft. In either case, stale bread was a ubiquitous ingredient in the past.

### 108. COUNTERFEIT SNOW

*France, 1555 (Livre fort excellent de cuisine, xlvii)*

*Take a quart of good fat milk. And it is necessary that it comes from a cow that has calved in the past year. Place within the said milk six egg whites and one or two ounces of rice flour, a quarter pound of powdered sugar beaten all together like butter. Skim what forms above. It is snow, place it in a plate.*

*Dish of apples and "trees" with snow.*

This was a popular dish everywhere in Europe in the mid-sixteenth century. In English cookbooks it is placed on a sprig of rosemary stuck in an apple to create a little winter scene. Recipes differ from place to place, though. The starch in this one helps a foam form on top when it is beaten. (Elsewhere the dish is to be made with cream and egg whites, though to beat egg whites and cream together proves nearly impossible. Either authors miscopied instructions, or it was assumed that the two would be beaten separately and then folded together afterward.)

### ❧ 109. FOR TO MAKE WARDENS IN CONSERVE ❧

*England, 1540s or 50s (A Proper Newe Booke of Cokerye, 78)*

*Fyrste make the syrope in this wyse, take a good quarte of good Romney, and putte a pynte of claryfyed honey, a pounde or a halfe of suger, and myngle all those together over the fyre, tyll tyme they seeth, and then set it to cole. And thys is a good sirope for many thinges, and will be kepte a year or two. Then take thy warden and scrape cleane awaye the barke, but pare them not, and seeth them in good redde wine so that they be wel soked and tender, that the wyne be nere hande soaked into them, then take and strayne them throughe a cloth or through a strainer into a vessel, then put to them of this syrope aforesayde tyll it be almost fylled, and then caste in the pouders, as fine canel, synamon, pouder of ginger, and such other, & put it in a boxes, and kepe it yf thou wylt, and make they Syrope as thou wylt worke in quantyte, as yf thou wylt worke twenty wardens, or lesse, as by experience.*

Wardens are a variety of pear—any hard variety such as Bosc or Anjou should work well. Romney or Rumney was a sweet golden Greek wine, probably stored in vessels coated with resin, which was imported to England through the Middle Ages. The resin taste would meld very nicely with the sweetness of the honey, so Retsina, still made in Greece, should be a good approximation. The syrup is brought just to the boil (to seethe) and cooled. The bark of the pear here means the peel; the seeds and core can also be removed by cutting a cone out of the base of each pear. Otherwise, they should be left whole, with stems attached. The author distinguishes between cinnamon and canella ("canel")—which probably refers here to cassia, though it is often difficult to be sure about which spice early authors were using. As long as the pears are covered in the syrup in a well-sealed glass jar, they can be kept at room temperature. The part of the recipe referring to boxes appears to be garbled. Only candied fruit or fruit paste could be kept in boxes.

## DRINK

### ⅋ 110. VERMILLION WINE ⅋

*Switzerland, 1565 (Grataroli, 191–2)*

*To make vermillion or red wine: for four sarcinis of wine take thirty wild parsnips, which are called carrots, that are red, cook them under coals, as you do for a salad, then clean off the exterior peel, when this is done, then grate finely until you find white and place the gratings into a little cloth bag, and from the bottom of a vessel of wine to be colored draw off a big pot of wine, and into the pot put the bag, and soak it well, then squeeze it, and put the wine into the top of the vessel. You always draw off wine from the bottom and put it in above, or else the bag will not emit enough color. It will be good, beautiful and red wine.*

This was a common trick, how to turn white wine red. Although it is not specifically stated here, the bag of grated carrots goes into the larger vessel with the smaller pot of wine. What *sarcinis* are is unknown. A barrel per se is not mentioned, but all wine containers would have had a spout to draw off wine and a "mouth" to add more. Carrots are not typically red today, so beets can be used. Grataroli also has many recipes for spiced and medicinal wines. One includes galangal, nutmeg, cloves, pepper, cinnamon, spikenard, citrus peel and honey. In others he includes long pepper, grains of paradise, and mace. Because so many combinations were possible, this seems to have been a matter of personal taste. He even has a recipe for instant wine, useful for sailors and travelers. It is basically fermented wine must cooked down, dried in the sun, and then pulverized. It is added to hot water and stirred and then ready to drink

# 4

## ☙ LATE RENAISSANCE AND ELIZABETHAN ERA

In the latter sixteenth century, cookbooks became much longer, even ency-clopedic. Bartolomeo Scappi, chef for several popes, wrote the monumental *Opera* (Works), which can be considered the first modern cookbook. Not only does it give directions for shopping by season, full menus, and extremely detailed recipes, but it is also illustrated. The work also influenced other cooks throughout Europe. Many recipes translated in the Spanish cookbook of Diego Granado *(Libro del Arte de Cocina)*, and it influenced the German of Marx Rumpolt *(Ein New Kochbuch*, 1581) and the Belgian one of Lance-lot de Casteau, *Overture de Cuisine* (1604). England produced several new cookbooks in the Elizabethan and Jacobean era, and although they borrow from each other incessantly, it is clear that a distinctive English style of cooking had emerged. The same can be said of Spanish cookbooks written about the same time as Cervantes's *Don Quixote*. In the early seventeenth century, these would exert great influence on cuisine throughout Europe, with Spanish recipes and ingredients appearing for decades to come.

## COLD FOODS

### ☙ 111. TO MAKE MORTADELLA FROM LEAN MEAT OF DOMESTIC PORK LEG, WRAPPED IN A CAUL ❧

*Italy, 1570 (Scappi, 46ᵛ–47)*

*Take ten pounds of the above-mentioned meat free of the bone, skin, and nerves, which has both fat and lean, and beat it with a knife on the table, adding eight ounces of fine salt, six ounces of dried sweet fennel, 4 ounces of crushed pepper, an ounce of pounded cinnamon, a half ounce of pounded nutmeg. When everything is well mixed together with the hand add four ounces of cold water, mint and marjoram beaten with a little wild thyme, and leave to rest in an earthenware or wooden vessel for four hours in a cool place. Take the caul from the pig, well cleaned of fibrous parts, and softened in tepid water, and make with this composition the mortadella as tommacelle are made. Being made, leave them to rest in the winter for two days in a dry place, then cook them on a grill, or in a pan with melted lard. You can also cook tommacelle on a spit separated by bay leaves, and the mortadella you can skewer through the middle surrounded with sprigs of rosemary. But in whatever way you cook them they must be served hot. With this composition you can also fill hog casings, which first have been kept in salt, once made in winter they can be left for two days, after which they can be boiled. From the lean meat that is well beaten you can also make cervelat with the caul, or in a casing, placing for each quantity of 10 pounds of the meat a pound and a half of grated parmigiano and an ounce and a half of pounded cinnamon, another ounce and a half of pounded pepper, an eighth of saffron, half a cup of cold water and three ounces of salt. And when everything is mixed together you make the cervelat in the caul or in casings, and cook them in the above mentioned mode. You can even make tomacelle in a caul adding eight ounces of raisins, and eight egg yolks, and the tomacelle you serve in winter will be much better if they are made after two days. Of mortadella and other salamis that are made from this meat, I will not speak because it has never been my profession.*

Mortadella is the ancestor of what we call bologna today, which is a pale imitation, in fact, baloney. Real mortadella is still made in Bologna and elsewhere today, studded with lumps of fat and peppercorns. The name supposedly comes from the myrtle berries that were once used to flavor the sausages. Judging from Scappi's comments at the end this recipe, preserved sausages were not something he would make; rather they would be bought. As a cook he is only responsible for freshly cooked sausage, but this nonetheless gives a good idea of how the original mortadella differed from those made today. The caul, offered as an alternative to hog casings, is a net of fat suspended in a membrane taken from the visceral lining of the pig. Scappi uses it often for wrapping delicate meats to keep them moist. Casings or intestines are easier to find today and any butcher that makes sausages can sell them. The key to making these properly is to thoroughly chop all the ingredients into a smooth paste; the cold water keeps the fat suspended in the mixture. Despite Scappi's comments, Mortadella is normally boiled and served cold in thin slices or in cubes. *Tommacelle* and *cervelat* are merely different kinds of sausages, the former with liver, the latter with cheese.

The following are sample lists of cold foods that might appear before a meal, as recorded in the banqueting management book of Giovanni Battista Rossetti *(Dello Scalco).* They would have been prepared by a *credenziero* in a separate kitchen from the space where the cook and his staff made the hot dishes. It is tempting to think, however, that some of these cold dishes could have been leftovers from the night before. All are meant to be dazzling and witty presentation pieces. Unlike the fashion today in Italy, salads were eaten at the start of a meal. Eating salad at the end of a meal, strangely enough, was the ancient custom and it seems that some people began to adopt the fashion in the Renaissance as well.

## Menu for 16th-Century Credenza Course
*Italy, 1584 (Rossetti, 68–69)*

*First Course*

*Eight elephants that had been eight suckling pigs big enough to cook in the oven, seemingly real elephants, as much as one can believe, with elephant heads made of pastry, with castles above of pastry, with armed figures that were beautiful to see*

*Stuffed Peacocks with white sauce loaded with white candies, in 8 plates*

*Hens in nests of pastry that are seen to be brooding, with peeled hard-boiled eggs and candied cloves, in 8 plates*

*Salad of pheasant meat with citron, in 8 plates*

*Blancmanger, in 8 plates [pounded chicken with almond milk, rice starch, and rosewater]*

*Loin of Hare, with royal sauce, in 4 plates*

*Pastries of veal rolls, in 8 plates*

*Flaky pastries of farro, cold, in 8 plates*

*Pork jowls with copudegi [?] split down the side, in 8 plates*

*Slices of pork loin with French mustard, in 8 plates*

*Endive salad with cheese around, in 8 plates*

*Cabbage salad with scallions and anchovies, in 8 plates*

Another fascinating source about salads is a book by Salvatore Massonio, written in Rome in the sixteenth century. Although his primary goal was to discuss the health benefits of eating salad, which again, was defined much more widely that we would today, he also reveals many of the common food preferences of his day. For example, he mentions a feast in Milan in 1559 at which the salad was the main nourishment and included both leafy green salads was well as fruits, flowers, cold salted meats, cold capon, livers, pastries, salted tongue, and so on.[1] But he also mentions common foods eaten before a meal that serve not as nourishment but as appetizers, or as he calls them foods that stimulate hunger. These include astringent and piquant foods like olives, sharp cheeses, and bitter greens. Massonio also gives his opinion about every salad ingredient. For example, he says rapunzel, the plant after which the fairy-tale princess is named and which she craves, is a white, slightly bitter root, eaten both raw and cooked, as are the leaves, but it has no known utility.[2] He means it has no medicinal value, but he also says that it is so common that it is known by all. So even though cookbooks do not mention it, we know it was a popular salad vegetable. Massonio also tells us about fava beans that "some are used to eating the first sprouts, while they are tender, when the plant has just begun to raise its stem, being a little point above the earth."[3] Elsewhere there are also recipes for hop sprouts and grapevine tendrils. Other banquet management guides give a good indication of the type of appetizers that would appear at the start of a meal. Domenico Romoli's extensive lists stretching back to 1546 include figs, nuts, lettuce and mint salad with capers, and three different fish, poached, marinated, and grilled, respectively.[4] Most of his antipasto courses offer a dried fruit or nuts, a salad, sometimes fritters or cheese, and a few fish dishes during Lent, or cold meat dishes or fowl at other times. Naturally starters were extremely variable according to the season, but they are very much like those offered to this day, although perhaps more varied.

### ❧ 112. TO PRESERVE CUCUMBERS ❧

*Liege, modern-day Belgium, 1604 (Lancelot de Casteau, 125)*

*Take little cucumbers and lay them on a table to sweat three or four days, then take some vinegar and boil it, and skim and let cool again, then throw in the cucumbers, and leave thus 15 days or three weeks, then pour off the vinegar and take another boiled and skimmed vinegar and let it cool, and throw it on your cucumbers and place in some ground alum, and take fennel seeds half bruised, and throw them in the barrel which should be well sealed, and keep it thus.*

Although cucumbers are considered quite ordinary today, this recipe was included among dishes for a banquet fit for princes. Cold foods like this were typical among appetizers, along with imported olives and capers. Alum (aluminum sulfate) is still sometimes used today to keep pickles green and firm and can be bought in grocery stores among spices. The cucumbers should be salted over the course of three or four days to "sweat" or let the water drain from them.

### ❧ 113. DIVERS SALLETS BOYLED ❧

*England, 1638 (Murrell, 23)*

*Parboile Spinage, and chop it fine, with the edges of two hard trenchers upon a board, or the backs of two Choppin-knives: then set them on a Chaffin-dish of Coales with Butter and vinegar. Season it with Sinamon, Ginger, Sugar, and a few parboyld Currans. Then cut hard Egges into quarters to garnish it withal, and serve it upon Sippets. So may you serve Burrage, Buglosse, Endiffe, Suckory, Coleflowers, Sorrell, Marigold-leaves, Winter-cresses, Leekes boyled Onions, Sporragus, Rocket, Alexanders. Parboyle them and season them all alike: whether it be with Oyle and Vinegar, or Butter and Vinegar, Sinamon, Ginger, Sugar, and Butter: Egges are necessary, or at least very good for all boyld Sallets.*

The idea of a salad was conceived somewhat differently in the past, though this was served cold as a starter. Presumably chopping with a blunt wooden plate or the back of a knife was to get a mushy rather than finely shredded texture. The spelling is quite erratic, but these are mostly common vegetables: borage and bugloss, endive, chicory, cabbage flowers (probably something like broccolini rather than cauliflower), cress, and then asparagus, arugula, and alexanders, which is *Smyrnium olustratum*, sometimes called black lovage or horse parsley. The marigold mentioned here is calendula, not the New World species. Sippets are toast points.

## SOUPS

### ❧ 114. TO MAKE A SOUP OF MELONS WITH MEAT BROTH ☙

*Italy, 1570 (Scappi, 80ᵛ)*

*Take melons in season, which begins in July and lasts through all August, though in Rome you find them even in September, and look for those that are not too mature, remove the peel and seeds and take the best part, cut in little mouthfuls and place in a pot in which is fresh butter, or melted chicken fat, with which you let it cook. When it is cooked pass through a strainer so in case there are any seeds they won't go in, then replace it in the pot with a bit of broth, gooseberries or whole unripe grapes and let it boil, and incorporate with beaten eggs and grated cheese. You can also cook the said melon with broth and when it is cooked, break up with a spoon and mix in as is said above, eggs cheese, spices, and not having gooseberries or unripe grapes, use verjuice.*

The season when this could be served is very short, not only for the melons but for the fruit garnish as well. This dish would have been classified by physicians as a cold and moist food, perfectly appropriate for counteracting the heat of late summer. Scappi offers variant procedures if a strainer is unavailable, and verjuice, presumably stored, can also supply the desired sourness. Although a hot fruit soup may not sound appealing, the meat broth base and combination of sweet, sour, and savory ingredients clearly mark this as a very typical Renaissance recipe. (Scappi also offers similar soup recipes using gourds or squash or even wild asparagus or hop sprouts.)

### ཏྠ 115. TO MAKE A LOMBARD SOUP WITH MEAT BROTH ཐྠ

*Italy, 1570 (Scappi, 81)*

*Take white bread cut in slices the thickness of a knife blade, remove the crust and let it cook in the oven or in a testa, and have rich broth, in which has been cooked beef, capons and cervelat sausages. Place the slices of bread in the plate and sprinkle on grated cheese, sugar, pepper and cinnamon, and place over each slice fresh provatura cheese, or fat cheese that is not too salty, and repeat this way three times. Bathe with the above written broth, which should not be too salty, so that it is well soaked. Cover with another plate and let it rest for a quarter of an hour in a hot place. Serve hot with the sausage cut in slices and with sugar and cinnamon over it.*

The testa was a covered earthenware crock used since ancient times for cooking food directly in the hearth over hot coals. Generally, slow-cooked braises work well in it, but pies and bread can also be baked inside. Here the idea is not to toast the bread, or it would be placed directly in front of the fire, but rather to dry it out thoroughly so it will absorb the broth better. Scappi distinguishes minestra, or a thick soup, from *zuppa*, which comes from the word meaning "to sop" up something with bread. The finished recipe is in structure and effect similar to a good French onion soup, though perhaps with much less liquid. The inverted soup plate placed on top was a typical way of keeping food warm and the two were brought to the table this way, sometimes wrapped with a ribbon as is depicted in Renaissance banquet scenes.

### ཏྠ 116. FOR WHITE PEASE POTTAGE ཐྠ

*England, 1596 (Dawson, 33)*

*Take a quart of white pease or more, and seethe them in fair water, close, until they do cast all their husks, the white cast away as long as any will come to the top. And when they be gone; then put into the pease two dishes of butter, and a little verjuice, with pepper and salt, and a little fine powder of march. And so let it stand till you will occupy it, and then serve it upon sops. You may seethe the porpoise and seal in your pease, serving it forth two pieces in a dish.*

Whole dried peas are called for here, specifically white pease which are a variety still common in Scandinavia. They are a pale green rather than pure white. It was generally agreed that they were superior to split peas in flavor. *Pease* is the original spelling of the word in English, and it was singular, the plural being *peases* or *peason*. Although the first seething (i.e., boiling) removed the skins, the recipe does not clearly specify any other cooking, but letting it stand may mean over the coals to cook gently. The soup is not pureed, though, as in a modern pea soup. Powder of march means spice powder. Porpoise and seal are not viable options today, but they were eaten in England in the past, though they became increasingly rare after the Middle Ages.

### ੬ੇ 117. CAULIFLOWER SOUP ੬ੇ

*Liege, modern-day Belgium, 1604 (Lancelot de Casteau, 10)*

*Place in the pottage cauliflower, sausages, some chicken or pigeon, or grilled mutton, and a bit of chopped mint.*

This brief recipe, adaptable to whatever leftovers are available, is best based on chicken broth. The cauliflower should be broken into florets and boiled in the broth just until tender. The mint should be added only at the very last minute. What is interesting is that this soup contains no spices, and it may be that the author intended the natural flavor of the vegetable to be highlighted. Cauliflower was a fairly new vegetable as well, selectively bred for large flowering heads from cabbage, as were Brussels sprouts and kohlrabi. They are all exactly the same species. White cauliflower, and it is not certain that this is what Lancelot had in mind, are made by tying up the outer leaves over the flower head, preventing chlorophyll from forming and thus leaving it white.

### ੬ੇ 118. HOW TO MAKE TRUFFLE BROTH ੬ੇ

*Spain, 1607 (Maceras, 79)*

*Toss the truffles in water, until it comes to a boil earth and all, so that it is washed better, and clean off the earth, and being clean, fry onions, garlic, parsley, mint in oil. Add to it salt, for it is a very flavorful dish. Season with salt, and crushed garlic and spices and bread crumbs, deglaze everything with water, and add the truffles. Have enough broth for your bowls, and cook well with caution. And after it is cooked and well seasoned with salt, vinegar, and spices, beat a couple of eggs, or two pair, considering how many truffles there are, and thicken with them, and serve in the bowls. This is the best pottage of all pottages, because often a little broth needs truffles for the aftertaste. You can cook these truffles in pantalones, cubilentes, English pasties, tarts and in casseroles.*

Although the author is very excited about truffles' flavor, there is no indication that they were very expensive in seventeenth-century Spain. Had they been it is unlikely that Maceras could have afforded many for his college refectory, which is where he worked. Today a soup like this with a few truffles, which here appear to be whole, could cost several hundred dollars. Like many soups throughout Europe, it is thickened with eggs. *Pantalones* means "pants" and these as well as *cublientes* were probably a shape of pastry or pasty (a little folded pie).

### ੩ 119. CAPIROTADA SOUP ੬

*Spain, 1611 (Martinez Montiño, 163–64)*

*Take pork loin and sausages and partridges all roasted, and make toast with the loins, sausages and partridges. Cut the partridges in quarters and the loin into pieces, and place all of this aside in layers, and when you add in the toast and the meat, toss on grated cheese and in this cheese add pepper and nutmeg, and ginger and place it on the layers, enough so that the sops are quite high. Next mash some eggs that are not very hard, and set them on each sop, next pound a bit of cheese with a clove of garlic and moisten with broth, then beat in a bowl eight eggs, four with the whites and the others without them, and beat it a lot, and moisten with broth. Next take the broth and the mashed cheese that is in the mortar with the eggs, and add in the broth that seems right to you to make the dish to soak the sops, and place it over the fire, and stir it with one hand so that it doesn't curdle. And when it's thickened, remove from the fire and add on top of the sops little by little, so that it soaks it up very well, and add cheese on top. Then comes what remains, the meat and the rest, cover with the sauce, add saffron so it becomes a little yellow. And when the sops become half cooked add very hot pork fat on top and grated cheese, and then finish cooking in an oven. In this capirotada you can also use birds and ducks when they are tender, because this is like an olla podrida, that has many things in it, but everything should be roasted first.*

What Martinez is hoping to achieve is a platter with a large mound of soaked bread, meat and cheese, moistened with broth thickened with eggs and then baked. It is almost a kind of solid soup and is meant to be a variation of the more typical *capirotada*, which is a sort of layered meat, bread, and cheese pudding. The *olla podrida* that he compares it with is also a hodgepodge of meats and vegetables, literally a "rotten pot" that can include nearly anything.

## MEAT

### ੩ 120. TO ROAST ON A SPIT OR BRAISE A LOIN OF BEEF, OR OF COW ੬

*Italy, 1570 (Scappi, 18)*

*Make sure above all that the said animals be fat and when they are of median age they will be so much better than if old, furthermore the animal should have been dead two days, more or less, according to the season, and so the meat will be tender enough, choose the inner loin which is attached to the tip of the shoulder and runs to the main bone which is much more tender than that which is above it which is called the back loin; when detached from the ribs and the membrane around it or silverskin removed, so that it will be even more soft and remain more tender, beat the entire length with a stick, splashing it all with malvasia, or Greco wine, rose vinegar, and crushed salt, pepper, cinnamon, ginger, nutmeg and cloves crushed with coriander or with fennel pollen, and let it rest for three hours under a weight with this composition, more or less according to its size. Having then large long slices of lardo, place them carefully around the loin with rosemary sprigs, tying it on with string, and letting it cook on a medium heat and catching whatever liquor falls from it, and when it is cooked remove from the spit and serve hot with a sauce made from the pan juices with vinegar, wine and sugar.*

*But if you want to braise it in a pot, remove from the spit while still very rare and remove the rosemary and lardo that's around it and place it in a pot or earthenware stewpot with the drippings that have collected in the pan, adding malvasia or Greco wine and cooked must or sugar with a bit of rose vinegar, and the same spices mentioned above, and seal the pot and let it finish cooking turning the pot occasionally. And when it is cooked serve hot with its own sauce over it, and in the pot you can also put raisins.*

For this magnificent recipe, buy a beef tenderloin, which is the whole piece from which filet mignon is usually cut. It is just about the most expensive cut of beef available, but, as Scappi notes, it is the most tender. *Malvasia* or malmsey is a sweet wine similar to marsala. *Greco* is the name of another sweet wine named for the "Greek" grape used to make it. Any sweet golden dessert wine will work—such as a muscat. Rose vinegar can be made by steeping clean and unsprayed rose petals in white wine vinegar for a few days or by adding some purchased rose water. The cooked must can be made by boiling down grape juice into a syrup. Any grape variety other than Concord would be preferable, even table grapes. For the spice mixture, the ginger should be dried. Whole spices freshly crushed are preferable. Lardo is cured and unsmoked pork fat rather than what is called lard in this country. Bacon will work perfectly fine, too. This cut of meat would have been cooked on a spit in front of the fire with a pan beneath to catch the drippings. It can also be done on a barbecue, threaded on shish kebab skewers mounted on the sides of the barbecue and turned slowly with a pan beneath. It can also be cooked directly on the grill, but then the drippings are lost. To braise thereafter use a cast-iron or earthenware pot that can withstand direct heat and seal it with a ring of dough made of flour and water, and place the pot directly in the hot coals or right in the barbecue if using. Turning in the hearth prevents the side facing the intense heat from cooking more quickly than the other side. Serve it in a long narrow serving plate with the sauce over, sprinkled with raisins if using and cut into thin slices across the grain.

### ੩ 121. TO POT ROAST A WHOLE STUFFED LEG OF LAMB ੨

*Italy, 1570 (Scappi, 36ᵛ–37)*

*Take a good leg. . .and beat it with a stick so that the meat separates from the bone that it has in the middle, then carefully remove the bone, which is the femur, but leaving the knee, and remove a part of the meat close to the bone and beat it with the same amount of lardo and raw prosciutto and garlic cloves, adding pepper, cinnamon, beaten herbs, some raisins and saffron, and invert the leg giving some cuts into the meat, avoiding cutting into the skin. Sprinkle the leg with rose vinegar and a powder of pepper, sugar and cinnamon, and then turn it back the way it was and fill with the said composition and sew shut with twine and place in a pot in which there is beaten lard and enough broth of another meat so that it is covered, adding clear verjuice, spices, prunes and dried sour cherries and seal the pot so that it can't leak steam and cook it on a slow fire for two hours; and when it's cooked serve hot with the broth over, removing the twine. But if you want to roast it on a spit, stuffed as it is, par boil it, remove and let cool, then stick with tiny bits of lardo, and place on the spit and cook just as you cook roasts. You can, after it is full of the same composition that is used to stuff it, cook it in an oven, adding less broth. Or you can equally put it on a spit raw.*

Because the final texture of this dish is similar to a pot roast, the name seemed appropriate here, though technically it is a whole leg slowly stewed. Scappi calls for a young castrato—a young castrated male sheep. Lamb is a good substitute. The stuffing is to be beaten in a large mortar, but chopping the meat and other ingredients together as finely as possible also works. The beaten lard called for in the pot is exactly what is available in this country as lard. Beef broth is also fine. The pot should be sealed with a ring of dough, and cooking it on the stovetop on the lowest flame is perfectly acceptable, though it can be cooked on coals in the fireplace as well. As with most of his recipes, Scappi offers options rather than dictating one single way of dealing with the ingredients and cooking methods.

### ੩ 122. TO MAKE SPANISH BALLES ੨

*England, 1588 (The Good Huswifes Handmaide for the Kitchen, 53)*

*Take a piece of a leg of Mutton, and pare away the skin from the flesh, chop the flesh verie small: then take marrow of beefe, and cut it as big as a hazell nut, and take as much of marrow in quantity as ye have of flesh, and put both in a faire platter, and some salt, and eight yolks of Egs, and stirre them well together: then take a litle eathern pot, and put in a pint, and a halfe of beefe broth that is not salt, or els Mutton broth and make it seeth: then make balles of your stuffe, and put them in boyling broth one after another, and let them stew softly the space of two houres. The lay them on sops three or foure in a dish, and of the uppermost of the broth on the sops, and make your balles as big as tennis balles.*

These are indeed meatballs, which can easily be made from ground lamb bought at the butcher. They are very gently simmered in broth, to prevent them from falling apart, though the eggs do hold them together. The "sops" are slices of bread, moistened with the broth and with a few meatballs placed on top. The size of tennis balls would have been a familiar reference since it was one of the most popular games among the wealthy.

### ✺ 123. HOW TO MAKE CHUETS ✺

*England, 1591 (A.W., 22ᵛ)*

*Take veale and perboyle it and chop it very fine, then take Prunes, Dates and Corance, wash them very clean and put them into your meat, then take Cloves, Mace, and pepper to season your meat withal and a little quantity of salt, verjious and Sugar, two ounces of biskets, and as many of Carowaies, this is the seasoning of your meat, then take fine flower, yolkes of Egs, and butter, a little quantitye of rosewater and sugar, then make little coffins for your Chewets and let them bake a quarter of an houre, then wet them over with butter, then strewe on Sugar and wet the Sugar with a little Rosewater, and set them into the Oven gain, then take them and serve five in a dish.*

These should be tiny appetizer-sized mouthfuls, hence the name chewet, of pastry with an open top. This can be done by cutting little disks of pastry dough and placing a ball of the filling in the center and then squeezing in the sides with the palm of your hand until it forms a little dumpling. The carowaies mentioned probably refer to a caraway-flavored biscuit rather than the spice alone; any regular biscuit or sugar cookie will work. The flavor combination, as with many other recipes, sounds perverse but is definitely worth trying.

### ✺ 124. HOW TO COOK ANOTHER DISH CALLED ALBUJAUANAS (MUTTON PATTIES) ✺

*Spain, 1607 (Maceras, 17)*

*Take a leg of mutton, two or three pounds, according to the number of guests, for each a half pound of meat. Take the meat and chop it very well with fat salt pork, parsley and mint, and after having chopped it with all this, put into a casserole, and take four or six maravedis of spices, and for each pound an egg, and you take these eggs and spices, fine salt, and vinegar and add all to the meat and knead it very well. Then being massaged, take a quarter pound of meat and place it in your hand and make a patty. Then take a greased casserole and place them in it. It should be cooked each one with a hole in the middle. Have a place to put the casserole on the fire, with a little fire underneath and above. When it is cooked beat a couple of eggs with a little vinegar and thicken a little broth, and place in the plates and add in the broth on top, and serve to the table.*

These are a kind of lamb patty with a hole in each, though why is not clear. The name suggests that this is a dish of Moorish origin because it seems to be a variant of an Arabic word. The sauce is a simple broth thickened with egg and made sour with vinegar, a standard soup when made in quantity. A *maravedi* was a coin and was also used as a unit of weight.

## FOWL

### ✥ 125. TO ROAST THE COCK AND HEN OF INDIA, WHICH IN SOME PLACES IN ITALY IS CALLED A PEACOCK OF INDIA (TURKEY) ✣

*Italy, 1570 (Scappi, 61)*

*The cock and the hen of India have bigger bodies than our own peacock, and the cock can spread its tail like our own peacock, and has black feathers, and white, and a neck of wrinkled skin, and on the head a horn of flesh, which when the cock gets angry, grows and gets big in a way that it covers all its moustache, and some others have a red comb mixed with blue; and a large breast and on the point of its breast it has a cluster of bristles like that of a pig, joined to the feathers, and it has flesh much more white and softer than our peacock, and so it becomes tender more quickly than capons and other similar birds. Wishing to roast it on a spit, don't let it sit too long after its death with the interior in the body more than 4 to 6 days in winter, or 2 in summer; pluck it dry or with hot water (thus you should do even the hen) and being plucked, and clean of its interior, prepare the breast, because it has a bone in the breast higher than other fowl, and cut the skin in a band near to this bone and carefully remove the flesh from the bone, and cut the edge of the bone with a razor sharp knife, and close up the skin again. Wishing to stuff it, fill it with the composition in chapter 115. Cut the wings, leave the head and feet, blanch it in water, and being blanched, let it cool again, then lard it finely, though if it's fat and stuffed you don't need to stick it with lard, but you will have to stick it with some cloves; put it on the spit and cook it quickly, such birds cook much quicker than our peacocks. From the meat of the breast you can make meat rolls, quenelles and all the dishes that can be made from lean veal. . . . The same goes for the hen and our peacock, but use these quickly after death, because being tenderized [i.e. hung] they're not as tasty; the cock and hen have the same season as our peacock; and it's true that in Rome they're used all year, the interior can be prepared like our peacock. . . .*

The stuffing Scappi refers to from an earlier chapter in his book is cured lard, liver, mint, marjoram, pimpernel, parsley, egg yolks, pepper, cinnamon, cloves, nutmeg, prunes, and cherries, or in summer gooseberries or unripe grapes, plus grated cheese, garlic, and fried onions. A modern turkey, bred for an enormous breast, is much larger than those used in the past, and consequently drier. A modern bird will not cook very quickly, and it would be a good idea to lard it, especially if it is baked in the oven. It is also not entirely clear why Scappi instructs to cut off the ridge on the breast bone; perhaps on a thin bird of the past it would protrude and look less elegant or even break through the skin. The other major difference in cooking method is that here the turkey is first blanched, that is, briefly immersed in boiling water, and then cooled before roasting. Interestingly, this is a typical procedure in Chinese cooking, and is said to remove some of the odor of the fowl. It may have been done in the past to remove what were called superfluities, the sort that rise up in a pot of chicken when it is boiled.

### ❧ 126. TO STEW LARKS OR SPARROWES ❧

*England, 1588 (The Good Huswifes Handmaide for the Kitchen, 19)*

*Take of your mutton broth the best, and put it in a pipkin, and put to it a litle whole Mace, whole pepper, Claret wine, marigolde leaves, Barberies, Rosewater, vergious, sugar, and Marrow, or else sweet butter: perboil the Larkes before, and then boyle them in the same broth and lay them upon sops.*

*Another way to stew Larkes: You must take them and draw them clean and cut of their feet, and then take a good deal of wine in a platter, and take a good deal of marrow, and put it in the wine, and set them on a Chafingdish, and let them stew there a good while: then take a quantity of small Raisins and wash them cleane, and put them into the broth, and take a litle Sugar and Synamon, and a few crums of Manchet bread and put them into the Larkes, and let them stew altogether. Then take and cut half a dozen tostes, and lay them in a platter, then put them into a dish with broth and serve them out.*

Both these recipes call for bone marrow to keep the tiny birds from drying out, though butter is an appropriate substitute, as the author states. In the past, no one would have been in the least squeamish about consuming a few little birds, especially stewed in a spicy sauce. To get an approximation of what these tasted like, quail is a decent substitute, or perhaps even Cornish game hens, though much lighter in flavor. The "manchet" in this recipe is fine white bread and the "tostes" are toast points.

### ❧ 127. TO STUE A CAPON IN LEMMONS ❧

*England, 1591 (A.W., 5)*

*Slice your Lemmons and put them in a Platter, and put to them white Wine and Rosewater, and so boile them and Sugar til they be tender. Then take the best of the broth wherein your Capon is boyled, and put thereto whole Mace, whole pepper & red Coraunte, barberries, a litle time, a good store of Marow. Let them boile wel togither til the broth be almost boiled away that you have no more then will wette your Sops. Then poure your Lemmons upon your Capon, & season your broth with Vergieus and Sugar, and put it upon your Capon also.*

The capon in this dish is actually not stewed but boiled separately and then the broth is used to make a very tart reduction that goes over bread, and the lemons are added at the end. The currants called for here are actual red currants rather than raisins. The "sops" are slices of toast. The final dish is both sour and sweet and from the lemon peel quite bitter as well. It should be served, after carving, with a piece of bread, the whole lemons, spices, and fruit on each plate.

### ❧ 128. HOW TO MAKE AN ESCABECHE OF PARTRIDGE ❧

*Spain, 1607 (Maceras, 37)*

*Roast the partridge such that it is half roasted, and divide it in the middle or in quarters, and fry it in oil, and pound all the spices, and bay leaves, white wine and vinegar judiciously, slices of lemon, and cook everything together, and then cool and put over the partridge, and it will keep all the time you like, and when you want to eat it, heat it up in the same escabeche, and don't forget to add salt into this escabeche.*

*Roast the partridge and remove the bones, pricking it very well, and add four maradevis of spices, cloves, pepper and saffron, white wine, and orange juice, and put the partridge in a casserole or plate and cook with all this for a quarter hour, and then you can serve.*

Two different versions of this sour and very traditional dish, which can be used for fish or other foods, are offered. The word *escabeche* means anything cooked and then marinated in vinegar or citrus and is probably the ancestor of the term *ceviche*, which today refers to marinated raw fish. The original idea was that the food would be preserved in the sour marinade until needed and the first version appears to be the older original one. The second version is meant to be eaten immediately and is somewhat more delicate, being boned. This version may reflect an increasing tendency to refine dishes while keeping the basic flavor profile.

### 129. TO MAKE BLANCMANGE

*Liege, modern-day Belgium, 1604 (Lancelot de Casteau, 32)*

*Take a capon or chicken which has been dead two or three days, and cook it, being cooked remove the breast meat and cut it into little pieces, and pound it in a mortar, adding two or three spoons of cow's milk. Then take seven pounds six ounces of cow's milk, a pound of rice flour which is very fine, and mix well your flour with the capon meat, and mix all the milk aforementioned with it. Then take a pound and a half of sugar, which is very white, place it in a cauldron on the fire and stir it well constantly with a wooden spoon, being boiled a quarter of an hour, place in eight ounces of rose water, a little salt, and let it boil again a little quarter hour, then remove from the fire and put in plates or in cups, or in square forms.*

The blancmange (meaning "white food") was one of the most popular dishes everywhere in Europe from the Middle Ages through the mid-seventeenth century. Originally it would have been made with almond milk and was specifically designed to be a light food appropriate for invalids. Nearly every cookbook written in these several hundred years includes a recipe, and some offer multiple variations. It could also be baked in a pie, colored with saffron, or cooked until fairly solid and sliced. The final texture should be like a very stiff pudding, and although a sweet chicken pudding scented with roses sounds a little strange today, the final taste is surprisingly pleasant. Today the term *blancmange* refers to a sweet almond and milk pudding thickened with gelatin.

### 130. A MALLARD SMORED, OR A HARE, OR OLD CONY

*England, 1615 (Markham, 81)*

*Take a mallard when it is clean dressed, washed, and trussed, and parboil it in water till it be scummed and purified; then take it up, and put it into a pipkin with the neck downward, and the tail upward, standing as it were upright; then fill the pipkin half full of water in which the mallard was parboiled, and fill up the other half with white wine; then peel and slice a good quantity of onions, and put them in with whole fine herbs, according to the time of year, as lettuce, strawberry leaves, violet leaves, vine leaves, spinach, endive, succory, and such like, which have no bitter or hard taste, and a pretty quantity of currants and dates sliced; then cover it close, and set it on a gentle fire, and let it stew, and smore until the herbs and onions be soft, and the mallard enough; then take out the mallard, and carve it as it were to go to the table; then to the broth put a good lump of butter, sugar, cinnamon; and if it be in summer, so many gooseberries as will give it a sharp taste, but in the winter as much wine vinegar; then heat it on the fire, and stir it all well together; then lay the mallard in a dish with sippets, and pour all this broth upon it; then trim the edges of the dish with sugar, and so serve it up. And in this manner you may also smore the hinder parts of a hare, or a whole cony, being trussed and close together.*

To "smore" means to braise or boil gently. The pipkin would have been a small pot with three legs and a handle placed over hot coals. Today any

kind of medium-sized pot with a cover will work, as long as it holds the entire bird. Mallards, male wild ducks, would have been fairly lean and probably tough, which is why this method was suggested. A modern domestic duck is probably much too fatty and delicate for boiling, though a "cony," meaning a rabbit, might work well. The final dish is set on toast with the sour green sauce over it, making a piquant contrast to the rich meat.

*Pipkin.*

## FISH AND SEAFOOD

### ⇥ 131. TO MAKE STUFFED CALAMARI SOUP ⇤

*Italy, 1570 (Scappi, 125)*

*Take a medium sized squid, which is not too big nor too small, cleaned . . . and parboil its tentacles in water and salt, and set aside the ink bladder, and stuff the body of the squid with a combination of parmigiano cheese grated, raw egg yolks, grated bread crumbs, chopped herbs, pepper, cinnamon, raisins and saffron. But if it is a fast day, in place of the cheese put in almonds or walnuts or pounded hazelnuts with a bit of bread soaked in verjuice, mixed with the materials above. When it is filled, place it in an earthenware or copper vessel with oil or butter, and enough water to cover, adding its beard cut into little mouthfuls, and let it boil very gently, adding common spices, and enough salt. When it is half cooked, add to it minutely chopped herbs, or mix into the broth pounded almonds tempered with white wine and clear verjuice and a bit of saffron. If you wish to give it a black color, add the ink which is in the bladder into the same broth. You can also, after the squid is stuffed, boil it gently in water for an hour with salt, so the filling doesn't fall out, remove from the broth, and while hot coat with flour and fry in butter or oil. When it's fried, serve with orange juice and sugar over it, or cover with various sauces.*

The method of cleaning squid Scappi recommends is to remove the eyes and the bone, a transparent cartilage quill inside along the back, while cleaning in several changes of water. You should also remove the beak, a tiny hard black nodule at the base of the tentacles, as well as all interior organs. He warns that the "mane," presumably the same thing he mentions here as "beard," is often full of sand. These must refer to the long trailing tentacles. Most squid available today have already been cleaned, but it is possible to buy squid ink separately, usually in Italian specialty stores. It has no flavor whatsoever but makes food a vibrant jet black. Squid must be cooked either very briefly or for a very long time. This recipe should take about an hour, as Scappi notes in the variation. The ends of the squid can also be secured with toothpicks to prevent the stuffed leaking out. Serve a squid or two, depending on the size, in a bowl with broth.

### ⊰ 132. TO MAKE STUFFED ROLLS OF TUNA MEAT COOKED ON A SPIT ⊱

*Italy, 1570 (Scappi, 111ᵛ)*

*Being ... much redder than all other fish, because of which redness it resembles veal, tuna flesh is made into rolls. ... Choose the leanest part and cut slices the length of the palm of your hand, and as thick as one finger. Then flatten them four or five times with the side of a knife blade and sprinkle with fennel pollen, salt and have a composition made from the belly, which is the fattiest part of the tuna, and one third that amount of salted tarantella softened, and beat everything together one with the other, as with a sausage, adding aromatic herbs. And if it is not a fasting day, in place of the tarantella add grated cheese, raw egg yolk, with pepper, cinnamon, cloves, nutmeg, and if you like garlic which is optional. Fill the rolls with the composition and let them cook on a spit, bathing from time to time with garlic mixed with verjuice and sapa. When it is cooked serve it hot with its sauce over. With tuna flesh you can make all those dishes that are made with sturgeon, and similarly with the organs, except that caviar can't be made from its eggs.*

Scappi calls these rolls *polpettoni*. If you use a tuna steak and cut it diagonally, you should be able to make four or five slices. These are pounded gently, either with the flat side of a knife or a flat-ended meat pounder, or even a rolling pin. Use the leftover bits for the filling, and ideally if you can find *tarantella*, a salted tuna belly, much like prosciutto in texture and even flavor, use that as well. It should be softened by soaking in hot water, and then the mixture pounded until smooth. Alternately the cheese and egg mixture works nicely, but be sure to add the spices, whichever filling is used. Four or five of these rolls can then be skewered like shish kebabs and either placed on a grill, or better, turned slowly without touching the grill. The basting material, both unripe grape juice and cooked-down grape juice, is the authentic way to do it. Wine alone also works but does not give quite the same sweet-and-sour glaze. The kind of sauce referred to here is not identified, but it could be the same garlic basting sauce.

### ❧ 133. TO SEETH STOCK FISH ❧

*England, 1588 (*The Good Huswifes Handmaide for the Kitchen, *43)*

*Take Stockfish and water it well, and then put out all the baste from the fish, then put it into a pipkin and put in no more water then will cover it, and set it on the fire, and as soon as it beginneth to boyle on the one side, then turn the other side to the fyre, and as soone as it beginneth to boyle on the side take it off and put it into a Colender, and let the water run out from it, but put in salte in the boyling of it, then take a litle fair water and sweete Butter, and let it boyle in a dish until it be something thicke, then poure it on the stockfish and so serve it in.*

Stockfish was a crucial Lenten staple across Europe and one of the most dependable sources of transportable protein because it never goes bad. Searching for cod to make stockfish led Europeans to first explore North American waters in the late fifteenth and early sixteenth centuries. Stockfish is essentially cod that is dried and must be beaten and soaked to become edible. Bacalao or salt cod is more common nowadays but is a fine substitute. It must be soaked for 24 hours and then picked over to remove the "best" from the fish, then lightly brought to the boil as described in this recipe. A pipkin is a small earthenware pot with three legs that is placed over hot coals, in which food "seethes" or gently boils. Stockfish is rarely mentioned in courtly cookbooks as it was considered food for common folk. The lack of spices here also indicates that this is a dish one might find in an ordinary household.

### ❧ 134. STUFFED CRAYFISH OR SEA CRABS ❧

*Liege, modern-day Belgium, 1604 (Lancelot de Casteau, 87–88)*

*Take crayfish or crabs and let them boil as with little crayfish, then take all the meat out, but do not break the upper shell. Then chop all the meat and add in chopped marjoram, nutmeg and pepper, three or four egg yolks, and fry everything in butter. Then return to the shell underneath, and place around all the little legs fried in butter.*

Other cookbook authors of the time suggest cooking the mixture in the shell; either way works fine. This recipe scarcely differs from modern ones except for the addition of nutmeg and the absence of breadcrumbs to hold the mixture together, but it is unnecessary if cooked in this fashion.

### ❧ 135. LITTLE FISH ❧

*Spain, 1607 (Maceras, 105)*

*Little fish you fry and put in escabeche like barbels, and you serve it hot with pepper and orange. Equally you can put it in a pot or earthenware casserole after washing. Be sure afterwards to add vinegar, spices, salt and chopped garlic, and toss everything and place it to cook. And don't add water, because enough falls from it and soaks everything, it will be very good this way. And cooked you can offer with salt, vinegar, water with parsley and verjuice, and serve with pepper.*

The *escabeche* is a classic way of both preserving and flavoring fish and normally involves frying and then marinating in a vinegar-based sauce. The method for barbel, a freshwater fish with beard-like protrusions on its chin, is to fry and then soak in vinegar, wine, spices, salt, garlic, bay leaves and water. It is reheated before serving. Appropriate for this dish are any small fish; fresh sardines work very well. The serving suggestions at the end of this recipe are to be combined as a sour sauce to accompany the fish.

### ⊰ 136. TO SOWCE OYSTERS ⊱

*England, 1634 (Murrell, A8b)*

*Take out the meat of the greatest oysters: save the liquor that commeth from them, and streine it into an earthen pipkin: put into it halfe a pint of white wine, and half a pint of wine vinegar: put in some whole pepper, and sliced ginger. Boyle all these together with two or three cloaves, when it hath boyled a little, put in your oysters, and let them boyle two or three walmes, but not too much. Then take them up, and let the sirrup stand until it be cold: then put in your oysters, and so may you keepe them all the yeere.*

Exactly what length of time a "walm" might be is unclear but the word means "to boil." It seems to suggest that it should be brought to the boil and very quickly cooked. Sousing means to pickle. Preserving all types of food was essential for making it through lean times, though the spices used here do not imply poverty. This recipe probably serves both as a way to keep food and to offer something tasty out of season. Oysters were a favorite in England at all levels of society and were also added to other recipes, as stuffing or in pies.

### ⊰ 137. FROG PIE ⊱

*Spain, 1611 (Martínez Montiño, 320)*

*From frogs you can make a pie, soak them in a bit of fresh fat and toss on top a bit of hot water, and a little bit of greens, salt and let it boil. Then take them out with a skimmer, and season with all spices and salt and place in a vessel with a little cow's butter, and when they are cooked, beat some egg yolks with lemon juice and add some broth in which you have purged the frogs, and fill your pie and thicken in the same way that you do to season English empanadas of frogs, soaking the frogs with your fat and onions and you can add all the spices and a little wine and a little verjuice, and stew them.*

*These frogs make a very good blancmange, purging the frogs in water which you boil a couple of times, and remove the little black veins that they have, and then take a quantity of these frogs equaling a breast and a half of chicken, and break up with your fingers very gently so that it will be very tender. Then beat in a bit of milk with a blancmange spoon and add in rice flour to make your blancmange of flesh.*

Although frogs are amphibians rather than fish, they were normally classified with sea creatures and sea mammals. From the directions given, it appears that the frogs are eaten whole, removed from the pie with other contents, thickened with egg yolks with which they have "stewed." In a sense, that is precisely what happens to them when baked in a pie, though it is an odd choice of cooking terms. The blancmange (meaning "white food") variation is no different from the typical chicken version except that the flesh is not pounded, but rather it seems gently stirred to retain the delicate bits of frog flesh.

## Vegetables

### ❧ 138. TO COOK STUFFED EGGPLANTS IN DAYS OF LENT ❧

*Italy, 1570 (Scappi, 151ᵛ)*

*Take the eggplants and peel the skin that they have around, and empty the interior through the narrow end, which can be done more easily by bringing them to a boil in hot water, reserve [the interior] and beat with knives together with little aromatic herbs and pounded mature walnuts and almonds, a bit of grated bread, pepper, nutmeg and cinnamon, a crushed clove of garlic, add a little oil and clear verjuice, and stuff the eggplants with this composition and place in a vessel of appropriate size to their bottoms with the mouths facing up. In the vase should be oil, water, salt and saffron, the above mentioned spices so that the eggplants are will be more than half covered. Close the pot and let it boil very gently, and when it is half cooked add to the broth a bit of grated bread, beaten herbs, making the broth piquant with spices and a little bitter. When it's cooked, serve hot with the same broth over it. But if you wish to cook it in an oven, you don't have to peel them, but only fill them with the same composition, or with oil, verjuice, pepper and a clove of garlic, and let it cook. And when it's cooked carefully lift the skin without breaking the eggplant, or cut them in half and with a knife remove the best part. You serve it hot with orange juice over, and if it's not a fast day, you add to the filling grated cheese and some egg.*

As usual, Scappi offers many variations in ingredients and in techniques. Hollowing out a peeled and parboiled eggplant is quite a trick, as is finding a pot just the right size for several eggplants. The ones Scappi was using may have been quite small and firm to survive this procedure whole.

### 139. TO MAKE A SOUP OF RED CHICKPEAS

*Italy, 1570 (Scappi, 155–55ᵛ)*

*Take red chickpeas, clean of all dirt, and place in clear lye, not too strong, or in tepid water with a bit of cinders in a cloth, and let soak for an hour in a hot place, then remove them and wash in clear water, and having avoided making the lye too strong as was said, because the chickpeas would shed their skins and would take up the odor of the lye. Then remove them from that and wash with tepid water, and place in a vessel with oil, salt, a bit of flour mixed with a spoon, and enough water so that they are covered by four fingers and more, and let them cook with sprigs of rosemary, and sage and whole heads of garlic, and pepper and serve in bowls. If you wish to make it without the flour and garlic, add minutely chopped herbs just when you want to serve it. But if you want to cook the chickpeas for a broth, you don't have to let them soak, it's enough to clean and wash them well, and place in a glazed earthenware vessel with plain tepid water, which you place for 6 hours over hot coals, keeping it covered, and when you want to cook them remove the scum that collects on top, and let them cook in the same water, adding a bit of oil and salt, and for aroma a few rosemary sprigs.*

Chickpeas, like most beans, come in "white" or beige as well as red and black varieties. These are dried. Although seemingly laborious and even dangerous, the first procedure, soaking in lye, an alkaline solution made from soaked ashes, does soften the skins. Baking soda has the same effect. The second method of slowly cooking the chickpeas in broth over hot coals is definitely preferred, as this makes the chickpeas tender, particularly when the salt is only added at the end in the final stages of cooking.

*Making red chickpea soup.*

### 140. TO MAKE FRIED TOAST OF SPINACH

*England, 1596 (Dawson, 112)*

*Take spinach and seethe it in water and salt. When it is tender, wring out the water between two trenchers. Then chop it small and set it on a chafing dish of coals. Put thereto butter, small raisins, cinnamon, ginger, sugar, a little of the juice of an orange, and two yolks of raw eggs. Let it boil till it be somewhat thick. Then toast your toast, soak them in a little butter and sugar and spread thin your spinach upon them. Set them on a dish before the fire a little while. So serve them with a little sugar upon them.*

This recipe makes excellent hors d'oeuvres, but the spinach must not be overcooked. A quick blanching in boiling water, and then wringing out, with bare hands actually works better than two boards or trenchers. The final effect is a kind of savory green cinnamon toast.

### ᕦ 141. FAVA BEAN TART ᕤ

*Liege, modern-day Belgium, 1604 (Lancelot de Casteau, 40)*

*Take cooked green fava beans and remove the skins, and pound them and add in two raw eggs, a quarter ounce of cinnamon, a bit of chopped mint, three ounces of sugar, four ounces of melted butter and make tarts. . . .*

This tart must be made with fresh fava beans, which are only available in the spring. You need about 2 pounds to make a small 8- or 9-inch tart. After removing the shells, blanch them for about 5 minutes in boiling water and remove the skins on each individual bean and proceed with the recipe. It is very time-consuming but well worth it. The pie crust should be very short (i.e., crisp), made of butter, flour and water. The filled shell should be baked until brown, about 45 minutes. This appears to have been a popular dish; it appears elsewhere through Europe in various forms. It also appears that while dried fava beans were considered lowly fare fit for peasants and difficult to digest, there was no such stigma associated with fresh beans.

On the Feast of the Epiphany, or Twelfth Night, 12 days after Christmas when the Three Magi were said to have come to visit the baby Jesus, there was a tradition of eating a cake that contained a whole dried bean. Whoever got the bean would be declared king for the day, or in French *Roi de La Fêve* (Bean King). This tradition survives in Louisiana among French-speaking Cajuns, though for Mardis Gras. The King Cake, eaten on this day, contains a little plastic baby rather than a bean, though.

### ᕦ 142. CARROT SALAD ᕤ

*Spain, 1611 (Martínez Montiño, 98)*

*The carrots for salad, you should look for the black ones, wash them, and clean off the rootlets, and cut the point and the tops, and put them in a pot, and press them to the bottom so they are very tight, and place the pot in the coals and put fire all around, and above and roast them very well. Then take them out and clean off the skin so they become very delicate and season with salt and serve with oil, vinegar while hot. And if you want to add sugar, you can. The pot should be shallow. You should set these carrots where there are coals, and make little slices.*

Carrots were first widely cultivated around the time this recipe was written. "Red" carrots, although we cannot be sure exactly what color that meant, and black carrots were more common than today's orange. This method of roasting will work in a covered casserole placed in the oven as well, set on high heat. The author seems to want the carrots to be kept warm. The word *salad* in the title merely means that this is a dish composed solely of vegetables, but not necessarily that it is cold.

## STARCHES AND PASTA

### ৺ 143. TO MAKE A MINESTRA OF CRACKED MILLET OR PANIC ৶

*Italy, 1570 (Scappi, 73)*

*Take millet or cracked panic, though panic is much better and more flavorful than millet, clean it of dust and any other dirt, that is, sift it the way you do semolina and place in a vessel of earthenware or tinned copper with meat broth and let it cook with cervelat sausage or with a piece of salted pork jowl to give it flavor, and when it is cooked add grated cheese and beaten eggs, pepper, cinnamon and saffron. You can even cook this grain with goat's milk or cow's in the way that you cook semolina. . . . When it is cooked in broth and still firm, you can remove it from the vessel and let it cool on a table or another vessel of wood or earthenware. And when it is cooled cut in slices and fry in fresh butter in a pan, and serve it hot with sugar and cinnamon over.*

Millet and its close relative panic are tiny round grains, familiar today as birdseed. In the past they were used to make polenta, and this dish is the exact equivalent of the recipe that is today made of corn. By the latter sixteenth century, corn was introduced from the New World and it began to replace millet, which was increasingly associated with poverty. Millet eventually became obsolete as food for humans and this is a pity, as it has a rich nutty flavor. Interestingly, Scappi had no qualms about serving it at the papal court. Although Scappi calls this dish a minestra (thick soup), it should be fairly firm like a porridge, or solid if sliced and fried.

### ৺ 144. TO MAKE A TART OF TAGLIATELLI OR LASAGNE COOKED IN FAT MEAT BROTH OR IN MILK ৶

*Italy, 1570 (Scappi, 358)*

*Take tagliatelli or lasagna made of fine flour, egg, milk, tepid goat's milk or tepid water and cook them in fat meat broth or in goat's milk, or cow's and when they are cooked remove them and let cool, so that you can cut them. Then have a pie plate buttered with a sheet of royal pastry made of fine flour, rose water, sugar and butter and above this sheet put a layer of provatura cheese, a sprinkling of sugar, pepper and canella with a few knobs of fresh butter and grated parmesan cheese. Then place over this the cut up tagliatelli or lasagna, and over the lasagna put a layer of the same ingredients that are below, in this way you can made more layers. Let it cook in the oven or in a testa without being covered, and when it is near being cooked sprinkle with sugar, cinnamon, and make it brimming with butter. In this way you can make every sort of macaroni made with a iron pin, cooked in the way mentioned above. You can also layer with mint, marjoram and pounded garlic cloves, and always serve it hot.*

This recipe is an ancestor of modern lasagna, without the tomatoes. The noodles are fresh, cooked whole and then cut after boiling. To make the pasta sheets, use Italian "00" flour, which has a low protein content and is easy to roll, or combine all-purpose flour with some pastry flour. Any cook in the past would have known how to make sheets of lasagna and there is no reason not to make them from scratch today. Measurements are completely unnecessary. In a bowl, or directly on a wooden board, pour a few cups of flour, and make a hollow depression in the top like a volcano or fountain, as the Italians referred to it. Add an egg or two into a hollow and then some water or milk. Stir until a firm dough forms and knead just until it is smooth. Let rest covered for about 15 minutes, divide into fist-size balls and then roll each out into thin sheets. Boil these in broth or milk for about two or three minutes. Hollow macaroni can be formed by rolling small knobs of dough around an iron pin into long tubes. A round chopstick floured also works. The provatura is a young fresh cheese. The cooking option offered is either baking in an oven or placing on hot coals in an earthenware testa (a kind of casserole) without a lid.

### 145. TO MAKE RAVIOLI

*Liege, modern-day Belgium (Lancelot de Casteau, 78–79)*

*Make a dough of white flour with eggs and butter, you will make little coverings. . . . Then you will take roasted flesh of veal, cold or other flesh of cooked veal. For a pound of meat, a half pound of beef fat, and chop it up well all together and you will add to it 3 raw eggs, three ounces of grated parmigiano, a half ounce of cinnamon and two of nutmeg, mix it all together well, and make your ravioli. . . . Then put them in boiling water, and you will take them out of the water and place five or six on a plate with a rich bouillon, and sprinkle on grated parmigiano and cinnamon, and bring it to the boil two or three times in the plate, then serve it. If you would like to make them smaller, it will be better to place a dozen in a plate.*

While we tend to think an obsession with things Italian is a modern phenomenon, through the Middle Ages and Renaissance, northern Europeans treasured goods from the south, including even ravioli, recipes for which appear in many cookbooks. The origin of the word is a little puzzling, and seems to be mean "a little turnip," which is what they would look like if each filled disk was pinched at the top like a purse.

### ❦ 146. HOW TO MAKE WHEAT STARCH ❦

*Spain, 1607 (Maceras, 79)*

*To Make eight plates of wheat starch, you take half a pound of starch and an açumbre of milk, and a pound of sugar. With a little of the milk, dissolve the starch, and being dissolved, strain through a fine thin cloth, and place in a casserole, and add the milk and sugar and place on the fire, stirring continuously with a spoon until it's thick. Then make each plate, and sprinkle with sugar and cinnamon on top. It's a good dish.*

Wheat starch was normally used to thicken other dishes, or to starch collars, but here it takes center stage in a kind of sweet starchy pudding. It was considered a rather fine and elegant ingredient, particularly because it was difficult to make, by soaking flour and drawing off the starch. An *azumbre* is about 2 quarts and a pound of starch is about 4 cups.

### ❦ 147. BUTTERED LOAVES ❦

*England, 1634 (Murrell, 24)*

*Season a little pottle of flour with Cloaves, Mace, and a little Pepper, mingle it with Milke warm from the cow, take halfe a pound of sweet Butter melted, half a pinte of Ale-yest, two or three raw Egges, temper your floure with these things, to the temper of a Manchet paste, then make them up in little Manchets about the bigness of an egge, flat them, cut them and pricke them, set them on a paper, and bake them like Manchet, let the Oven-lidde be downe: but if something be in the Oven that requireth longer or more heate, then cover them with a paper, in an houre they will be thorowly soakt: then melt a pound of sweete Butter, with some Rose-water in it, draw froth your loaves, and pare away the crusts, slit them throrow betwixt the top and bottome, in two places, and they will be like round toasts: put them into the melted Butter, and turne them over and over in the Butter, then take a warme dish and put in the bottome peeces of the loaves, strew on Sugar of a good thicknesse, then set on the middle peeces, and serve them likewise: lastly put on the tops, and scrape on Sugar on them also: so you may set on three, foure, five, sixe or more in a dish. If you be not ready to send them in, then set them in the Ovens mouth, with a paper over them, to keep them from drying.*

This perplexing recipe results in something like an extremely buttery stack of fluffy bread rounds and is actually quite simple and well worth trying. The dough, significantly reduced in quantity, can be made with 6 cups of flour to 2 cups of warm milk in which a packet of yeast has been

*Buttered loaves.*

dissolved. One egg and spices are mixed in along with a stick of melted butter and a dash of rosewater. Add enough flour if necessary to make a soft, biscuit-like dough. Form into little flat rounds, either by flattening balls of dough or rolling out and cutting with a biscuit cutter. Poke the top with a fork, let rise about an hour and bake on parchment paper or a greased cookie sheet at 350 degrees for about 40 minutes. Let cool and then carefully cut off the upper crust and again divide the insides two or three times if you can. Soak these in butter and stack as high as you can with sugar in between each layer. Murrell specified to scrape the sugar, which means he was using a sugar loaf or solid cone, which is how sugar was sold. A similar recipe in *The Good Hus-wifes Handmaide for the Kitchen* calls these Restons and includes ginger between the layers.

## Eggs and Dairy

### ❧ 148. TO MAKE CANNONCINI OF FRESH EGGS ❧

*Italy, 1570 (Scappi, 422ᵛ)*

*Beat ten eggs and take a spoon that holds no more than one egg, and a frying pan, not too large anointed with butter. Into this put your full spoon of egg and make a frittata as large as the pan. Place on the frittata sugar, cinnamon, cooked raisins and roll it around like cannoli. In this way do the others and place one on the other, sprinkled with sugar, cinnamon and orange juice. Cut the ends of the cannoli so that they're all equal and stew them between two plates with a bit of butter, sugar and orange juice, plus rosewater and serve hot.*

These rolled omelets are made from scrambled eggs. The quantity can easily be limited to two eggs per person. As plates nowadays are rarely flameproof or deep enough to hold 10 omelets, the best way to do this is to cook each very thin omelet first in a small frying pan. Then assemble them, sugar and spices first and the raisins having been boiled in wine, and then return the omelets to the pan until the liquid thickens a bit. Scappi clearly preferred to use plates so that the rolls would be presented on a hot platter, still nice and even.

### ❧ 149. TO POACH EGG YOLKS IN SUGAR ❧

*Italy, 1570 (Scappi, 422)*

*The sugar being clarified, place in a pan of silver or copper well lined with tin or in a silver plate and let it scald. When the sugar is hot, place in it egg yolks and sprinkle on a bit of rosewater. Heat from above with an oven peel or a pan cover. Serve the eggs in its own pan with sugar and cinnamon over it. You can even cook it with the whites.*

Scappi's range of egg recipes is remarkable, particularly those poached. Normally this is done in water, but he also does it in goat's milk, sweetened white wine and then sugar in another unusual dish. For this recipe, clarifying sugar is unnecessary; merely use white sugar. The best results happen when the sugar has begun to melt and caramelize, but it should not become too dark. The syrup that forms beneath the egg yolks can be poured on before serving. A stainless steel pan also works fine. The peel is precisely the sort used to move pizzas in and out of the oven, with a metal end that can be heated. Sometimes a special device called a salamander was used. It is a flat metal rectangle on the end of a rod heated in the flame and then held over the food. It is much safer today to use the broiler. The yolks can be cooked alone but the variation of whole eggs may be more palatable to modern tastes. Six eggs will fit comfortably in a pan with a 1/4 inch of sugar covering the entire bottom surface. They should be cooked until "loose" or *sparse* in Italian, that is, soft.

### ᘓ 150. HUEVOS RELLENOS (STUFFED EGGS) ᘓ

*Spain, 1607 (Maceras, 91)*

*For a dozen eggs, take half a pound of peeled almonds and half a pound of sugar, and make a marzipan well beaten. Beat the eggs well, and make omelets very thin like paper, and as wide as the pan. Then take a bit of marzipan and make it the length of the tortilla, and roll each one up. After you have filled them all up, make in each one two or three holes, to make the tortilla big, and beat four eggs reserved and fill up the holes in the tortillas and fry without burning. Put them on plates and serve with sugar and cinnamon. Sometimes these are called arrolados, it is a regal dish, though costly.*

This dish of eggs, though it includes expensive ingredients, could probably have been made in simpler versions for everyday meals in the college refectory. Eggs were one of the most frequently used ingredients in Spanish cooking both at court and in ordinary households.

### ᘓ 151. TO MAKE STUFFED EGGS ᘓ

*Liege, modern-day Belgium, 1604 (Lancelot de Casteau, 133)*

*Hard boil the eggs, and cut them in two pieces. Then take the yellow out of both sides and chop them well with parsley, marjoram and a bit of salt and add in raw egg yolks, chopping it well together. Then fill the whites with this. After, fry them in butter, then put a little pepper on them, which will be sweet and sharp, and serve thus.*

*Another*

*Take the same eggs, place them in boiling water with butter and place in parmesan or another good fat cheese, cinnamon, pepper, with some butter and serve thus.*

The second variation picks up after the eggs have already been cooked and stuffed; the only difference is then they are cooked again with cheese rather than merely fried. Contrary to what one might expect, the eggs are not arranged face up as with modern devilled eggs, but rather are cooked with the yolk side down so that it solidifies and takes on the flavor either of the butter or the spiced cheese and poaching liquid.

### ⇥ 152. FRIED QUESADILLAS OF CURDS ⇤

*Spain, 1611 (Martínez Montiño, 204–5)*

*Curdle the milk, and when it is curdled put it on the fire so that it is hot, and then amass it with your hands little by little, and let it come completely together. Then remove it from the whey and press it very well, and place it in the mortar and mash well, and add a bit of flour and add eggs enough so that it's soft, and add a bit of chopped mint, or dried ground and season with salt, and then knead a fine dough without sugar and make a big delicate sheet and extend over a table and with a little spoon place little spoonfuls of this mixture over the dough, each separate from the other, and moisten the fingers of your hands in water, and flatten everything, so they become broadened. Then take the pastry cutter and cut around so that you don't come too near the filling. Then remove the cutting scraps, and make your quesadillas like little oil lamps, so you give each five or six pinches. To make these don't wet them, because they're better when you make these pinches, so they are joined with the filling itself, and with this they stick very well. Then you take a frying pan and put the pan on the fire, so that the fat is not too hot, and place them in the bottom and fry little by little, and turn them over, so they don't toast too much. And season with a little skimmed honey drizzled over them, and put them judiciously in a plate and for each layer sprinkle on sugar and cinnamon. The result you can keep many days, and the honey should contain a little water when you skim it. The quesadillas should not be bigger than pieces of eight. And notice that when you finish making the filling, make one quesadilla to test the fat, and if the filling disperses in the fat, add a bit more flour.*

These are a direct ancestor of the quesadillas made in Mexico today with corn-based dough, though they are smaller—in fact the size of large coins or "pieces of eight." The directions here are remarkably precise and so flawless that any beginner should be able to follow them without any trouble. The cheese curds need not be made fresh, though it is actually very easy to do. Buy powdered rennet, which was traditionally made with the lining of a calf's stomach, though is today mostly genetically engineered, and follow the directions on the packet for curdling the cheese or separating the curds and whey. The pot should then be heated very gently and stirred with the hand to bring together the curds, which can then be strained from the liquid. Cottage cheese drained of some liquid or farmer cheese will work best. A regular butter-based pastry dough works well, and the shape should be like a little purse gathered at the top and then flattened slightly into a disk. Honey sold today is already clarified.

## SAUCES

### ⤙ 153. ROYAL SAUCE ⤚

*Italy, 1570 (Scappi, 93ᵛ)*

*Take three pounds of fine sugar and a foglietta of white vinegar without rose, and a half foglietta of white wine and a bit of whole cinnamon sticks. Let everything together boil in a new glazed pot until it begins to cook, and put a cover on the pan, so that it does not steam. To know when it's cooked, place a drop on a plate or platter, and if the little ball is compact, when touching it doesn't spread, it will be cooked. Then serve it cold, being careful that it does not burn, because you must remove it the moment it makes a little ball, as is said above. When you cook it, you may add in nutmeg and cloves and in place of the pan you can cook it in a casserole.*

This is a simple sweet-and-sour sauce bordering on a jelly. It is normally served with roasts. Notice that Scappi's technique is essentially that of candy makers, boiling sugar and other ingredients to the soft-ball stage, which will make the sauce thick. The *foglietta* is a wine measurement equaling 1/3 liter, which is about 10 ounces or a cup and a quarter. If you do not have a scale to measure 3 pounds of sugar, keeping in mind a pound troy equals 12 ounces rather than 16, the Renaissance 3 pounds equals 36 ounces of sugar or about 4½ cups. White wine vinegar is what should be used here rather than rose-flavored vinegar, which was one of Scappi's favorite ingredients. This would normally serve a large crowd, so the recipe can be roughly quartered, using 1 cup of sugar, a quarter cup of vinegar, an eighth of wine, a bit of cinnamon stick, a few cloves, and a sliver of nutmeg. Let it cool with the whole spices so their flavor permeates the sauce. Similar sauces are also made with a base of apples juice or orange juice, quince or pomegranate.

### ⤙ 154. CARROT SAUCE ⤚

*Italy, 1570 (Scappi, 92ᵛ)*

*Choose the most colored part of the carrot, which is cleaned, and let it cook more than half way in water. Next take it out, put it in an earthenware pot and for every pound of carrots place seven ounces of sugar and four of quince, half [an ounce] of cinnamon, a quarter of pepper, a quarter of cloves and nutmeg, and boil everything together with 10 ounces of clear verjuice, and 4 ounces of rose vinegar, and when it's cooked pass it through a sieve. This sauce should have a bit of body, and after it's sieved, let it cool and serve.*

Although this recipe sounds like something invented by a modern avant-garde chef, Renaissance cooks were much more creative with new sauces, not being constrained by expectations of how a sauce should blend with a main ingredient, or be of a liquid consistency. Rather, the intention here was to offer sharp and vibrant contrasts in both flavor and texture. For this sauce, color was also an interest. Most contemporary authors refer to carrots as red, and this has led many food historians to assume that orange carrots were not yet "invented," so to speak, by gardeners. It may also be the case that just as they used the word *red* to refer to egg yolks, it was a manner of speech, or even possibly that the word *orange*, denoting color, which derives from the fruit and not the other way around, had not yet been used to describe carrots. In any case, you will get an interesting thick cold sauce/jam colored orange with this recipe. It was typically used as a condiment for meats.

### ❧ 155. TO MAKE A GREEN SAUCE ❧

*Italy, 1570 (Scappi, 431 [mispaginated 421])*

*Take parsley, spinach leaves, sorrel, pimpernel, arugula, a bit of mint and chop everything finely. Pound it in a mortar with toasted slices of bread, and if you want put in almonds or hazelnuts, which is optional, but if it is without, it remains greener. When it's pounded, place in sugar, salt and temper everything with vinegar. And when it's well pounded, you don't need to sieve it. In this way you can make it with caprioli, which are fresh vine tendrils.*

This is essentially a medieval ancestor of pesto, though not oil-based, but rather sweet and sour, and thickened with bread, which as a general rule is how sauces were made before they evolved. The combination of savory, sour, and bitter herbs seems intentional, but the recipe will work with almost any combination. The sourness of sorrel, bitterness of arugula, and sweetness of mint contrast very nicely though. Vine tendrils are the little curly shoots with which grapevines anchor themselves. Eventually they become tough and sturdy, but when fresh they are crisp and pleasantly sour, like grape leaves. A sauce like this could be served either over a large piece of meat in a platter or placed in small individual bowls from which each diner could take what he or she pleased.

### ⇥ 156. MUSTARD OF CREMONA ⇤

*Liege, modern-day Belgium, 1604 (Lancelot de Casteau, 65–66)*

*Take two pounds of orange peel candied in sugar, half a pound of quinces candied in sugar or marmalade, and chop everything well together finely. Then take half a pint of very thick mustard, then take sugar melted with rosewater and place in it tournesol, and let it boil to give it a good red color. Mix in what you have chopped, and mix the mustard in, adding enough syrup and place in plates with three or four spoons to place on the table with the roast.*

This kind of sweet fruit mustard has a long history and is still made in Cremona, Italy, normally with many varied candied fruits. It is of particular interest in a cookbook written in present-day Belgium, as evidence of the popularity of Italian recipes across Europe. You might consider this Europe's first infatuation with Mediterranean foods, the second occurring right now around the world. The original version of mustard would have been made with must, or grape juice, as the sweetener, and oddly, our word for the mustard plant comes from the sauce rather than the plant, *sinapis* in Latin. Tournesol is a red flower, used as a dye.

## FRUIT

### ⇥ 157. TO CONSERVE CHERRIES IN JELLY ⇤

*Italy, 1570 (Scappi, 432ᵛ)*

*Take ten pounds of fresh marasche cherries or visciole, picked that day, that have not been bruised, leave the stem in the middle and gather them into bundles of ten. Get a casserole with a pound of clear water and place in these cherries and as they begin to scald, add in ten pounds of fine sugar pounded and sieved and let it boil very gently, skimming with a spoon. When the cherries split and everything is colored remove them and put them on a plate to dry, and let the liquid boil by itself, until it becomes cooked, not forgetting however to skim it. Test it on a plate, when it forms a little ball that doesn't spread out, remove from the fire. Pour out the cherry solids into cups or silver plates with the tepid liquid over and put it in a cool place to congeal. In this same way you can make sour cherries, and in the same liquid you can cook fresh damson plums.*

The recipe calls for marasco cherries, which are a dark, sweet variety (from which the liqueur Maraschino is made) similar to morellos or bings. He also says that you can use *visciola*, which are sour cherries. Any type will work in the recipe. It is not entirely clear why he suggests gathering into bundles of ten. If he intends that the cherries should be cooked this way, and ultimately conserved this way, it is not specified, but this would be a very elegant way to do it, with the little clusters neatly tied together. A pound of water is about a pint, so it seems that the liquid cooked here is mostly cherry juice and sugar. Pounding and sieving would create powdered sugar, and it seems that this is what would work best. This kind of conserve was not eaten in the morning the way we eat preserves, but rather was served as a kind of dessert, and eaten with a spoon, especially when these fruits were out of season. Although pasteurizing conserves for long storage was not yet invented, such preparations were stored for many months, usually by sealing in a ceramic jar with a layer of fat on top to keep out air and mold.

### ⅋ 158. TO BAKE PEACHES ℰ

*England, 1588 (*The Good Huswifes Handmaide for the Kitchen, *34)*

*Take peaches, pare them, and cut them into two peeces, & take out the stones as cleane as you can for breaching of the Peach: then make your pie three square to bake fowre in a pie, let your paste be very fine, then make your dredge with fine Sugar, Synamon and Ginger: and first lay a little dredge in the bottom of your pies: then put in Peaches, and fill up your coffins with your Dredge, and put into every coffin three spoonfuls of Rosewater. Let not your oven be too hot, etc.*

These appear to be little square open tarts rather than closed pies, each containing four peeled peach halves, which is what the term "breaching" refers to. The great amount of sugar and spices is what thickens the contents while it bakes.

*Peach tarts.*

### ⅋ 159. A PLATE OF ALL FRUITS (WITH EGGS) ℰ

*Spain, 1611 (Martínez Montiño, 133)*

*Take half a pound of sour cherries in conserve, and some pears, peaches, and apricots, some plums. All these should be conserved by hand, for of all the ingredients that you must work with, it is necessary to know how to make this. Make a dozen and a half scrambled eggs, and with these conserves and scrambled eggs, and some very delicate wafers, assemble a plate, arranged very well, interposing the conserves with the wafers so that you use up everything. This plate you can make many ways, changing the conserves, as with cermenas pears, lemons and quinces when in season; but at all times include scrambled eggs, or encanutados so these adorn the plate better.*

This combination seems perfectly bizarre on first sight, but not necessarily if you think of jam on toast with eggs for breakfast. This was most likely served at the end of a meal as a kind of dessert. The author is more concerned with adornment than any particular combination of preserved fruit, so include any moist fruit conserve you can find, preferably whole or in slices to create a decorative effect. In the recipe, *ojuelas* or little crispy fried wafers are called for, but any light, flaky biscuit will work as well. Presumably the *encanutados*, meaning "enchanters," are another kind of biscuit.

### ⇥ 160. APPLE TART ⇤

*Liege, modern-day Belgium, 1604 (Lancelot de Casteau, 42)*

*Take a dozen apples chopped, fry in butter, three ounces of sugar, a satin of cinnamon and four egg yolks, a bit of pounded anise, and make a tart of short pastry dough.*

The short crust is essentially a pastry dough made with a lot of butter and a little water, which here would have been sweetened as well. The egg yolks hold the chopped apples together so it can be sliced and served. A satin is a Walloon (Belgian) measurement equaling 1/4 ounce. In a shallow tart pan this should take about 35 to 40 minutes at 350 degrees to bake, or merely remove when the crust is golden brown.

### ⇥ 161. TO MAKE A MARMALADE OF ORANGES ⇤

*England, 1615 (Markham, 117)*

*To make an excellent marmalade of oranges, take the oranges, and with a knife pare off as thin as is possible the uppermost rind of the orange; yet in such sort as by no means you alter the colour of the orange; then steep them in fair water, changing the water twice a day till you find no bitterness of taste therein; then take them forth, and first boil them in fair running water, and, when they are soft, remove them into rose water, and boil them therein till they break: then to every pound of the pulp put a pound of refined sugar, and so, having mashed and stirred them all well together, strain it through very fine strainers into boxes, and so use it as you shall see occasion.*

Marmalade was originally made with quince, and from the directions to keep it in a box, we can assume that it was somewhat thicker than would be common today—probably more like a paste. It was also considered, in the past, to be a medicinal kind of food, eaten on its own rather than spread on toast.

## SWEETS

### ⇥ 162. TO MAKE FRITTERS, IN THE ROMAN DIALECT CALLED ZEPPOLLE ⇤

*Italy, 1570 (Scappi, 371)*

*Take a pound of red chickpeas, soaked, with the skins removed, and boil them in good meat broth with six ounces of cleaned chestnuts and then remove from the broth and drain. Pound in a mortar with six ounces of cleaned aged walnuts, that are not rancid, adding 4 ounces of sugar, an ounce of cinnamon, half an ounce of cloves and nutmeg, then take an ounce and a half of yeast, tempered in a cup of tepid white wine and a bit of rosewater, and mix everything together, adding mint, marjoram, pimpernel and wild thyme beaten with a knife, and of this composition make balls and fry in fat or butter. When fried, sprinkle with rosewater and serve hot with sugar and cinnamon on top. If the composition is left to rest for an hour after they are made, covered in a warm place, to let the yeast work, it will be much better. Not having yeast, in its place use six egg whites.*

These are really more like falafel than what is today called *zeppole* in Italy, which is a puffy, batter-based fritter. Chickpeas come in both red and black varieties. Those available in the United States are tan, but they will work fine. Use dried chickpeas soaked overnight and remove the skins by rubbing them gently in a dishtowel. Dried chestnuts may also be hard to find, but preserved, sweetened whole chestnuts in a can or jar should be suitable. The yeast Scappi would have used was probably a leaven left over from a batch of dough broken up in water or a sour frothy starter. That is, dried yeast and cakes of yeast were not available, and his 1 1/2 ounces refers to liquid weight. If using dried yeast, one teaspoon dissolved in the warm wine and rosewater should suffice. If frying in butter, use clarified butter or ghee, which is available in Indian groceries. It has a much higher smoking point than regular butter, which will probably burn at temperatures high enough to fry. The egg whites, if used, should probably be beaten to stiff peaks and then folded into the chickpea mixture. Fry about three or four balls at a time and remove with a slotted spoon and drain on paper towels before sprinkling with sugar and cinnamon.

### ❧ 163. TO MAKE MANUS CHRISTI ❧

*England, 1573 (John Partridge, Eiv^v–Di)*

*Take halfe a pownde of white Suger, put thereto iiii ounces of Rosewater, seethe them upon a softe tier of Coales, tyll the water be consumed, and the Sugre is become hard, then put therein a quarter of an ounce of the powder of Pearles, stirre them well together, put for every spoonful, a peece of a leafe of Golde cut of purpose: caste them upon a leafe of white Paper, anointed fyrste with the Oyle of sweete Almonds, or sweete butter for cleaving too.*

The name of this recipe means Hand of Christ, and although it is really just rose-flavored candy, the pearls and gold were thought to have medicinal qualities. Of course they would also be very impressive for their cost alone. Another variant suggests pouring the entire mixture on parchment paper and then scoring it with a knife into diamonds, or lozenges. These

can be made today without the gold and pearls, by merely cooking powdered sugar and rosewater together and then dropping them onto oiled
parchment paper.

### ⊰ 164. TO MAKE FARTS OF PORTINGALE ⊱

*England, 1591 (A.W., 33)*

*Take a quart of life Hony, and set it upon the fire and when it seetheth scum
it clean, and then put in a certaine of fine Biskets well serced [sieved], and
some pouder of Cloves, some Ginger, and powder of sinamon, Annis seeds and
some Sugar, and let all these be well stirred upon the fire, til it be as thicke as
you thinke needful, and for the paste for them take Flower as finelye dressed
as may be, and a good peece of sweet Butter, and woorke all these same well
togither, and not knead it.*

Although the typesetter seems to have made a few mistakes here (as in
a certain what of fine Biskets), the name of these cookies is indeed Farts
of Portugal, and similar recipes appear in other cookbooks as well. It may
seem redundant to make cookies out of crushed and sieved biscuits, but
the intention is to make something light and crumbly. They should be
baked.

### ⊰ 165. BUÑUELOS ⊱

*Spain, 1599 (Granado, 413)*

*Take a quart of milk in a saucepan and with flour make a porridge-like
mixture on a very small flame and cook until it is stiff. Then put it aside,
and add as many eggs as you like, and beat them in well until it is soft. Drop
from a spoon to fry well. Then dip them in honey and toss on cinnamon and
sugar.*

These donuts are simple and still very popular in Spain and were made
with much the same dough used for *churros*, a long, ridged donut, commonly eaten with hot chocolate. This type of sweet could have been enjoyed
by practically anyone, as the ingredients were relatively inexpensive.

### ⊰ 166. TO MAKE FLAKY SPANISH PASTRY ⊱

*Liege, modern-day Belgium, 1604 (Lancelot de Casteau, 66–69)*

*Make a dough of white flour, the finest you can find, place in two eggs, a bit
of butter and make the dough with cold water, so that it is a bit soft and beat
well a half hour. Then let it rest. Then roll your dough on a long board and
extend the dough as thin as paper the size of a half foot, then take pork fat,*

*melted on a gentle fire and grease your dough so that it is greased the entire length and roll your dough, then extend again the dough like the other and grease and roll on the other dough until you have a roll as thick as an arm. Then let it cool. When the dough is well chilled you cut it in pieces the size of three fingers, then have a piece of paper the size of [a] hand or bigger and place the dough on and press twice in the middle of the dough and enlarge the dough to a little patty, so it is just as thick as part of a little finger, then take flesh of mutton chopped with beef fat. Note for a pound of meat, half a pound of fat. Add in pepper, nutmeg, a bit of salt, and verjuice or vinegar and mix everything well together and fill your pastry with this meat and cut your pastry a covering which is not as thick, and cover your pastry thus, and grease well on top. Take some paper and cut a band which is not as high as the pastry and turn it around the pastry and fasten the end with egg yolk so the paper sticks together, then let it cook in an oven which is very hot. The pastry having been in the oven a quarter of an hour, remove it and remove the paper, replace the pastry in the oven until it is cooked enough, having removed the paper the leaves open up much better.*

This complex puff pastry is baked freeform, the ribbon of dough providing a temporary support for the edge of the dough so that it becomes firm without spreading, and after it is removed the flaky leaves expand. The dough is similar to a modern puff pastry, except that lard rather than butter separates the leaves. Lancelot may have seen this recipe in a Spanish translation by Granado of Scappi's Italian cookbook, which may have led him to call the pastry Spanish. In any case, it shows that cookbooks freely influenced each other, even across language barriers.

### ⊰ 167. A TART OF MILK ⊱

*Spain, 1607 (Maceras, 127)*

*To make this tart, you need half a quart of milk, and two ounces of flour in a saucepan and mix with eggs as when you make custard, and throw in six eggs with salt and mint and mix in with the milk, and add half a pound of sugar, and form the tart from this mixture, placing it to cook on a small fire, so that it congeals little by little, and it should not stick to the lid, and add sugar and cinnamon on top.*

This is the ancestor of the modern-day flan (egg custard). As the directions suggest, it is cooked over a gentle flame with a lid, probably in a round earthenware casserole. Today flans are usually made in a moderate oven with the tart pan set into a larger vessel with a little water or a *bain marie*. This prevents the set custard from either burning or becoming too dense. The Early Modern cook would have probably needed to watch the tart pan very carefully to prevent this. The addition of mint, very unusual today, makes for a pleasant variation.

## ☙ 168. A MOST DELICATE AND STIFFE SUGAR-PASTE, WHEREOF TO CAST RABETS, PIGEONS, OR ANY OTHER LITTLE BIRD OR BEAST, EITHER FROM THE LIFE, OR CARV'D MOLDS ☙

*England, 1608 (Plat, B3ᵛ)*

*First dissolve Isinglass in faire water with some Rosewater in the latter ende, then beate blanched almonds as you would for marchpane stuffe [marzipan], and drawe the same with creame, and Rosewater (milke will serve, but creame is more delicate) then put therein some powdered sugar, into which you may dissolve your Isinglass being first made into a gellie, in faire warme water (note, the more Isinglass you put therein, the stiffer our worke will prove) then having your rabbets, woodcoke &c. molded either in plaister from life, or else carved in wood (first anointing your wodden moldes with oyle of sweete almonds, and your plaister or stone moldes with barrowes grease) poure your sugar paste thereon. A quarte of creame, a quarterne [1/4 lb.] of almonds, 2 ounces of Isinglass, and 4 or 6 ounces of sugar, is reasonable good proportion for this stuffe. . . . For so your moulds will last long. You may dredge over your foule with crums of bread, cinnamon and sugar boyled together, and so they will seem as if they were rosted and breaded. Leach [sliced foods] & gelly may be cast in this manner. This paste you may also drive with a fine rowling pin, as smooth & as thin as you please; it lasteth not long, & therefore it must be eaten within a fewe dayes after the making thereof. By this meanes a banquet may be presented in the form of a supper, being a verie rare and strange devise.*

Plat is here explaining how to make one of the "conceits" of which English courtiers were so fond. The directions specify that a plaster cast can be made from an actual animal or it can be carved in wood. The former would then yield an exact replica of the animal, which, especially after coating with bread crumbs, was meant to look like roast fowl, but is in fact candy. These were the types of tricks that appeared in the dessert course, or in England called a banquet. This one uses isinglass, a clear gelatin made from the bladder of fish, though regular gelatin will work also. Sugar paste was also made of sugar held together with gum Arabic or tragacanth, and then molded by hand into any desired shape. Such "subtleties," as they were also called, could appear at the very start of a formal meal, or at the end.

## DRINKS

## ☙ 169. TO COOK WATER WITH ANISE, SUGAR AND CINNAMON ☙

*Italy, 1570 (Scappi, 391ᵛ)*

*Take the quantity of water that you want and let it boil in a vessel of glazed earthenware or in a double carafe of glass for more than a quarter of an hour, and for every boccale an ounce of anise, and when it's boiled another quarter hour, place in two ounces of fine sugar, skimming it diligently, so you don't take out the anise, and when it's boiled another quarter of an hour, put in a quarter of whole cinnamon removing the vessel at once from the fire, and keeping it covered until it is half cooled. This is so the water can soak up the substance of the cinnamon, and when it's cold, strain it through a white cloth, but it will be better if you strain it through a cone shaped sieve with cheese cloth and a bit of sponge at the bottom. This water will have the color of cinnamon.*

This recipe is intended for invalids. The spicy cinnamon water was probably intended to warm people suffering from chills and colds, but it can make a very pleasant drink today as well, even if drunk cooled. The boccale is about 3 quarts, but precise measurements are not important here. Scappi probably intends a quarter of an *ounce* of cinnamon stick. A 4-inch stick weighs about 1/4 ounce.

### ⇨ 170. TO MAKE HIPPOCRAS ⇦

*England, 1615 (Markham, 111)*

*To make hippocras, take a pottle [bottle] of wine, two ounces of good cinnamon, half an ounce of ginger, nine cloves, and six pepper corns, and a nutmeg, and bruise them and put them into the wine with some rosemary flowers, and so let them steep all night, and then put in sugar a pound at least; and when it is well settled, let it run through a woolen bag made for that purpose; thus if your wine be claret, the hippocras will be red; if white then of that color also.*

Hippocras.

Hippocras was one of the most universally enjoyed of flavored wines, and recipes ultimately go back to classical times—there is a recipe for what is called *conditum paradoxum* that is not terribly different from this except that sugar, cloves, and nutmeg were introduced in the Middle Ages. The name refers to the ancient Greek physician Hippocrates, and this was considered to have medicinal properties. The conical strainer, if not the recipe itself, was supposed to have been invented by Hippocrates.

### ⇨ 171. HOW TO HELP BASTARD BEING EAGER ⇦

*England, 1615 (Markham, 138)*

*Take two gallons of the best stoned honey, and two gallons of white wine, and boil them in a fair pan; skim it clean, and strain it through a fair cloth that there be no motes in it; then put to it one ounce of corianders, and one ounce of aniseeds, four or five orange peels dry and beaten to a powder, let them lie three days; then draw your bastard into a clean pipe, then put your honey in with the rest, and beat it well; then let it lie a week and touch it not, after draw it at pleasure.*

Despite the ridiculous-sounding title, this recipe was a way to correct bastard, a sweet wine, if it happened to turn sour. "Stoned honey" means crystallized and spreadable honey, something that happens naturally to honey if unprocessed. "Motes" means solid specks, and a pipe is a barrel holding about 100 gallons. (Other remedies offered in this cookbook are how "To make white bastard" and "A remedy for bastard if it prick.")

# ✒ NOTES

### 1. Introduction

1. Giovanni Battista Rossetti, *Dello Scalco* (Ferrara: Domenico Mammarello, 1584), 215.
2. Bartolomeo Scappi, *Opera* (Venice: Michele Tramezino, 1570), 54.

### 2. The Middle Ages, 1300–1450

1. *Le Menagier de Paris,* Tr. Eileen Power (London: The Folio Society, 1992), 162–63.
2. Johannes of Bockenheim, *Registrum coquine.* In "Le 'Registre de cuisine' de Jean De Bockenheim, Cuisinier du Pape Martin V," by Bruno Laurioux, Vol. 100, no. 2 (1988), 737.

### 3. The Renaissance

1. Platina, *On Right Pleasure and Good Health,* Mary Ella Milham, ed. (Tempe, AZ: Medieval and Renaissance Text and Studies, 1988), 322.
2. Ibid., 278.
3. Ibid., 136–37.
4. Ibid., 409.
5. Wynkyn de Worde, *The Book of Kervynge* (Lewes, East Sussex, UK: Southover Press, 2003), 54.

6. Martino of Como, *Libro de Arte Coquinaria*, trans. Jeremy Parzen as *The Art of Cooking* (Berkeley: University of California Press, 2005), 109.

7. Robert May, *The Compleat Cook* (Totnes, Devon, UK: Prospect Books, 2000), 37.

8. Iodoco Willich, *Ars Magirica. Hoc est, coquinaria* (Zurich: Jacob Gesner, 1563), 11.

9. Ibid., 22–30.

## 4. Late Renaissance and Elizabethan Era

1. Salvatore Massonio, *Archidipno overo dell'insalata* (Venice: Marc'antonio Brogiollo, 1627), 10–12.

2. Ibid., 161–63.

3. Ibid., 338–39.

4. Domenico Romoli, *La Singolare Dottrina* (Venice: Gio. Battista Bonfadino), 1593), 33$^v$.

# BIBLIOGRAPHY

A.W. *A book of cokrye very necessary for all such as delight therein.* London: Edward Allde, 1591.

Adamson, Melitta Weiss. *Food in Medieval Times.* Westport, CT: Greenwood Press, 2004.

———. *Regional Cuisines of Medieval Europe.* New York: Routledge, 2002.

Albala, Ken. *Eating Right in the Renaissance.* Berkeley: University of California Press, 2002.

———. *Food in Early Modern Europe.* Westport, CT: Greenwood Press, 2003.

Anonimo Toscano. *Libro della Cocina.* staff-www.uni-marburg.de/-gloning/an-tosc.htm

[Anonimo Veneziano]. *Libro di Cucina del Secolo XIV.* Edited by Ludovico Frati. Bologna: Arnaldo Forni, 1986.

———. *Libro di cucina/Libro per cuoco.* Translated by Louise Smithson, http://www.geocities.com/helewyse/libro.html?200521.

Beebe, Ruth Anne. *Sallets, Humbles and Shrewsbery Cakes.* Jaffrey, N H: David R. Godine, 1976.

Bensoussan, Maurice. *Les Particules alimentaires: Naissance de la gastronomie au XVIe siêcle.* Paris: Maisonneuve et Larose, 2002.

Black, Maggie. *The Medieval Cookbook.* New York: Thames and Hudson, 1992.

Bober, Phyllis Pray. *Art, Culture and Cuisine.* Chicago: University of Chicago Press, 1999.

Cappatti, Montanari. *Italian Cuisine.* New York: Columbia University Press, 2003.

Carlin, Martha, and Joel T. Rosenthal, eds. *Food and Eating in Medieval Europe.* London: The Hambledon Press, 1998.

Castelvetro, Giacomo. *Breve racconto di tutte le radici, di tutte l'erbe e di tutti i frutti che crudi o cotti in Italia si mangiano,* http://www.liberliber.it/biblioteca/c/castelvetro/index.htm.

——. *The Fruit, Herbs and Vegetables of Italy.* Tr. Gillian Riley. London: Viking, 1989.

Caton, Mary Anne, ed. *Fooles and Fricasees: Food in Shakespeare's England.* Washington, DC: Folger Shakespeare Library, 1999.

*Chiquart's "On Cookery": A Fifteenth Century Savoyard Culinary Treatise.* Tr. Terence Scully. New York: Peter Lang, 1986.

*Curye on Inglysch: English Culinary Manuscripts of the Fourteenth Century (Including the Forme of Cury).* Constance B. Heiatt and Sharon Butler, eds. Published for the Early English Text Society. London: Oxford University Press, 1985.

Davidson, Alan. *The Oxford Companion to Food.* Oxford: Oxford University Press, 1999.

Dawson, Thomas. *The Good Housewife's Jewel.* Introduction by Maggie Black. Lewes, East Sussex, UK: Southover Press, 1996 (*The good huswifes Iewell.* London: Edward White, 1596).

Fernández-Armesto, Felipe. *Food: A History.* Oxford: Macmillan, 2001.

Fiorato, Adelin Charles, and Anna Fones Baratto. *La Table et ses dessous.* Paris: Presses de la Sorbonne Nouvelle, 1999.

Flandrin, Jean Louis. *L'Ordre de Mets.* Paris: Odile Jacob, 2002.

Flandrin, Jean-Louis, and Carole Lambert. *Fetes Gourmandes au Moyen Âge.* Paris: Imprimerie Nationale, 1998.

Flandrin, Jean-Louis, and Massimo Montanari. *Food: A Culinary History.* New York: Columbia University Press, 1999.

Garcia, L. Jacinto. *Carlos V a la mesa.* Toledo, Spain: Ediciones Bremen, 2000.

Gillet, Philip. *Par Mets et par vins.* Paris: Payot, 1985.

Glanville, Phillipa, and Hilary Young, eds. *Elegant Eating.* London: V&A Publications, 2002.

*The Good Huswifes Handmaide for the Kitchen.* Bristol: Stuart Press, 1992 (*The good Huswifes Handmaide for the Kitchin.* London: Richard Fish, 1588).

Granado, Diego. *Libro del Arte de Cocina.* Madrid: Sociedad de Bibliófilos Españoles, 1971. (1st ed. 1599).

Grataroli, Guglielmo. *De vini natura.* Strassbourg: Theodosius Ribelius, 1565.

Harleian Mss: See *Two Fifteenth Century Cookbooks.*

Hartley, Dorothy. *Food in England.* Boston: Little, Brown, 1999.

Heiatt, Constance, Brenda Hosington, and Sharon Butler. *Pleyn Delit.* Toronto: University of Toronto Press, 1996.

Henisch, Bridget Ann. *Fast and Feast.* University Park: Pennsylvania State University Press, 1976.

Hollingsworth, Mary. *The Cardinal's Hat.* London: Profile Books, 2004.

Jeanneret, Michel. *A Feast of Words.* Chicago: University of Chicago Press, 1991.

Johannes of Bockenheim. *Registrum coquine.* In "Le 'Registre de cuisine' de Jean de Bockenheim, Cuisinier du Pape Martin V" by Bruno Laurioux. Mélanges de l'Ecole française de Rome. Moyen âge, temps modernes. Vol. 100, no. 2, 1988, pp. 709–760.

Katz, Solomon H., ed. *Encyclopedia of Food and Culture.* New York: Charles Scribner's Sons, 2003.

Kiple, Kenneth F., ed. *The Cambridge World History of Food.* Cambridge: Cambridge University Press, 2000.

La Varenne, François Pierre. *Le Cuisinier François.* Paris: Montalba, 1983.

———. *The French Cook.* Lewes, East Sussex, UK: Southover Press, 2001.

Lancelot de Casteau. *Overture de Cuisine.* Anvers/Bruxelles: De Schutter, 1983 (Liege: Leonard Streel, 1604).

*Larousse Gastronomique.* New York: Clarkson Potter, 2001.

Laurioux, Bruno. *Manger au Moyen Âge.* Paris: Hachette, 2002.

*Libellus de arte coquinaria.* Rudolph Grewe and Constance B. Heiatt, eds. Tempe: Arizona Center for Medieval and Renaissance Studies, 2001.

*Liber Cure Cocorum.* Richard Morris, ed. Trans. Cindy Renfrow. Berlin: A. Asher, 1862. http://www.pbm.com/lindahl/lcc/parallel.html.

*Liber de coquina.* http://staff-www.uni-marburg.de/-gloning/mul2-lib.htm Page numbers refer to the edition of Marianne Mulon. "Deux traits inédits d'art culinaire medieval." In *Bulletin philologique et historique (jusqu'au 1610) du Comité des Travaux historiques et scientifiques 1968*, Vol. 1. Paris, 1971.

*Libre de Sent Sovi.* Rudolph Grewe, ed. Barcelona: Editorial Barcino, 1979.

*Livre fort excellent de cuisine.* Lyon: Olivier Arnoulet, 1555.

*Livres en bouche: Cinq siècles d'art culinaire français.* Paris: Bibliotèque national de France/Hermann, 2001.

Llopis, Manual Martínez. *Historia de la Gastronomia Española.* Madrid: Editora Nacional, 1981.

Maceras, Domingo Hernandez de. *Libro del arte de Cozina.* Salamanca: Ediciones Universidad de Salamanca, 1999 (Salamanca: antonia Ramirez, 1607).

Markham, Gervase. *The English Housewife.* Michael R. Best, ed. Montreal: McGill-Queen's University Press, 1986 (*The English Hus-wife.* London: John Beale, 1615).

*Martha Washington's Booke of Cookery*. Karen Hess, ed. New York: Columbia University Press, 1981, 1995.

Martínez Montiño, Francisco. *Arte de Cocina*. Barcelona: Maria Angela Marti, 1763. http://www.bib.ub.es/grewe/showbook.pl?gw57. (1st ed. 1611).

Martino, Maestro [of Como]. *Libro de arte coquinaria*. Luigi Ballerini and Jeremy Parzen, eds. Milan: Guido Tommasi, 2001. Translated by Jeremy Parzen as *The Art of Cooking*. Berkeley: University of California Press, 2005.

Massonio, Salvatore. *Archidipno overo dell'insalata*. Venice: Marc'antonio Brogiollo, 1627.

May, Robert. *The Compleat Cook*. Totnes, Devon, UK: Prospect Books, 2000.

Meads, Chris. *Banquets Set Forth*. Manchester: Manchester University Press, 2001.

*Le Ménagier de Paris. The Goodman of Paris*. Tr. Eileen Power. London: The Folio Society, 1992.

Mennell, Stephen. *All Manners of Food*. Oxford: Blackwell, 1985.

Messisbugo, Christoforo di. *Banchetti*. Ferrara: Giovanni de Buglhat and Antonio Hucher, 1549.

Messisbugo, Cristofaro [sic] di. *Libro Novo*. Bologna: Arnaldo Forni, 2001.

Montanari, Massimo. *Alimentazione e cultura nel Medioevo*. Rome: Laterza, 1992.

———. *The Culture of Food*. Oxford: Blackwell, 1994.

Murrell, John. *Murrell's Two Books of Cookery and Carving*. Stuart Peachy, ed. Bristol, UK: Stuart Press, 1993 (5th edition, London: John Marriot, 1638).

Naso, Irma. *La cultura del Cibo*. Turin: Paravia, 1999.

Partridge, John. *The treasurie of commodious conceits*. London: Richard Iones, 1573.

Paston-Williams, Sara. *The Art of Dining*. London: The National Trust, 1993.

Pérez Samper, María de los Ángeles. *La alimentación en la Espana del Siglo de Oro*. Huesca: La Val de Onsera, 1998.

Peterson, T. Sarah. *Acquired Taste*. Ithaca, NY: Cornell University Press, 1994.

Plat, Hugh. *Delightes for ladies*. London: H. Lownes, 1608.

Platina (Bartolomeo Sacchi). *On Right Pleasure and Good Health*. Mary Ella Milham, ed. Tempe, AZ: Medieval and Renaissance Texts and Studies, 1998.

Pleij, Herman. *Dreaming of Cockaigne*. New York: Columbia University Press, 2001.

Plouvier, Liliane. *L'Europe a table*. Brussels: Editions Labor, 2003.

*A Proper Newe Booke of Cokerye*. Jane Hugget, ed. Bristol: Stuart Press, 1995 (London: John Kynge and Thomas Marche, n.d.).

*A Proper Newe Booke of Cokerye.* Anne Ahmed, ed. Cambridge: Corpus Christi College, 2002.

Redon, Odile, Françoise Sabban, and Silvano Serventi. *The Medieval Kitchen.* Chicago: University of Chicago Press, 1998.

Revel, Jean-François. *Culture and Cuisine.* New York: Da Capo, 1982.

Riley, Gillian. *Renaissance Recipes.* San Francisco: Pomegranate Artbooks, 1993.

Romoli, Domenico. *La Singolare Dottrina.* Venice: Gio. Battista Bonfadino, 1593. (1st ed. 1560).

Rossetti, Giovanni Battista. *Dello Scalco.* Ferrara: Domenico Mammarello, 1584. Reprint: Bologna: Arnaldo Forni, 1991.

Rubel, William. *The Magic of Fire.* Berkeley: Ten Speed Press, 2002.

Rupert of Nola. *Libre de doctrina per a ben server, de taller y del art de coch.* . . . http://www.cervantesvirtual.com/servlet/SirveObras/5791539 7105571162900080/index.htm.

———. *Libre del Coch.* Translated from Spanish version by Robin Caroll-Mann. http://www.Florilegium.org/files/FOOD-Manuscripts/Guisados1-art. html.

Sabban, Françoise, and Silvano Serventi. *A Tavola nel Rinascimento.* Rome: Laterza, 1996.

Santich, Barbara. *The Original Mediterranean Cuisine.* Chicago: Chicago Review Press, 1995.

Scappi, Bartolomeo. *Opera.* Venice, 1570. Reprint: Bologna: Arnaldo Forni, 2002.

Schivelbusch, Wolfgang. *Tastes of Paradise.* New York: Pantheon Books, 1992.

Scully, Terence. *The Art of Cookery in the Middle Ages.* Woodbridge, Suffolk, UK: Boydell Press, 1995.

———. *Early French Cookery.* Ann Arbor: University of Michigan Press, 1995.

Segan, Francine. *Shakespeare's Kitchen.* New York: Random House, 2003.

Serradilla Muñoz, Jose V. *La mesa del emperador.* San Sebastian: R&B Ediciones, 1997.

Serventi, Silvano, and Françoise Sabban. *Pasta.* New York: Columbia University Press, 2002.

Sim, Alison. *Food and Feast in Tudor England.* New York: St. Martin's Press, 1997.

Spencer, Colin. *British Food.* London: Grub Street, 2002.

Strong, Roy. *Feast.* London: Jonathan Cape, 2002.

Symons, Michael. *A History of Cooks and Cooking.* Urbana: University of Illinois Press, 2000.

Syngrapheus, Polyonimus. *Schola Apiciana.* Frankfort: Christian Egenolffs, 1534.

Tannahill, Ray. *Food in History.* New York: Crown Publishers, 1998.

Toussaint-Samat, Maguelonne. *History of Food.* Oxford: Basil Blackwell, 1992.

*Tractatus de modo preparandi et condiendi omnia cibaria.* http://www. staff.uni-marburg.de/-gloning/mul1-tra.htm. Page numbers refer to the edition of Marianne Mulon. "Deux traits inédits d'art culinaire medieval" In *Bulletin philologique et historique (jusqu'au 1610) du Comité des Travaux historiques et scientifiques 1968,* Vol. 1 Paris, 1971.

*Two Fifteenth Century Cookbooks,* Thomas Austin, ed. Early English Text Society. Rochester, NY: Boydell and Brewer, 2000 reprint.

*Viandier,* tr. James Prescott. http://www.telusplanet.net/public/prescotj/data/viandier/viandier1.html.

*The Viandier of Taillevent.* Terence Scully, ed. Ottowa, Canada: University of Ottowa Press, 1988.

Visser, Margaret. *The Rituals of Dinner.* New York: Grove Weidenfeld, 1991.

*The Vivendier.* Terence Scully, ed. Totnes, Devon, UK: Prospect Books, 1997.

Wheaton, Barbara Ketcham. *Savoring the Past.* New York: Touchstone, 1983.

Willich, Iodoco. *Ars magirica. Hoc est, coquinaria.* Zurich: Jacob Gesner, 1563.

Wilson, C. Anne. *Food and Drink in Britain.* Chicago: Academy Chicago Publishers, 1991.

Wright, Clifford. *A Mediterranean Feast.* New York: William Morrow, 1999.

Wynkyn de Worde. *The Boke of Kervyng.* Lewes, East Sussex, UK: Southover Press, 2003.

Young, Carolin C. *Apples of Gold in Settings of Silver.* New York: Simon and Schuster, 2002.

# INDEX

adaptations of recipes, xxxvi–xxxvii

Agliata (Garlic Sauce), 88

Albujauanas (Mutton Patties), 107

ale. *See* beer

alexanders (*Smyrnium olustratum*), 101

alkanet, 3, 44, 63–64

almond milk, xxxvii, 4, 44, 45, 54, 57, 82, 111

almonds, 21, 65, 88

alum (aluminum sulfate), 100

ambergris, 4, 86

Anonimo Toscano, 41, 56

Anonimo Veneziano, 31, 51, 59, 61, 65, 69

appetizers, 9, 18, 99

apples, 20–21, 62, 66–67, 129; juice, 125

apricots, 128

Arab influence, 2, 33–34, 40, 61, 108

Armored Chicken, 44

artichokes, 2, 13, 21, 81

arugula, 101, 126

asparagus, 13, 49, 81, 101

aspic. *See* gelatin

A.W., 107, 110, 131

azaroles, 16

*azumbre* (measurement), 121

*bain marie* (water bath), 132

barbecue grill. *See* grill

barbel (fish), 114–15

barding, 25–26

barley, 54

bastard. *See* wine

batticarne (meat pounder), 75, 113

beans, 8, 81. *See also* fava; lupins

beef, 11, 20, 39, 104; sauce for, 89

beer, 8, 17; in sauces, 78

beets, 95; juice, 39

Belgium. *See* Liege

Blanche Brawen (White Pork Pâté), 30

blanching, 109

blancmange, 44, 20, 99, 111; of frogs, 116

boar, 11, 20

*boccale* (measurement), 133–34

Bockenheim, Johannes of, 49, 137

Bologna, Italy, 98

borage, 101

Boswell, James, xxv

bouillon. *See* broth

bozolati, 66

braise, 39–40, 102, 105, 112

brazier, 26–27

bread, 8–9, 25, 93, 102; buttered loaves, 121–22; crumbs, 14, 56, 80, 88; pudding, 55–56

bream, 90

Brie (cheese), 35

broth, 10, 32, 43, 57, 74, 77, 89, 102; variations by nationality, 33–34

Brouet rousset (Russet Broth), 32

Brussels sprouts, 103

bugloss, 101

Buñeulos, 131

burdock, 82

butter, 15, 56, 85, 90, 130

cabbage, 50, 99, 103; flowers, 101

calamari (squid), 112

calendula, 101

Cameline Sauce, 37, 45, 87

candy, 16, 18, 21, 51–52, 55; soft-ball stage, 125

canella. *See* cinnamon

cannabis, 73

cannelloni, 21

Canoncini of Fresh Eggs, 122

capers, 100

capon, 11, 20, 28, 76, 82, 99, 110–11

caraway, 107

cardoons, 21

carp, 12, 90; fritters, 79

carrots, 95, 118–19, 125–26

carving, 7, 18

cassia. *See* cinnamon

cassia buds, 3, 32

cast iron. *See* iron

cat, viii, 40

Catalonia (or Catalunya), 29, 40–41, 57, 58–59, 67–68, 76, 83

caul, 20, 41, 97–98

cauliflower, 49, 101, 103

caviar, 20, 79

Cervantes Saavedra, Miguel de, 97

*cervelat* (sausage), 98, 119

chafing dish, 82, 109

Charles V, king of France, 29–30

chawdron, 35, 82

cheese, 14, 20–21, 57–58, 90, 100, 109, 124–25

cherries, 20–21, 90, 109, 127–28; with shrimp, 80

chestnuts, 21, 74, 91, 130

chicken, xxxv, 32–33, 42, 43, 44, 75, 82, 99, 111; sauce for, 61. *See also* capon

chickpeas, 117, 129–30

chicory, 101, 111

chili peppers, xxxvii, 2, 8, 61

chine bone, 49

Chiquart Amiczo, xxxviii, 29, 35–36, 38, 49

chocolate, 1

chowder, 35, 45

Chuets, 107

*churros*, 131

Chykonys in bruette (Chickens in Broth), 43

cider (hard), 17

cinnamon, 3, 77, 88–89, 91, 93–95, 109; water, 134

citron, 21, 93, 95

cleanliness, 7

cloves, 77, 89, 91, 95, 109

cochineal, 4

cod. *See* stockfish

Codonyat, 64

coffee, 1

Cold flounder, 31

Cold Sage (chicken Salad), 30

college refectory, 103, 123

coloring (food), 4

Columbus, Christopher, 37

compost (compote), 51–52, 62, 91

conceits. *See* subtleties

cony. *See* rabbit

cookbooks, xxxvi

cooks (professional), xxxvi, 28, 43

copyists, 49

Cordial sauce, 89

corn, xxxvii, 8, 84, 119, 124

crabs, 114

Crampone (cheese), 35

cranberry sauce, 15

crane, 11, 43

crayfish, 114

cream, 14, 94

*credenza*, 9, 18, 99

*credenziero*, (cook of cold foods), 99

crepes, 64

cress, 101

crusaders and spices, 3

cubebs, xxxvii, 3; sources, 26

cucumbers, 100

currants, 39, 111; *Ribes*, 110

custard, 132

cutlery, 7

cutting boards, 27

dairy products, 2, 12, 14

dates, 16, 111

Dawson, Thomas, 102, 117

defrutum (cooked wine), 69

*De honesta voluptate*, 71, 73

dietary theory, 5–6, 12, 14, 15–16, 68, 78, 81, 101, 134

diet of the poor, xxxviii, 8, 48, 81, 114, 119

Digestive Pottage, 73

Dish of Roasted Cat, 40

distillation. *See* spirits

Dodine blanche (Ducks in White Sauce), 77

donuts, 131

*dragée. See* candy

drippings, 89

duck, 11, 77, 111–12

*Du fait de cuisine. See* Chiquart

earthenware, 24, 78, 105, 132

eels, 12, 46–47, 90

eggplants, 2; casserole, 52; stuffed, 116

eggs, 13–14, 57–59, 85–87, 122–23, 128; egg whites, 94

endive, 20, 99, 101, 111

England: Elizabethan Era, 97, 100, 102, 106–7, 109–11, 115, 117, 121, 128–31, 133–34; feast menu, 82; Middle Ages, 30, 34, 38, 39, 43, 46, 50, 54–55, 58, 60, 63, 65–66; Renaissance, 74, 78, 81, 84, 86, 90, 94

*entremets*, 9, 54

Epiphany (Twelfth Night), 118

escabeche, of fish, 114–15; of partridge, 110

experimentation, xxxvi

exploration of North America, 114

falafel, 130

faro, 99; Farro of Spelt, 56

Farts of Portingale, 131

fasts. *See* Lent

fava beans, 47–48, 53, 81, 118

fennel, 51; pollen, 105, 113

Ferrara, x–xi, 71–72, 74, 77, 79, 81, 83–84, 87, 91–93

*fideos. See* pasta

fig peckers, 11, 20

figs, 16, 65, 100

fingers (eating with), 7

fish, 12, 89, 100; dangers of eating cold, 31; little, 114; pickled, 9. *See also* Lent

flan, 21, 132

flavors, evolution of preferences, 77–78

Florence, 71, 75, 80, 89. *See also* Tuscany

flounder, 12, 31

flowers, edible, 99

fluke, 90

foccaccia, 20

foglietta (measurement), 125

forks, 7–8

*Forme of Cury*, 29, 58, 63, 65

fowl, 11–12. *See also individual species*

France: Middle Ages, 30, 36, 41, 42, 45, 47, 57–61, 64, 68; Renaissance, 73, 76–79, 85–86, 88–89, 91, 93

frittatas, 87, 122
fritters, 66, 79, 82, 100, 129
Frog Pie, 115
fruit, 15–16; with eggs, 128
funnel cakes, 64–65
Furmente or frumenty, 54–55, 82
*fusticellos*, 33–34

galangal, xxxvii, 3, 63, 95
game, 11. *See also* venison
Garbies a la Catalana, 67
garlic, 88, 109, 113; Garlic Soup, 73
garrotxa (cheese), 59
gazpacho (white), 36
gelatin, 31–32, 133; of Every Meat, 20
ghee, 130
ginger, 3, 77, 89, 91
gluttony, 47
gnocchi, 83–84
goat, 20, 40
gold leaf, 130–31
*Good Huswifes Handmaide for the Kitchen*, 81, 84, 106, 109, 114, 122, 128
goose, 42
gooseberries, 109
gourds, 91, 101
grains of paradise (meleguetta pepper), xxxvii, 2–3, 61, 77, 95; sources, 26
Granado, Diego, 97, 131–32
grapes, 21; leaves, 111; unripe, 109; vine tendrils, 100, 126
Grataroli, Guglielmo, 95
graters, 25, 83
*Greco* (wine), 105
greens, 51, 84, 99
green sauce, 60
grill, xxxvii, 23, 78, 85–86, 105, 113
Gruyau (Barley Gruel), 54
guinea fowl, 9

halibut, 60
hare, 75–76, 99, 111

Harleian Manuscripts #279 and #4016, 30, 43, 46, 50, 63, 66
hazelnuts, 112
health. *See* dietary theory
hearth (cooking), xxxvii, 23–24, 26–27
Hell Sauce, 88
Hemp Seed Soup, 72
herbs. *See* leaves
Hercules, 39
Hericoc of Mutton, 36
heron, 11, 82
herring, 12
hippocras, 91, 134
Hippocrates, 134
holidays, 48, 65, 84, 91, 114, 116. *See also* Lent
honey, 74, 93, 95, 124–25, 135
hop sprouts, 101
Huevos rellenos, 123
humoral physiology. *See* dietary theory
hyssop, 36

illness, dishes for, 34, 54, 111, 133
illustrations in cookbooks, 97
India, 2
Indonesia, 2
ingredients: expense, 2; hard to find, xxxv, xxxvii; illegal, xxxv; substitutions, xxxvii
iron (cast), 23, 76, 105
isinglass, 133
Italian Pottage, 74
Italy: xv; Late Renaissance, 97, 101–2, 104–6, 108, 112–13, 116–17, 119, 122, 125–27, 129, 133; Middle Ages, 33, 41, 48, 51, 56, 59, 61, 65–66, 69; Renaissance, 72, 74–85, 87–93

Jacobin Soup, 35
Janet of Young Goat, 40
Jasper of Milk, 86–87
jaunette sauce for fish, 45, 59

kid, 11, 19, 75

knives, 25

lamb, 11, 20, 38, 106

lamprey, 46–47

Lancelot de Casteau, 97, 100, 103, 111, 114, 118, 120, 123, 127, 129, 131

larding, 37, 44–45, 109. *See also* barding

lardo, 75, 105

larks, 109

leach or leche meats (sliced), 30, 133

leaves, 48, 51

leeks, 49

lemons, 2, 6, 12, 110

Lent, 4–5, 11–12, 48, 54, 57, 65, 84–85, 91, 100, 114, 116

lettuce, 20, 100

*Libellus de arte coquinaria*, 29

*Liber Cure Coquorum*, 34, 38, 54–55, 60

*Liber de Coquina*, 33, 48

*Liber de doctrina per a ben server, de taller y del art del coch. See* Rupert of Nola

*Libre de Sent Sovi*, 29

Liege, Belgium, 97, 100, 103, 111, 114, 118, 120, 123, 127, 129, 131

liver, 20, 99, 109

*Livre fort excellent de cuisine*, 71, 73, 76–79, 85, 88–89, 91, 93

Lombardy, 62

long pepper. *See* pepper, long

Lord's Prayer, as cooking timer, 66, 80

Low Countries. *See* Liege

lupins, 21, 81

lye, 117

macaroni. *See* pasta

mace, 95

Maceras, Domingo Hernandez de, 103, 107, 110, 114, 121, 123, 132

Malaches white (Egg Tart), 58

*malvasia* or malmsey (wine), 105

Manchego (cheese), 52, 57

manchet, 9, 92, 109, 121

manners, 7–8

Manus Christi (sweets), 130

*maravedi*, coin and unit of measurement, 108

marigold, 101

marjoram, 109

Markham, Gervase, 111, 129, 134

marmalade, 21, 129

marrow, 50

Martínez Montiño, Francisco, 104, 115, 118, 124

Martino (dei' Rossi) of Como, 71–72, 75–76, 78, 80–81, 85, 87–88, 90, 137

marzipan, 20–21, 123, 133

Massonio, Salvatore, 99–100, 138

mastic, 37

May, Robert, 86, 137

mead, 17

meal structure, 17–18

meal times, 19

measurements, 27–28, 43, 71, 93

meat: balls, 107; in late medieval diet, 11; and status, 8, 10–11

medicine. *See* dietary theory

medlars, 16

meleguetta pepper. *See* grains of paradise

melons, 91, 101

*membrillo*, 64

Menagier de Paris, 29, 32–33, 137

menu (16th century), 19–21

*merenda*, 19

Messisbugo, Christoforo di, 71–72, 74, 77, 79, 81, 83–84, 87, 91–93

Mexico, 2

mezzaluna, 26

Middle Eastern cuisine. *See* Arab influence

milk, xxxvi, 2, 21, 77, 86, 111, 132

millet, 119

minestra, 10, 82–83, 102, 119

mint, 100, 103, 109, 126, 132

mortadella, 51, 97–98

mortar and pestle, 22, 44, 88, 106

Mostaccioli, 92–93

motes (specks) in wine, 135
mozzarella, 84, 87
Murrell, John, 100, 115, 121
mushrooms, 80
musk, 4, 93
must, 3–4, 93. *See also* sapa
mustard, 60, 62, 99, 127
mutton, 41, 82, 107
myrtle berries, 98

napkins, 7
Naples, 29, 31, 36, 40, 44, 52–53, 57–58, 64, 67
New World foods, 8–9
noodles. *See* pasta
Nun's Bozolati, 66
nutmeg, 77, 89, 95, 109, 114
nuts, 100. *See also individual species*

ojuelas (wafers), 128–29
olives, 15, 18, 20–21, 99
*olla podrida*, 104
Olney, Buckinghamshire, England, 85
omelet, 49
onions, 81, 109
orache, 51
oranges, 46, 129; color, 126; juice, 125
organ meats, xxxv
ovens, 24–25
oysters, 34, 45, 115

pancakes, 84–85
*pancetta*, 41
*pan forte*, 93
panic (grain), 119
*pan pepato*, 93
*pantalones* (pies), 103–4
*pappardelle. See* pasta
parboil, 28
parchment paper, 86
Paris, vii
parmigiano, 14, 90, 112, 120
parsley, 39, 109
partridge, 20, 73, 104, 110

Partridge, John, 130
*passum* (cooked raising wine), 69
pasta, 13; *fideos*, 57; lasagna, 119; maccheroni, 83, 120; *pappardelle*, 75–76; ravioli, 84, 120–21; tagliatelli, 119
pastry, 20, 78, 92, 99, 118, 125; flaky Spanish, 131–32
paternoster. *See* Lord's prayer
peaches: baked, 128; conserves, 128; unripe, 65, 91
peacock, xxxv, 12, 20, 41–42, 99
pearls, powdered, 130–31
pears, 21, 94, 128
peas, 57, 102–3
peel (baker's), 25, 123
pellitory, 60
pepper, 2, 77, 93, 95; long, 3, 61, 95; sources, 26
perch, 90
perfumes in food, 4
pesto, 15, 60
pheasant, 11–12, 77–78, 99
pies, 9, 13–14, 18, 46–47, 82, 102, 104, 115. *See also* tarts
pig, suckling. *See* pork
pigeon, 75, 77, 82
pike: in English Sauce, 78; sauce for, 90
pimpernel, 109
Pinyonata (Pine Nut Soup), 36
pipkin, 24, 109, 111–12, 114
pistachios, 21
pizza (puff pastry), 93
Plat, Hugh, 133
Platina (Bartolomeo Sacchi), 71, 73, 75, 80, 137
plums, 127–28
poison in mushrooms, 79–80
polenta, 56, 84, 119
*polpettoni* (tuna rolls), 113
pomegranate, 20, 61, 125
pork, 20, 30, 37–38, 72, 82, 88, 97, 104; suckling pig, 99
porpoise, xxxv, 2, 103

Portuguese and spice trade, 2

potatoes, 8, 82, 84

pot roast, 106

pots and pans, 23–24

poverty. *See* diet of poor

powme dorrys (Golden Apples of Pork), 38

pregnancy and tansy, 51

printing, 1, 8

*Proper Newe Booke of Cokerye*, 74, 86, 90–91, 94

prosciutto, 9, 20, 72

*provatura* (cheese), 120

prunes, 15, 91, 109

pudding, 13, 56, 65

quailing (curdling), 74

quails, 20

Quesadillas of Curds, 124

quince, 21, 64, 125

rabbit, 111–12. *See also* hare

*raclette*, 58

raisins, 15–16, 106; in Cameline Sauce, 87–88

rapunzel, 100

ravioli. *See* pasta

recipe format, 27–28; variations and options, 106, 116

*Regimen Sanitatis* of Salerno, 81

*Registrum coquine*, 49

rennet, 124–25

restons, 122

retsina (wine), 94

ribs (braised beef), 39

rice, 2, 13, 56, 82–83

rice flour, 43–44, 111

Richard II, king of England, 29

roach (fish, *Rutilus rutilus*), 90

rolling pins, 26

Rome, 49, 72, 75–76, 78, 80, 82, 85, 87–88, 90, 97, 99, 101, 104–6, 108, 112–13, 116–17, 119, 122, 125–27, 129, 133

Romoli, Domenico, 71, 75, 80, 89, 138

rose, 90; vinegar, 4, 105

rosewater, 3, 86

Rossetti, Giovanni Battista, 99–100, 137

roux, 14

rumney (wine), 94

Rumpolt, Marx, 97

Rupert of Nola, 29, 31, 36, 40, 44, 45, 52–53, 57–58, 64, 67, 71; and Martino, 83

rye, 9

Rysshews of fruyt, 63

safety, 26–27

saffron, 60, 69, 93, 111

salad, 9, 13, 20, 99–101, 118–19

salamander, 123

salami, 20, 72, 98

salmon, 45, 89–90

sandalwood, 3, 39–40, 44

sapa, 3, 28, 60, 91–92, 105, 113

sardines, 12, 115

satin (measurement), 129

sauces, 14–15; Cameline, 87; carrot, 125; chicken, 61; Civet or Black for Boar, 61; Cordial for fish, 89; green, 60, 126; Hell, 88; jaunette, 59; mustard, 60, 127; Pyke, 90; roast beef, 89; Royal, 99, 125; White Agliata (Garlic Sauce), 88

Savoy, 29, 35–36, 38, 49

scalco (banquet manager), 99

Scandinavia, 102

Scappi, Bartolomeo, 97, 101–2, 104–6, 108, 112–13, 116–17, 119, 122, 125–27, 129, 132–33, 137

sea bass, 78

seal, 102

semolina, 119

serving food, 18

Shakespeare, William, 82

shrimp, 80

Shrove Tuesday, 85

sieves, 22, 101; conical, 134

sippets (toast points), 101, 109

smoke and burnt food, to remove odor, 53, 82–83

smore. *See* braise

snow (counterfeit), 93

soffrito, 76

sops, 107, 110. *See also* sippets

sorrel, 126

soup, 10, 32–36, 72–74, 101–4, 112, 116, 119

souse (pickle), 115

Spain, Late Renaissance, 97, 103–4, 107, 110, 114, 118, 121, 123, 124, 131–32; Middle Ages, 31, 36, 40, 44, 52–53, 57–58, 64, 67

Spanish balles, 106

sparrows, 81, 109

spelt, 56

spiced water, 133

spices, xxxv, 2–3, 63, 77, 79, 85, 88; absence of, 90, 103, 114; suppliers, xxxvii, 26. *See also individual spices*

spikenard, 3, 95

spinach, 2, 39, 111, 117

spirits, 17–18

spit (roasting), xxxvii, 22–23, 105

spoons (cooking), 25

sprouts, 20; bean, 100

squash, 8, 92, 101

squid, 112–13; ink, 113

stockfish (dried cod), 12, 114

strainer. *See* sieves

strawberry, 63; leaves, 111

Stuff a Shoulder or Other Part (Mutton), 41

Stuffed Goose Neck, 42

sturgeon, 113

Stwed Beeff (Beef Stew), viii, 39

subtleties (novelty dishes), 4–5, 38, 40, 86, 93, 133

sugar, 2–3, 15–16, 76–77, 86, 122; powdered, 128

sugar paste (sculptures), 5, 9, 133

sumac, 51–52, 62

supper, 73–74

swan, 11, 43, 82

sweet and sour, xxxv, 2, 6, 39, 101, 110, 113, 125

sweet potatoes, 9

Switzerland, 58, 95

syringes, 26

Taillevent. See *Viandier*

*tamis. See* sieve

tansy, 50–51

*tarantella* (salted tuna belly), 113

tarragon, 36

tarts, 20, 80–81, 90–92, 118, 128–29, 132

tea, 1

techniques (cooking), and dietary theory, 6

temperature (cooking), xxxvi, 28

tempering, 6, 38

testa (or testo in Italian), 102

texture of food, xxxv

thrushes, 11

Tirel, Guillaume. See *Viandier*

tomacella (sausage), 48, 98

tomatoes, 8, 120

tongue, 20, 99

toothpicks, 21

*Tractatus de modo preparandi et condiendi omnia cibaria*, 37, 42, 45, 47, 58, 60–61, 68

translations, xxxviii

trencher, 7; wooden, 117–18

truffles, 21, 103

tuna, 89; casserole, 45–46; rolls, 113

turkey, xxxvii, 9, 11, 20, 108–9

turnips, 91–92

turtle doves, 20

Tuscany, 41, 51, 56

vanilla, 4

veal, viii, 11, 20, 38, 75, 82, 99, 120; calves' heads, xxxv

vegetables, 13

Venice, 31, 51, 59, 61, 65–66, 69; spice trade, 3

venison, 2; Venoison of fresh deer, 37

verjuice, 3, 14, 32, 74, 101, 113
Viandier, 29, 30, 32, 36–37, 45, 54, 57,
    59, 64, 68, 71, 85
vinegar, 4, 14, 110
vine tendrils. *See* grapes
violet leaves, 111

wafers, 21
walnuts (green), 65
wardens. *See* pears
water, 17
wheat berries, 54–55
wheat starch, 35, 121

whisk, 25
Willich, Iodoco, 138
wine, 8, 16–17, 68, 95, 134; flavored, 17;
    instant, 95. *See also* hippocras
Wynkyn de Worde, 82, 137

yeast, 121, 130

zabaglione, 89
zeppole, 129
*zuppa* (soup), 102

## About the Author

KEN ALBALA is Professor of History and Chair of the History Department at University of the Pacific, Stockton, California. He is a prolific author who specializes in Early Modern Europe food history, authoring such titles as *Eating Right in the Renaissance* (2002) and *Food in Early Modern Europe* (Greenwood, 2003) and serving as series editor for Greenwood's series Food Culture around the World and Cooking Up History.

## About the Author

KEN ALBALA is Professor of History and Chair of the History Department at University of the Pacific, Stockton, California. He is a prolific author who specializes in Early Modern Europe food history, authoring such titles as *Eating Right in the Renaissance* (2002) and *Food in Early Modern Europe* (Greenwood, 2003) and serving as series editor for Greenwood's series *Food Culture around the World* and *Cooking Up History*.